C-2667   CAREER EXAMINATION SERIES

This is your
PASSBOOK for...

Chief Budget Examiner

Test Preparation Study Guide
Questions & Answers

COPYRIGHT NOTICE

This book is SOLELY intended for, is sold ONLY to, and its use is RESTRICTED to individual, bona fide applicants or candidates who qualify by virtue of having seriously filed applications for appropriate license, certificate, professional and/or promotional advancement, higher school matriculation, scholarship, or other legitimate requirements of education and/or governmental authorities.

This book is NOT intended for use, class instruction, tutoring, training, duplication, copying, reprinting, excerption, or adaptation, etc., by:

1) Other publishers
2) Proprietors and/or Instructors of "Coaching" and/or Preparatory Courses
3) Personnel and/or Training Divisions of commercial, industrial, and governmental organizations
4) Schools, colleges, or universities and/or their departments and staffs, including teachers and other personnel
5) Testing Agencies or Bureaus
6) Study groups which seek by the purchase of a single volume to copy and/or duplicate and/or adapt this material for use by the group as a whole without having purchased individual volumes for each of the members of the group
7) Et al.

Such persons would be in violation of appropriate Federal and State statutes.

PROVISION OF LICENSING AGREEMENTS – Recognized educational, commercial, industrial, and governmental institutions and organizations, and others legitimately engaged in educational pursuits, including training, testing, and measurement activities, may address request for a licensing agreement to the copyright owners, who will determine whether, and under what conditions, including fees and charges, the materials in this book may be used them. In other words, a licensing facility exists for the legitimate use of the material in this book on other than an individual basis. However, it is asseverated and affirmed here that the material in this book CANNOT be used without the receipt of the express permission of such a licensing agreement from the Publishers. Inquiries re licensing should be addressed to the company, attention rights and permissions department.

All rights reserved, including the right of reproduction in whole or in part, in any form or by any means, electronic or mechanical, including photocopying, recording, or by any information storage and retrieval system, without permission in writing from the Publisher.

Copyright © 2025 by
National Learning Corporation

212 Michael Drive, Syosset, NY 11791
(516) 921-8888 • www.passbooks.com
E-mail: info@passbooks.com

PASSBOOK® SERIES

THE *PASSBOOK® SERIES* has been created to prepare applicants and candidates for the ultimate academic battlefield – the examination room.

At some time in our lives, each and every one of us may be required to take an examination – for validation, matriculation, admission, qualification, registration, certification, or licensure.

Based on the assumption that every applicant or candidate has met the basic formal educational standards, has taken the required number of courses, and read the necessary texts, the *PASSBOOK® SERIES* furnishes the one special preparation which may assure passing with confidence, instead of failing with insecurity. Examination questions – together with answers – are furnished as the basic vehicle for study so that the mysteries of the examination and its compounding difficulties may be eliminated or diminished by a sure method.

This book is meant to help you pass your examination provided that you qualify and are serious in your objective.

The entire field is reviewed through the huge store of content information which is succinctly presented through a provocative and challenging approach – the question-and-answer method.

A climate of success is established by furnishing the correct answers at the end of each test.

You soon learn to recognize types of questions, forms of questions, and patterns of questioning. You may even begin to anticipate expected outcomes.

You perceive that many questions are repeated or adapted so that you can gain acute insights, which may enable you to score many sure points.

You learn how to confront new questions, or types of questions, and to attack them confidently and work out the correct answers.

You note objectives and emphases, and recognize pitfalls and dangers, so that you may make positive educational adjustments.

Moreover, you are kept fully informed in relation to new concepts, methods, practices, and directions in the field.

You discover that you are actually taking the examination all the time: you are preparing for the examination by "taking" an examination, not by reading extraneous and/or supererogatory textbooks.

In short, this PASSBOOK®, used directedly, should be an important factor in helping you to pass your test.

CHIEF BUDGET EXAMINER

DUTIES
An employee in this class is responsible for performing highly specialized administrative work supervising the budget unit in a large department in the analysis of departmental budget requests, the preparation of the operating and capital budgets and the implementation of budget procedures in departments. The incumbent works closely with departmental executives who are responsible for finalizing policy decisions and who review work through frequent conferences, reports and observations of the effectiveness of budgetary programs. Does related work as required.

SCOPE OF THE EXAMINATION
The <u>written test</u> will cover knowledge, skills and/or abilities in such areas as:

1. Administration;
2. Administrative analysis;
3. Budgeting;
4. Preparing written material;
5. Supervision;
6. Understanding and interpreting tabular material; and
7. Understanding and interpreting written material.

HOW TO TAKE A TEST

I. YOU MUST PASS AN EXAMINATION

A. WHAT EVERY CANDIDATE SHOULD KNOW

Examination applicants often ask us for help in preparing for the written test. What can I study in advance? What kinds of questions will be asked? How will the test be given? How will the papers be graded?

As an applicant for a civil service examination, you may be wondering about some of these things. Our purpose here is to suggest effective methods of advance study and to describe civil service examinations.

Your chances for success on this examination can be increased if you know how to prepare. Those "pre-examination jitters" can be reduced if you know what to expect. You can even experience an adventure in good citizenship if you know why civil service exams are given.

B. WHY ARE CIVIL SERVICE EXAMINATIONS GIVEN?

Civil service examinations are important to you in two ways. As a citizen, you want public jobs filled by employees who know how to do their work. As a job seeker, you want a fair chance to compete for that job on an equal footing with other candidates. The best-known means of accomplishing this two-fold goal is the competitive examination.

Exams are widely publicized throughout the nation. They may be administered for jobs in federal, state, city, municipal, town or village governments or agencies.

Any citizen may apply, with some limitations, such as the age or residence of applicants. Your experience and education may be reviewed to see whether you meet the requirements for the particular examination. When these requirements exist, they are reasonable and applied consistently to all applicants. Thus, a competitive examination may cause you some uneasiness now, but it is your privilege and safeguard.

C. HOW ARE CIVIL SERVICE EXAMS DEVELOPED?

Examinations are carefully written by trained technicians who are specialists in the field known as "psychological measurement," in consultation with recognized authorities in the field of work that the test will cover. These experts recommend the subject matter areas or skills to be tested; only those knowledges or skills important to your success on the job are included. The most reliable books and source materials available are used as references. Together, the experts and technicians judge the difficulty level of the questions.

Test technicians know how to phrase questions so that the problem is clearly stated. Their ethics do not permit "trick" or "catch" questions. Questions may have been tried out on sample groups, or subjected to statistical analysis, to determine their usefulness.

Written tests are often used in combination with performance tests, ratings of training and experience, and oral interviews. All of these measures combine to form the best-known means of finding the right person for the right job.

II. HOW TO PASS THE WRITTEN TEST

A. NATURE OF THE EXAMINATION

To prepare intelligently for civil service examinations, you should know how they differ from school examinations you have taken. In school you were assigned certain definite pages to read or subjects to cover. The examination questions were quite detailed and usually emphasized memory. Civil service exams, on the other hand, try to discover your present ability to perform the duties of a position, plus your potentiality to learn these duties. In other words, a civil service exam attempts to predict how successful you will be. Questions cover such a broad area that they cannot be as minute and detailed as school exam questions.

In the public service similar kinds of work, or positions, are grouped together in one "class." This process is known as *position-classification*. All the positions in a class are paid according to the salary range for that class. One class title covers all of these positions, and they are all tested by the same examination.

B. FOUR BASIC STEPS

1) Study the announcement

How, then, can you know what subjects to study? Our best answer is: "Learn as much as possible about the class of positions for which you've applied." The exam will test the knowledge, skills and abilities needed to do the work.

Your most valuable source of information about the position you want is the official exam announcement. This announcement lists the training and experience qualifications. Check these standards and apply only if you come reasonably close to meeting them.

The brief description of the position in the examination announcement offers some clues to the subjects which will be tested. Think about the job itself. Review the duties in your mind. Can you perform them, or are there some in which you are rusty? Fill in the blank spots in your preparation.

Many jurisdictions preview the written test in the exam announcement by including a section called "Knowledge and Abilities Required," "Scope of the Examination," or some similar heading. Here you will find out specifically what fields will be tested.

2) Review your own background

Once you learn in general what the position is all about, and what you need to know to do the work, ask yourself which subjects you already know fairly well and which need improvement. You may wonder whether to concentrate on improving your strong areas or on building some background in your fields of weakness. When the announcement has specified "some knowledge" or "considerable knowledge," or has used adjectives like "beginning principles of…" or "advanced … methods," you can get a clue as to the number and difficulty of questions to be asked in any given field. More questions, and hence broader coverage, would be included for those subjects which are more important in the work. Now weigh your strengths and weaknesses against the job requirements and prepare accordingly.

3) Determine the level of the position

Another way to tell how intensively you should prepare is to understand the level of the job for which you are applying. Is it the entering level? In other words, is this the position in which beginners in a field of work are hired? Or is it an intermediate or advanced level? Sometimes this is indicated by such words as "Junior" or "Senior" in the class title. Other jurisdictions use Roman numerals to designate the level – Clerk I, Clerk II, for example. The word "Supervisor" sometimes appears in the title. If the level is not indicated by the title, check the description of duties. Will you be working under very close supervision, or will you have responsibility for independent decisions in this work?

4) Choose appropriate study materials

Now that you know the subjects to be examined and the relative amount of each subject to be covered, you can choose suitable study materials. For beginning level jobs, or even advanced ones, if you have a pronounced weakness in some aspect of your training, read a modern, standard textbook in that field. Be sure it is up to date and has general coverage. Such books are normally available at your library, and the librarian will be glad to help you locate one. For entry-level positions, questions of appropriate difficulty are chosen – neither highly advanced questions, nor those too simple. Such questions require careful thought but not advanced training.

If the position for which you are applying is technical or advanced, you will read more advanced, specialized material. If you are already familiar with the basic principles of your field, elementary textbooks would waste your time. Concentrate on advanced textbooks and technical periodicals. Think through the concepts and review difficult problems in your field.

These are all general sources. You can get more ideas on your own initiative, following these leads. For example, training manuals and publications of the government agency which employs workers in your field can be useful, particularly for technical and professional positions. A letter or visit to the government department involved may result in more specific study suggestions, and certainly will provide you with a more definite idea of the exact nature of the position you are seeking.

III. KINDS OF TESTS

Tests are used for purposes other than measuring knowledge and ability to perform specified duties. For some positions, it is equally important to test ability to make adjustments to new situations or to profit from training. In others, basic mental abilities not dependent on information are essential. Questions which test these things may not appear as pertinent to the duties of the position as those which test for knowledge and information. Yet they are often highly important parts of a fair examination. For very general questions, it is almost impossible to help you direct your study efforts. What we can do is to point out some of the more common of these general abilities needed in public service positions and describe some typical questions.

1) General information

Broad, general information has been found useful for predicting job success in some kinds of work. This is tested in a variety of ways, from vocabulary lists to questions about current events. Basic background in some field of work, such as sociology or economics, may be sampled in a group of questions. Often these are principles which have become familiar to most persons through exposure rather than through formal training. It is difficult to advise you how to study for these questions; being alert to the world around you is our best suggestion.

2) Verbal ability

An example of an ability needed in many positions is verbal or language ability. Verbal ability is, in brief, the ability to use and understand words. Vocabulary and grammar tests are typical measures of this ability. Reading comprehension or paragraph interpretation questions are common in many kinds of civil service tests. You are given a paragraph of written material and asked to find its central meaning.

3) Numerical ability

Number skills can be tested by the familiar arithmetic problem, by checking paired lists of numbers to see which are alike and which are different, or by interpreting charts and graphs. In the latter test, a graph may be printed in the test booklet which you are asked to use as the basis for answering questions.

4) Observation

A popular test for law-enforcement positions is the observation test. A picture is shown to you for several minutes, then taken away. Questions about the picture test your ability to observe both details and larger elements.

5) Following directions

In many positions in the public service, the employee must be able to carry out written instructions dependably and accurately. You may be given a chart with several columns, each column listing a variety of information. The questions require you to carry out directions involving the information given in the chart.

6) Skills and aptitudes

Performance tests effectively measure some manual skills and aptitudes. When the skill is one in which you are trained, such as typing or shorthand, you can practice. These tests are often very much like those given in business school or high school courses. For many of the other skills and aptitudes, however, no short-time preparation can be made. Skills and abilities natural to you or that you have developed throughout your lifetime are being tested.

Many of the general questions just described provide all the data needed to answer the questions and ask you to use your reasoning ability to find the answers. Your best preparation for these tests, as well as for tests of facts and ideas, is to be at your physical and mental best. You, no doubt, have your own methods of getting into an exam-taking mood and keeping "in shape." The next section lists some ideas on this subject.

IV. KINDS OF QUESTIONS

Only rarely is the "essay" question, which you answer in narrative form, used in civil service tests. Civil service tests are usually of the short-answer type. Full instructions for answering these questions will be given to you at the examination. But in case this is your first experience with short-answer questions and separate answer sheets, here is what you need to know:

1) Multiple-choice Questions

Most popular of the short-answer questions is the "multiple choice" or "best answer" question. It can be used, for example, to test for factual knowledge, ability to solve problems or judgment in meeting situations found at work.

A multiple-choice question is normally one of three types—
- It can begin with an incomplete statement followed by several possible endings. You are to find the one ending which *best* completes the statement, although some of the others may not be entirely wrong.
- It can also be a complete statement in the form of a question which is answered by choosing one of the statements listed.

- It can be in the form of a problem – again you select the best answer.

Here is an example of a multiple-choice question with a discussion which should give you some clues as to the method for choosing the right answer:

When an employee has a complaint about his assignment, the action which will *best* help him overcome his difficulty is to
    A. discuss his difficulty with his coworkers
    B. take the problem to the head of the organization
    C. take the problem to the person who gave him the assignment
    D. say nothing to anyone about his complaint

In answering this question, you should study each of the choices to find which is best. Consider choice "A" – Certainly an employee may discuss his complaint with fellow employees, but no change or improvement can result, and the complaint remains unresolved. Choice "B" is a poor choice since the head of the organization probably does not know what assignment you have been given, and taking your problem to him is known as "going over the head" of the supervisor. The supervisor, or person who made the assignment, is the person who can clarify it or correct any injustice. Choice "C" is, therefore, correct. To say nothing, as in choice "D," is unwise. Supervisors have and interest in knowing the problems employees are facing, and the employee is seeking a solution to his problem.

2) True/False Questions

The "true/false" or "right/wrong" form of question is sometimes used. Here a complete statement is given. Your job is to decide whether the statement is right or wrong.

SAMPLE: A roaming cell-phone call to a nearby city costs less than a non-roaming call to a distant city.

This statement is wrong, or false, since roaming calls are more expensive.

This is not a complete list of all possible question forms, although most of the others are variations of these common types. You will always get complete directions for answering questions. Be sure you understand *how* to mark your answers – ask questions until you do.

V. RECORDING YOUR ANSWERS

Computer terminals are used more and more today for many different kinds of exams.

For an examination with very few applicants, you may be told to record your answers in the test booklet itself. Separate answer sheets are much more common. If this separate answer sheet is to be scored by machine – and this is often the case – it is highly important that you mark your answers correctly in order to get credit.

An electronic scoring machine is often used in civil service offices because of the speed with which papers can be scored. Machine-scored answer sheets must be marked with a pencil, which will be given to you. This pencil has a high graphite content which responds to the electronic scoring machine. As a matter of fact, stray dots may register as answers, so do not let your pencil rest on the answer sheet while you are pondering the correct answer. Also, if your pencil lead breaks or is otherwise defective, ask for another.

Since the answer sheet will be dropped in a slot in the scoring machine, be careful not to bend the corners or get the paper crumpled.

The answer sheet normally has five vertical columns of numbers, with 30 numbers to a column. These numbers correspond to the question numbers in your test booklet. After each number, going across the page are four or five pairs of dotted lines. These short dotted lines have small letters or numbers above them. The first two pairs may also have a "T" or "F" above the letters. This indicates that the first two pairs only are to be used if the questions are of the true-false type. If the questions are multiple choice, disregard the "T" and "F" and pay attention only to the small letters or numbers.

Answer your questions in the manner of the sample that follows:

32. The largest city in the United States is
    A. Washington, D.C.
    B. New York City
    C. Chicago
    D. Detroit
    E. San Francisco

1) Choose the answer you think is best. (New York City is the largest, so "B" is correct.)
2) Find the row of dotted lines numbered the same as the question you are answering. (Find row number 32)
3) Find the pair of dotted lines corresponding to the answer. (Find the pair of lines under the mark "B.")
4) Make a solid black mark between the dotted lines.

VI. BEFORE THE TEST

Common sense will help you find procedures to follow to get ready for an examination. Too many of us, however, overlook these sensible measures. Indeed, nervousness and fatigue have been found to be the most serious reasons why applicants fail to do their best on civil service tests. Here is a list of reminders:

- Begin your preparation early – Don't wait until the last minute to go scurrying around for books and materials or to find out what the position is all about.
- Prepare continuously – An hour a night for a week is better than an all-night cram session. This has been definitely established. What is more, a night a week for a month will return better dividends than crowding your study into a shorter period of time.
- Locate the place of the exam – You have been sent a notice telling you when and where to report for the examination. If the location is in a different town or otherwise unfamiliar to you, it would be well to inquire the best route and learn something about the building.
- Relax the night before the test – Allow your mind to rest. Do not study at all that night. Plan some mild recreation or diversion; then go to bed early and get a good night's sleep.
- Get up early enough to make a leisurely trip to the place for the test – This way unforeseen events, traffic snarls, unfamiliar buildings, etc. will not upset you.
- Dress comfortably – A written test is not a fashion show. You will be known by number and not by name, so wear something comfortable.

- Leave excess paraphernalia at home – Shopping bags and odd bundles will get in your way. You need bring only the items mentioned in the official notice you received; usually everything you need is provided. Do not bring reference books to the exam. They will only confuse those last minutes and be taken away from you when in the test room.
- Arrive somewhat ahead of time – If because of transportation schedules you must get there very early, bring a newspaper or magazine to take your mind off yourself while waiting.
- Locate the examination room – When you have found the proper room, you will be directed to the seat or part of the room where you will sit. Sometimes you are given a sheet of instructions to read while you are waiting. Do not fill out any forms until you are told to do so; just read them and be prepared.
- Relax and prepare to listen to the instructions
- If you have any physical problem that may keep you from doing your best, be sure to tell the test administrator. If you are sick or in poor health, you really cannot do your best on the exam. You can come back and take the test some other time.

VII. AT THE TEST

The day of the test is here and you have the test booklet in your hand. The temptation to get going is very strong. Caution! There is more to success than knowing the right answers. You must know how to identify your papers and understand variations in the type of short-answer question used in this particular examination. Follow these suggestions for maximum results from your efforts:

1) Cooperate with the monitor

The test administrator has a duty to create a situation in which you can be as much at ease as possible. He will give instructions, tell you when to begin, check to see that you are marking your answer sheet correctly, and so on. He is not there to guard you, although he will see that your competitors do not take unfair advantage. He wants to help you do your best.

2) Listen to all instructions

Don't jump the gun! Wait until you understand all directions. In most civil service tests you get more time than you need to answer the questions. So don't be in a hurry. Read each word of instructions until you clearly understand the meaning. Study the examples, listen to all announcements and follow directions. Ask questions if you do not understand what to do.

3) Identify your papers

Civil service exams are usually identified by number only. You will be assigned a number; you must not put your name on your test papers. Be sure to copy your number correctly. Since more than one exam may be given, copy your exact examination title.

4) Plan your time

Unless you are told that a test is a "speed" or "rate of work" test, speed itself is usually not important. Time enough to answer all the questions will be provided, but this does not mean that you have all day. An overall time limit has been set. Divide the total time (in minutes) by the number of questions to determine the approximate time you have for each question.

5) **Do not linger over difficult questions**

If you come across a difficult question, mark it with a paper clip (useful to have along) and come back to it when you have been through the booklet. One caution if you do this – be sure to skip a number on your answer sheet as well. Check often to be sure that you have not lost your place and that you are marking in the row numbered the same as the question you are answering.

6) **Read the questions**

Be sure you know what the question asks! Many capable people are unsuccessful because they failed to *read* the questions correctly.

7) **Answer all questions**

Unless you have been instructed that a penalty will be deducted for incorrect answers, it is better to guess than to omit a question.

8) **Speed tests**

It is often better NOT to guess on speed tests. It has been found that on timed tests people are tempted to spend the last few seconds before time is called in marking answers at random – without even reading them – in the hope of picking up a few extra points. To discourage this practice, the instructions may warn you that your score will be "corrected" for guessing. That is, a penalty will be applied. The incorrect answers will be deducted from the correct ones, or some other penalty formula will be used.

9) **Review your answers**

If you finish before time is called, go back to the questions you guessed or omitted to give them further thought. Review other answers if you have time.

10) **Return your test materials**

If you are ready to leave before others have finished or time is called, take ALL your materials to the monitor and leave quietly. Never take any test material with you. The monitor can discover whose papers are not complete, and taking a test booklet may be grounds for disqualification.

VIII. EXAMINATION TECHNIQUES

1) Read the general instructions carefully. These are usually printed on the first page of the exam booklet. As a rule, these instructions refer to the timing of the examination; the fact that you should not start work until the signal and must stop work at a signal, etc. If there are any *special* instructions, such as a choice of questions to be answered, make sure that you note this instruction carefully.

2) When you are ready to start work on the examination, that is as soon as the signal has been given, read the instructions to each question booklet, underline any key words or phrases, such as *least, best, outline, describe* and the like. In this way you will tend to answer as requested rather than discover on reviewing your paper that you *listed without describing*, that you selected the *worst* choice rather than the *best* choice, etc.

3) If the examination is of the objective or multiple-choice type – that is, each question will also give a series of possible answers: A, B, C or D, and you are called upon to select the best answer and write the letter next to that answer on your answer paper – it is advisable to start answering each question in turn. There may be anywhere from 50 to 100 such questions in the three or four hours allotted and you can see how much time would be taken if you read through all the questions before beginning to answer any. Furthermore, if you come across a question or group of questions which you know would be difficult to answer, it would undoubtedly affect your handling of all the other questions.

4) If the examination is of the essay type and contains but a few questions, it is a moot point as to whether you should read all the questions before starting to answer any one. Of course, if you are given a choice – say five out of seven and the like – then it is essential to read all the questions so you can eliminate the two that are most difficult. If, however, you are asked to answer all the questions, there may be danger in trying to answer the easiest one first because you may find that you will spend too much time on it. The best technique is to answer the first question, then proceed to the second, etc.

5) Time your answers. Before the exam begins, write down the time it started, then add the time allowed for the examination and write down the time it must be completed, then divide the time available somewhat as follows:
    - If 3-1/2 hours are allowed, that would be 210 minutes. If you have 80 objective-type questions, that would be an average of 2-1/2 minutes per question. Allow yourself no more than 2 minutes per question, or a total of 160 minutes, which will permit about 50 minutes to review.
    - If for the time allotment of 210 minutes there are 7 essay questions to answer, that would average about 30 minutes a question. Give yourself only 25 minutes per question so that you have about 35 minutes to review.

6) The most important instruction is to *read each question* and make sure you know what is wanted. The second most important instruction is to *time yourself properly* so that you answer every question. The third most important instruction is to *answer every question*. Guess if you have to but include something for each question. Remember that you will receive no credit for a blank and will probably receive some credit if you write something in answer to an essay question. If you guess a letter – say "B" for a multiple-choice question – you may have guessed right. If you leave a blank as an answer to a multiple-choice question, the examiners may respect your feelings but it will not add a point to your score. Some exams may penalize you for wrong answers, so in such cases *only*, you may not want to guess unless you have some basis for your answer.

7) Suggestions
    a. Objective-type questions
        1. Examine the question booklet for proper sequence of pages and questions
        2. Read all instructions carefully
        3. Skip any question which seems too difficult; return to it after all other questions have been answered
        4. Apportion your time properly; do not spend too much time on any single question or group of questions

5. Note and underline key words – *all, most, fewest, least, best, worst, same, opposite*, etc.
6. Pay particular attention to negatives
7. Note unusual option, e.g., unduly long, short, complex, different or similar in content to the body of the question
8. Observe the use of "hedging" words – *probably, may, most likely*, etc.
9. Make sure that your answer is put next to the same number as the question
10. Do not second-guess unless you have good reason to believe the second answer is definitely more correct
11. Cross out original answer if you decide another answer is more accurate; do not erase until you are ready to hand your paper in
12. Answer all questions; guess unless instructed otherwise
13. Leave time for review

b. Essay questions
 1. Read each question carefully
 2. Determine exactly what is wanted. Underline key words or phrases.
 3. Decide on outline or paragraph answer
 4. Include many different points and elements unless asked to develop any one or two points or elements
 5. Show impartiality by giving pros and cons unless directed to select one side only
 6. Make and write down any assumptions you find necessary to answer the questions
 7. Watch your English, grammar, punctuation and choice of words
 8. Time your answers; don't crowd material

8) Answering the essay question

Most essay questions can be answered by framing the specific response around several key words or ideas. Here are a few such key words or ideas:

M's: manpower, materials, methods, money, management
P's: purpose, program, policy, plan, procedure, practice, problems, pitfalls, personnel, public relations

a. Six basic steps in handling problems:
 1. Preliminary plan and background development
 2. Collect information, data and facts
 3. Analyze and interpret information, data and facts
 4. Analyze and develop solutions as well as make recommendations
 5. Prepare report and sell recommendations
 6. Install recommendations and follow up effectiveness

b. Pitfalls to avoid
 1. *Taking things for granted* – A statement of the situation does not necessarily imply that each of the elements is necessarily true; for example, a complaint may be invalid and biased so that all that can be taken for granted is that a complaint has been registered

2. *Considering only one side of a situation* – Wherever possible, indicate several alternatives and then point out the reasons you selected the best one
3. *Failing to indicate follow up* – Whenever your answer indicates action on your part, make certain that you will take proper follow-up action to see how successful your recommendations, procedures or actions turn out to be
4. *Taking too long in answering any single question* – Remember to time your answers properly

IX. AFTER THE TEST

Scoring procedures differ in detail among civil service jurisdictions although the general principles are the same. Whether the papers are hand-scored or graded by machine we have described, they are nearly always graded by number. That is, the person who marks the paper knows only the number – never the name – of the applicant. Not until all the papers have been graded will they be matched with names. If other tests, such as training and experience or oral interview ratings have been given, scores will be combined. Different parts of the examination usually have different weights. For example, the written test might count 60 percent of the final grade, and a rating of training and experience 40 percent. In many jurisdictions, veterans will have a certain number of points added to their grades.

After the final grade has been determined, the names are placed in grade order and an eligible list is established. There are various methods for resolving ties between those who get the same final grade – probably the most common is to place first the name of the person whose application was received first. Job offers are made from the eligible list in the order the names appear on it. You will be notified of your grade and your rank as soon as all these computations have been made. This will be done as rapidly as possible.

People who are found to meet the requirements in the announcement are called "eligibles." Their names are put on a list of eligible candidates. An eligible's chances of getting a job depend on how high he stands on this list and how fast agencies are filling jobs from the list.

When a job is to be filled from a list of eligibles, the agency asks for the names of people on the list of eligibles for that job. When the civil service commission receives this request, it sends to the agency the names of the three people highest on this list. Or, if the job to be filled has specialized requirements, the office sends the agency the names of the top three persons who meet these requirements from the general list.

The appointing officer makes a choice from among the three people whose names were sent to him. If the selected person accepts the appointment, the names of the others are put back on the list to be considered for future openings.

That is the rule in hiring from all kinds of eligible lists, whether they are for typist, carpenter, chemist, or something else. For every vacancy, the appointing officer has his choice of any one of the top three eligibles on the list. This explains why the person whose name is on top of the list sometimes does not get an appointment when some of the persons lower on the list do. If the appointing officer chooses the second or third eligible, the No. 1 eligible does not get a job at once, but stays on the list until he is appointed or the list is terminated.

X. HOW TO PASS THE INTERVIEW TEST

The examination for which you applied requires an oral interview test. You have already taken the written test and you are now being called for the interview test – the final part of the formal examination.

You may think that it is not possible to prepare for an interview test and that there are no procedures to follow during an interview. Our purpose is to point out some things you can do in advance that will help you and some good rules to follow and pitfalls to avoid while you are being interviewed.

What is an interview supposed to test?

The written examination is designed to test the technical knowledge and competence of the candidate; the oral is designed to evaluate intangible qualities, not readily measured otherwise, and to establish a list showing the relative fitness of each candidate – as measured against his competitors – for the position sought. Scoring is not on the basis of "right" and "wrong," but on a sliding scale of values ranging from "not passable" to "outstanding." As a matter of fact, it is possible to achieve a relatively low score without a single "incorrect" answer because of evident weakness in the qualities being measured.

Occasionally, an examination may consist entirely of an oral test – either an individual or a group oral. In such cases, information is sought concerning the technical knowledges and abilities of the candidate, since there has been no written examination for this purpose. More commonly, however, an oral test is used to supplement a written examination.

Who conducts interviews?

The composition of oral boards varies among different jurisdictions. In nearly all, a representative of the personnel department serves as chairman. One of the members of the board may be a representative of the department in which the candidate would work. In some cases, "outside experts" are used, and, frequently, a businessman or some other representative of the general public is asked to serve. Labor and management or other special groups may be represented. The aim is to secure the services of experts in the appropriate field.

However the board is composed, it is a good idea (and not at all improper or unethical) to ascertain in advance of the interview who the members are and what groups they represent. When you are introduced to them, you will have some idea of their backgrounds and interests, and at least you will not stutter and stammer over their names.

What should be done before the interview?

While knowledge about the board members is useful and takes some of the surprise element out of the interview, there is other preparation which is more substantive. It *is* possible to prepare for an oral interview – in several ways:

1) Keep a copy of your application and review it carefully before the interview

This may be the only document before the oral board, and the starting point of the interview. Know what education and experience you have listed there, and the sequence and dates of all of it. Sometimes the board will ask you to review the highlights of your experience for them; you should not have to hem and haw doing it.

2) Study the class specification and the examination announcement

Usually, the oral board has one or both of these to guide them. The qualities, characteristics or knowledges required by the position sought are stated in these documents. They offer valuable clues as to the nature of the oral interview. For example, if the job involves supervisory responsibilities, the announcement will usually indicate that knowledge of modern supervisory methods and the qualifications of the candidate as a supervisor will be tested. If so, you can expect such questions, frequently in the form of a hypothetical situation which you are expected to solve. NEVER go into an oral without knowledge of the duties and responsibilities of the job you seek.

3) Think through each qualification required

Try to visualize the kind of questions you would ask if you were a board member. How well could you answer them? Try especially to appraise your own knowledge and background in each area, *measured against the job sought*, and identify any areas in which you are weak. Be critical and realistic – do not flatter yourself.

4) Do some general reading in areas in which you feel you may be weak

For example, if the job involves supervision and your past experience has NOT, some general reading in supervisory methods and practices, particularly in the field of human relations, might be useful. Do NOT study agency procedures or detailed manuals. The oral board will be testing your understanding and capacity, not your memory.

5) Get a good night's sleep and watch your general health and mental attitude

You will want a clear head at the interview. Take care of a cold or any other minor ailment, and of course, no hangovers.

What should be done on the day of the interview?

Now comes the day of the interview itself. Give yourself plenty of time to get there. Plan to arrive somewhat ahead of the scheduled time, particularly if your appointment is in the fore part of the day. If a previous candidate fails to appear, the board might be ready for you a bit early. By early afternoon an oral board is almost invariably behind schedule if there are many candidates, and you may have to wait. Take along a book or magazine to read, or your application to review, but leave any extraneous material in the waiting room when you go in for your interview. In any event, relax and compose yourself.

The matter of dress is important. The board is forming impressions about you – from your experience, your manners, your attitude, and your appearance. Give your personal appearance careful attention. Dress your best, but not your flashiest. Choose conservative, appropriate clothing, and be sure it is immaculate. This is a business interview, and your appearance should indicate that you regard it as such. Besides, being well groomed and properly dressed will help boost your confidence.

Sooner or later, someone will call your name and escort you into the interview room. *This is it.* From here on you are on your own. It is too late for any more preparation. But remember, you asked for this opportunity to prove your fitness, and you are here because your request was granted.

What happens when you go in?

The usual sequence of events will be as follows: The clerk (who is often the board stenographer) will introduce you to the chairman of the oral board, who will introduce you to the other members of the board. Acknowledge the introductions before you sit down. Do not be surprised if you find a microphone facing you or a stenotypist sitting by. Oral interviews are usually recorded in the event of an appeal or other review.

Usually the chairman of the board will open the interview by reviewing the highlights of your education and work experience from your application – primarily for the benefit of the other members of the board, as well as to get the material into the record. Do not interrupt or comment unless there is an error or significant misinterpretation; if that is the case, do not hesitate. But do not quibble about insignificant matters. Also, he will usually ask you some question about your education, experience or your present job – partly to get you to start talking and to establish the interviewing "rapport." He may start the actual questioning, or turn it over to one of the other members. Frequently, each member undertakes the questioning on a particular area, one in which he is perhaps most competent, so you can expect each member to participate in the examination. Because time is limited, you may also expect some rather abrupt switches in the direction the questioning takes, so do not be upset by it. Normally, a board member will not pursue a single line of questioning unless he discovers a particular strength or weakness.

After each member has participated, the chairman will usually ask whether any member has any further questions, then will ask you if you have anything you wish to add. Unless you are expecting this question, it may floor you. Worse, it may start you off on an extended, extemporaneous speech. The board is not usually seeking more information. The question is principally to offer you a last opportunity to present further qualifications or to indicate that you have nothing to add. So, if you feel that a significant qualification or characteristic has been overlooked, it is proper to point it out in a sentence or so. Do not compliment the board on the thoroughness of their examination – they have been sketchy, and you know it. If you wish, merely say, "No thank you, I have nothing further to add." This is a point where you can "talk yourself out" of a good impression or fail to present an important bit of information. Remember, *you close the interview yourself*.

The chairman will then say, "That is all, Mr. _____, thank you." Do not be startled; the interview is over, and quicker than you think. Thank him, gather your belongings and take your leave. Save your sigh of relief for the other side of the door.

How to put your best foot forward

Throughout this entire process, you may feel that the board individually and collectively is trying to pierce your defenses, seek out your hidden weaknesses and embarrass and confuse you. Actually, this is not true. They are obliged to make an appraisal of your qualifications for the job you are seeking, and they want to see you in your best light. Remember, they must interview all candidates and a non-cooperative candidate may become a failure in spite of their best efforts to bring out his qualifications. Here are 15 suggestions that will help you:

1) Be natural – Keep your attitude confident, not cocky

If you are not confident that you can do the job, do not expect the board to be. Do not apologize for your weaknesses, try to bring out your strong points. The board is interested in a positive, not negative, presentation. Cockiness will antagonize any board member and make him wonder if you are covering up a weakness by a false show of strength.

2) Get comfortable, but don't lounge or sprawl

Sit erectly but not stiffly. A careless posture may lead the board to conclude that you are careless in other things, or at least that you are not impressed by the importance of the occasion. Either conclusion is natural, even if incorrect. Do not fuss with your clothing, a pencil or an ashtray. Your hands may occasionally be useful to emphasize a point; do not let them become a point of distraction.

3) Do not wisecrack or make small talk

This is a serious situation, and your attitude should show that you consider it as such. Further, the time of the board is limited – they do not want to waste it, and neither should you.

4) Do not exaggerate your experience or abilities
In the first place, from information in the application or other interviews and sources, the board may know more about you than you think. Secondly, you probably will not get away with it. An experienced board is rather adept at spotting such a situation, so do not take the chance.

5) If you know a board member, do not make a point of it, yet do not hide it
Certainly you are not fooling him, and probably not the other members of the board. Do not try to take advantage of your acquaintanceship – it will probably do you little good.

6) Do not dominate the interview
Let the board do that. They will give you the clues – do not assume that you have to do all the talking. Realize that the board has a number of questions to ask you, and do not try to take up all the interview time by showing off your extensive knowledge of the answer to the first one.

7) Be attentive
You only have 20 minutes or so, and you should keep your attention at its sharpest throughout. When a member is addressing a problem or question to you, give him your undivided attention. Address your reply principally to him, but do not exclude the other board members.

8) Do not interrupt
A board member may be stating a problem for you to analyze. He will ask you a question when the time comes. Let him state the problem, and wait for the question.

9) Make sure you understand the question
Do not try to answer until you are sure what the question is. If it is not clear, restate it in your own words or ask the board member to clarify it for you. However, do not haggle about minor elements.

10) Reply promptly but not hastily
A common entry on oral board rating sheets is "candidate responded readily," or "candidate hesitated in replies." Respond as promptly and quickly as you can, but do not jump to a hasty, ill-considered answer.

11) Do not be peremptory in your answers
A brief answer is proper – but do not fire your answer back. That is a losing game from your point of view. The board member can probably ask questions much faster than you can answer them.

12) Do not try to create the answer you think the board member wants
He is interested in what kind of mind you have and how it works – not in playing games. Furthermore, he can usually spot this practice and will actually grade you down on it.

13) Do not switch sides in your reply merely to agree with a board member
Frequently, a member will take a contrary position merely to draw you out and to see if you are willing and able to defend your point of view. Do not start a debate, yet do not surrender a good position. If a position is worth taking, it is worth defending.

14) Do not be afraid to admit an error in judgment if you are shown to be wrong

The board knows that you are forced to reply without any opportunity for careful consideration. Your answer may be demonstrably wrong. If so, admit it and get on with the interview.

15) Do not dwell at length on your present job

The opening question may relate to your present assignment. Answer the question but do not go into an extended discussion. You are being examined for a *new* job, not your present one. As a matter of fact, try to phrase ALL your answers in terms of the job for which you are being examined.

Basis of Rating

Probably you will forget most of these "do's" and "don'ts" when you walk into the oral interview room. Even remembering them all will not ensure you a passing grade. Perhaps you did not have the qualifications in the first place. But remembering them will help you to put your best foot forward, without treading on the toes of the board members.

Rumor and popular opinion to the contrary notwithstanding, an oral board wants you to make the best appearance possible. They know you are under pressure – but they also want to see how you respond to it as a guide to what your reaction would be under the pressures of the job you seek. They will be influenced by the degree of poise you display, the personal traits you show and the manner in which you respond.

ABOUT THIS BOOK

This book contains tests divided into Examination Sections. Go through each test, answering every question in the margin. We have also attached a sample answer sheet at the back of the book that can be removed and used. At the end of each test look at the answer key and check your answers. On the ones you got wrong, look at the right answer choice and learn. Do not fill in the answers first. Do not memorize the questions and answers, but understand the answer and principles involved. On your test, the questions will likely be different from the samples. Questions are changed and new ones added. If you understand these past questions you should have success with any changes that arise. Tests may consist of several types of questions. We have additional books on each subject should more study be advisable or necessary for you. Finally, the more you study, the better prepared you will be. This book is intended to be the last thing you study before you walk into the examination room. Prior study of relevant texts is also recommended. NLC publishes some of these in our Fundamental Series. Knowledge and good sense are important factors in passing your exam. Good luck also helps. So now study this Passbook, absorb the material contained within and take that knowledge into the examination. Then do your best to pass that exam.

EXAMINATION SECTION

EXAMINATION SECTION
TEST 1

DIRECTIONS: Each question or incomplete statement is followed by several suggested answers or completions. Select the one that BEST answers the question or completes the statement. *PRINT THE LETTER OF THE CORRECT ANSWER IN THE SPACE AT THE RIGHT.*

1. The one of the following which BEST characterizes an agency in which delegation of authority is practiced on an organization-wide level is that the agency is
   A. autocratic
   B. authoritarian
   C. centralized
   D. decentralized

2. The concept of the *chain of command* is MOST similar to which one of the following concepts?
   A. Span of control
   B. Matrix or task-force organization
   C. Scalar principle
   D. Functional departmentation

3. The one of the following techniques which is NOT conducive to the establishment of an effective working relationship between employees and supervisors is
   A. periodic discussion of job performance with employees
   B. listening to employees when they discuss their job difficulties
   C. observation of employees on the job, in both individual and group situations, in order to help them with job performance
   D. treating all employees the same with respect to job performance and individual behavior

4. Which of the following is a valid, commonly-raised objection to the establishment of work standards for office clerical workers?
   A. Routine clerical work is not subject to accurate measurement.
   B. Clerical work standards can only lower employee morale by creating undue pressure to produce work rapidly.
   C. Work standards are not effective tools for planning, scheduling, and routing clerical work.
   D. Some phases of many clerical jobs, such as telephone answering or information gathering, cannot be readily or accurately measured.

5. Of the following, the feature which is LEAST characteristic of almost all successful staff relationships with line managers is that the staff employee
   A. is primarily a representative of his supervisor
   B. receives a salary at least equal to the average salary of his supervisor's direct line subordinates
   C. relies largely on persuasion to get his ideas put into effect
   D. is prepared to submerge his own personality and his own desire for recognition and see others often receive more recognition than he receives

6. The one of the following systems which has, as its principal objective, the storage of items in files so that they may be readily found when needed is called
   A. information retrieval
   B. simulation
   C. critical path
   D. PERT

6.____

7. A detailed description of the steps to be taken in order to accomplish a job is MOST appropriately called a
   A. policy
   B. rule
   C. procedure
   D. principle

7.____

8. In choosing the best place in the executive hierarchy to which to assign the task of making a certain type of decision, which one of the following should normally be LEAST important?
   A. Who knows the facts on which the decision will be based, or who can obtain them most readily?
   B. Who has the most adequate supply of current forms on which the decision is normally recorded?
   C. Who has the capacity to make sound decisions?
   D. How significant is the decision?

8.____

9. Of the following, the action which is LEAST likely to be either expressed or implied every time a manager delegates work to a subordinate is that the manager
   A. creates a need for a new class of positions
   B. indicates what work the subordinate is to do
   C. grants the subordinate some authority
   D. creates an obligation for the subordinate who accepts the work to try to complete it

9.____

10. Of the following, the LEAST appropriate use of organizational charts is to
    A. depict standard operating procedures
    B. indicate lines of responsibility
    C. indicate the relative level of key positions
    D. portray organizations graphically

10.____

11. The one of the following considerations which is generally LEAST important in deciding whether to automate a management operation by using a computer is whether the computer
    A. possesses a suitable array of programmed actions that might be taken
    B. can draw upon available data for information as to which alternative is best
    C. is already familiar to the staff of the organization
    D. can issue findings in a way that will facilitate the decision-making process

11.____

12. In evaluating a proposal to establish a library in your agency, it is generally considered LEAST necessary to determine
    A. the average time staff members spend on preparatory research when assigned to projects
    B. how often junior professional and technical staff members are sent out to *look something up* in a local library
    C. how much time and money agency executives devote to telephoning around the country seeking information before making decisions
    D. the quality of the research done by executives and scientists in the agency

12.____

13. In determining the number and type of tasks that should be combined into a single job, the one of the following which is normally the LEAST useful factor to consider is the
    A. benefit of functional specialization
    B. benefit of tall pyramid organization structures in increasing decentralization
    C. need for coordination of tasks with each other
    D. effect of the tasks assigned on the morale of the employee

13.____

14. Of the following, the one which is LEAST likely to be an objective of systems and procedures analysis is to
    A. eliminate as many unessential forms and records as feasible
    B. simplify forms in content and method of preparation
    C. mechanize repetitive, routine tasks
    D. expand as many of the forms as possible

14.____

15. A specific managerial function encompasses all of the following: The establishment of an intentional structure of roles through determination and enumeration of the activities required to achieve the goals of an enterprise and each part of it, the grouping of these activities, the assignment of such groups of activities to a manager, the delegation of authority to carry them out, and provision for coordination of authority and informational relationships horizontally and vertically in the organization structure.
    Of the following, the MOST appropriate term for this entire managerial function is
    A. organizing   B. directing   C. controlling   D. staffing

15.____

16. The optimum number of subordinates that a supervisor can supervise effectively generally tends to vary INVERSELY with the
    A. percentage of the supervisor's time devoted to supervision rather than operations
    B. repetition of activities
    C. degree of centralization of decision-making within the supervisor's unit
    D. ability of subordinates

16.____

17. Under certain circumstances, a top manager may desire to strengthen the position of his staff people by granting them concurring authority, so that no action may be taken in a functional area by subordinate line officials until a designated staff employee agrees to the action. For example, office manages may have to get the approval of the agency personnel officer before hiring a new employee.
    This approach is likely to be MOST valid under which one of the following conditions?
    A. The top manager refrains from indicating the grounds on which the staff employee may grant or withhold his approval of line proposals.
    B. The point of view represented by the staff employee is particularly important, and the possible delay in action will not be serious.
    C. It is more important to fix specific accountability for failure to take appropriate action than for wrong actions taken.
    D. The top manager gives speed priority over prudence.

17._____

18. The inclusion of the reason why a superior in his written orders to his subordinates normally is MOST likely to
    A. encourage belief by the subordinates in the meaning and intent of the order
    B. be a waste of valuable time for both superior and subordinates
    C. be useful principally where the superior has no power to enforce the order
    D. discourage effective two-way communication between superior and subordinates

18._____

19. The one of the following which is generally LEAST justification for an administrator's search for alternative methods of attaining a given objective of the unit he heads is that such search
    A. always turns up a better method of attaining objectives than that currently in use
    B. helps to make certain that the best method has a chance to be found and evaluated
    C. helps to insure that his peers realize that the existing method of attaining the objective is not the best
    D. is a good way to train the unit's staff in the organization's operational procedures

19._____

20. *Managing-by-Objectives* tends to place PRINCIPAL emphasis upon which of the following?
    A. Use of primarily qualitative goals at all management levels
    B. Use of trait-appraisal systems based upon personality factors
    C. Use of primarily qualitative goals at lower management levels as contrasted with primarily quantitative goals at higher management levels
    D. Goals which are clear and verifiable

20._____

21. Which one of the following BEST identifies the two most important considerations which generally should determine the degree of management decentralization desirable in a given situation? The
    A. age of the subordinate executives to whom decisions may be delegated and the number of courses in management that they have completed
    B. number of skills and the competence possessed by subordinate executives and the distribution of the necessary information to the points of decision
    C. ratio of the salary of the superior executives to the salary of the subordinate executives and the number of titles on the executive staff
    D. number of titles in the executive staff and the distribution of information to those various titles

22. Which one of the following is generally LEAST likely to occur at mid-level management as a result of installing an electronic data processing system?
    A. The time that managers will be required to spend on the controlling function will increase.
    B. The number of contacts that managers will have with subordinates will increase.
    C. Additional time will be needed to train people for managerial positions.
    D. There will be an increase in the volume of information presented to managers for analysis.

23. The concept that the major source of managerial authority is derived from the subordinate's acceptance of the manager's power is MOST closely identified with
    A. Luther Gulick
    B. John D. Mooney
    C. Frederick W. Taylor
    D. Chester I. Barnard

24. The one of the following which is generally the principal objection to a pure *functional organization*, as compared with a pure *line organization*, is that
    A. there is a tendency to overload intermediate and supervisory management at each succeeding level of organization with wide and varied duties
    B. authority flows in an unbroken line from top management to the worker
    C. workers must often report to two or more supervisors
    D. there is a lack of specialization at the supervisory level

25. The appraisal of subordinates and their performance is an integral part of the supervisor's job. There is wide agreement that several basic principles must be taken into account by supervisors involved in the appraisal process in order to perform this function correctly.
    The one of the following statements which LEAST represents a basic principle of the appraisal process is:
    Appraisal(s)
    A. should be based more on performance of definite tasks than on personality considerations
    B. of long-range potential should rely most heavily on subjective judgment of that potential

C. involves the use of value judgments by the supervisor and does, therefore, require reference to pre-established standards
D. should aim at emphasizing subordinates' strengths rather than weaknesses

26. Of the following, the INITIAL step in the decision-making procedure normally is
    A. evaluation of alternatives
    B. implementing the chosen course of action
    C. listing potential solutions
    D. diagnosis and problem definition

26.____

27. Management textbooks are LEAST likely to define coordination as
    A. a concern for harmonious and unified action directed toward a common objective
    B. the essence of management, since the basic purpose of management is the achievement of harmony of individual effort toward the accomplishment of group goals
    C. the orderly arrangement of group effort to provide unity of action in pursuit of common purpose
    D. the transmittal of messages from senders to receivers, involving acts of persuasion of regulation, or simply the rendering of information

27.____

28. A number of important assumptions underlie the modern human relations approach to management and administration.
The one of the following which is NOT an assumption integral to the human relations school of thought is that
    A. employee participation is essential to higher productivity
    B. employees are motivated solely by monetary factors
    C. teamwork is indispensable for organization growth and survival
    D. free-flow communications must be established and maintained for organizational effectiveness

28.____

29. Of the following, the MAIN purpose of systematic manpower planning is to
    A. analyze the levels of skill needed by each worker
    B. analyze causes of current vacancies, such as resignations, discharges, retirements, transfers, or promotions
    C. save money by eliminating useless jobs
    D. provide for the continuous and proper staffing of the workforce

29.____

30. A Planning-Programming-Budget System (PPBS) is PRIMARILY intended to do which of the following?
    A. Improve control through a budgeting-by-line-item system
    B. Plan and program budgets by objective rather than by function
    C. Raise money for social welfare programs
    D. Reduce budgets by planning and programming unspent funds

30.____

KEY (CORRECT ANSWERS)

1.	D	11.	C	21.	B
2.	C	12.	D	22.	A
3.	D	13.	B	23.	D
4.	D	14.	D	24.	C
5.	B	15.	A	25.	B
6.	A	16.	C	26.	D
7.	C	17.	B	27.	D
8.	B	18.	A	28.	B
9.	A	19.	B	29.	D
10.	A	20.	D	30.	B

TEST 2

DIRECTIONS: Each question or incomplete statement is followed by several suggested answers or completions. Select the one that BEST answers the question or completes the statement. *PRINT THE LETTER OF THE CORRECT ANSWER IN THE SPACE AT THE RIGHT.*

1. An administrative office is designed so that several administrative associates can log on to Microsoft Outlook and use an e-mail inbox that syncs in real time. Each associate can also send jobs to a central office printer. This is an example of
   A. network connectivity
   B. cloud connectivity
   C. office integration
   D. employee training

   1.____

2. In the planning of office space for the various bureaus and divisions of an agency, the one of the following arrangements which is generally considered to be MOST desirable in a conventional layout is to
   A. locate offices where employees do close and tedious work, such as accounting, and also offices of high-level executives away from windows so that distractions will be minimal
   B. locate *housekeeping* offices such as data processing and the mailroom very close to the high executive offices to increase convenience for the executives
   C. locate departments so that the work flow proceeds in an uninterrupted manner
   D. centralize the executive suite for maximum availability and public exposure

   2.____

3. Generally, the one of the following that is LEAST likely to be an essential step in a records retention plan is
   A. storing inactive records
   B. checking for accuracy of all records to be retained
   C. classification of all records
   D. making an inventory of all agency records

   3.____

4. The PRINCIPAL asset of an office layout diagram, as contrasted with the more abstract organization charts and flowcharts, is that an office layout diagram is
   A. more readily adaptable to strictly conceptual studies
   B. pictorial and therefore easier to understand
   C. suitable for showing both manual and machine processing operations, whereas organization charts and flowcharts may only be used for manual processing operations
   D. better suited for summarizing the number of work units produced at each step

   4.____

5. One of the assistants whom you supervise displays apparent familiarity toward a businessman who deals with your agency. This assistant spends more time with this person than the nature of his business would warrant, and you have observed that they are occasionally seen leaving the office together for lunch. In several instances, when this businessman comes into the office and this assistant is not at his desk, the businessman will not deal with any other staff member but will, instead, leave the office and return later when that particular employee is available.
Of the following courses of action, the FIRST one you should take is to
   A. audit the agency's books and records pertaining to this businessman
   B. rebuke the assistant for unprofessional conduct at the next staff meeting and warn him of disciplinary action if the practice is not discontinued forthwith
   C. advise your agency head of the action by the businessman and the assistant that has been described in the above paragraph
   D. reassign the assistant to duties that will not bring him into contact with any businessman

5.____

6. The one of the following factors which generally is the BEST justification for keeping higher inventories of supplies and equipment is an expected
   A. decline in demand
   B. price increase
   C. decline in prices
   D. increase in interest charges and storage costs

6.____

7. Statistical sampling is often used in administrative operations PRIMARILY because it enables
   A. administrators to determine the characteristics of appointed or elected officials
   B. decisions to be made based on mathematical and scientific fact
   C. courses of action to be determined by scientifically-based computer programs
   D. useful predictions to be made from relatively small samples

7.____

8. According to United States Department of Labor figures, the PRINCIPAL source of disabling injuries to office workers is
   A. flying objects and falling objects
   B. striking against equipment
   C. falls and slips
   D. handling materials

8.____

9. To expedite the processing of applications issued by your agency, you ask your assistant to design a form that will be used by your typists. After several discussions, he presents you with a draft that requires the typist to use 23 tabular-stop positions.
Such a form would PROBABLY be considered
   A. *undesirable*; typists would now have to soft-roll the platen to make the typing fall on the lines
   B. *desirable*; the fill-in operation by typists would be speeded up

9.____

C. *undesirable*; proper vertical alignment of data would be made difficult by the number of tabular-stop positions required
D. *desirable*; it would force the typists to utilize the tabular-stop device

Question 10.

DIRECTIONS: Following are five general instructions to file clerks which might appear in the proposed filing manual for an agency.

I. Follow instructions generally; if you have a suggestion for improvement in the filing methods, install it after notifying the file supervisor who will duly authorize a change in the manual.
II. You may discuss the contents of files with fellow employees or outsiders, but do NOT give papers from the file to any person whose duties have no relation to the material requested.
III. All special instructions must be given by the file supervisor. Any problems that arise outside the regular routine of filing must be decided by the file supervisor, not by a fellow clerk.
IV. You will not be held responsible for your own errors; thus, refrain from asking other workers for instructions. No one is more interested in helping you in your training than your file supervisor.
V. Speed is the first essential in filing; make it your primary consideration—quick finding of filed material is the real test of your efficiency.

10. Which of the choices listed below BEST identifies those of the above statements that should or should not be followed by agencies in the functioning of their filing sections?
Instruction(s) _____ should be followed; instructions _____ should not be followed.
   A. I, II, III; IV, V
   B. III; I, II, IV, V
   C. II, IV; I, III, V
   D. I, III; II, IV, V

11. Listed below are five steps in the process of staffing:
   I. Authorization for staffing
   II. Manpower planning
   III. Development of applicant sources
   IV. Evaluation of applicants
   V. Employment decisions and offers
The one of the following sequences which is generally the MOST logical arrangement of the above steps is:
   A. I, II, III, IV, V
   B. II, I, III, IV, V
   C. III, I, II, IV, V
   D. II, III, I, IV, V

12. Job enrichment is LEAST likely to lead to
   A. fewer employee grievances
   B. increased employee productivity
   C. people acting as adjuncts of increased automation
   D. increased employee morale

13. Of the following, programmed instruction would usually be MOST effective in teaching
    A. principles of decision-making
    B. technical skills and knowledge
    C. good judgment
    D. executive management ability

14. Assume that a group has been working effectively with a contributing nonconformist in its midst.
    The BEST of the following reasons for the group to retain the nonconformist generally is that
    A. nonconformists stimulate groups to think
    B. he may be their boss some day
    C. nonconformists usually are fun to work with
    D. another nonconformist will usurp his role

15. The *grievance-arbitration* process involves systematic union-management deliberation regarding a complaint that work- or contract-related.
    An outcome that does NOT result from this process is
    A. a communications channel from the rank-and-file workers to higher management is developed or improved
    B. the contract is immediately changed to provide justice for both parties
    C. both labor and management identify those parts of the contract that need to be clarified and modified in subsequent negotiations
    D. the language of the agreement is informally translated into understandable terms for the parties bound by it

16. In government, job evaluation is the process of determining the relative worth of the various jobs in an organization so that differential wages can be paid. Job evaluation is based on several basic assumptions.
    Of the assumptions listed below, the MOST questionable is that
    A. the cash payments in government should be substantially higher than those in local private industry
    B. it is logical to pay the most for jobs that contribute most to the organization
    C. people feel more fairly treated if wages are based on the relative worth of their jobs
    D. the best way to achieve the goals of the enterprise is to maintain a wage structure based on job worth

17. Of the following, the training method that normally provides the instructor with the LEAST *feedback* from the trainees is
    A. the lecture method
    B. the conference method
    C. simulation or gaming techniques
    D. seminar instruction

18. Insufficient and inappropriate delegation of work assignments is MOST often the fault of
    A. subordinates who are unwilling to accept responsibility for their own mistakes
    B. a paternal attitude on the part of management

C. the immediate supervisor
D. subordinates who are too willing to take on extra responsibility

19. As contrasted with expense budgets, capital budgets are MORE likely to   19.____
   A. be used for construction of physical facilities
   B. be designed for a shorter time period
   C. include personal service expenditures
   D. include fringe benefits

20. During the first quarter of a year, a division's production rate was 1.26 man-   20.____
   hours per work unit produced. For the second quarter of that year, all other
   factors (e.g., size of staff, character of work unit, etc.) remained constant,
   except that the manner of reporting production rate was changed to work units
   per man-hour instead of man-hours per work unit. During that second quarter,
   the unit's production rate was .89 work units per man-hour.
   On the basis of the above information, it would be MOST NEARLY CORRECT
   to conclude that the division's production rate during the second quarter was
   approximately _____ than during the first quarter.
   A. 30% lower   B. 10% lower   C. 10% higher   D. 30% higher

Questions 21-22.

DIRECTIONS: Questions 21 and 22 are to be answered on the basis of the following
information.

The five bureaus within a department sent the following budget requests to the department head:

   Bureau A: $10 million
   Bureau B: $12 million
   Bureau C: $18 million
   Bureau D: $6 million
   Bureau E: $4 million

After reviewing all of these requests, the department head decided to reduce these requests so that they would total only $40 million. He considered the following two options to accomplish this:

   Option I: Reduce the requests of Bureaus A, B, and D by an equal dollar amount.
               Reduce the dollar amount request of Bureau C by 2½ times the dollar
               amount that he reduces the request of Bureau B. Reduce the dollar
               amount request of Bureau E by ½ of the dollar amount that he reduces
               the request of Bureau B.
   Option II: First, reduce the dollar amount request of all five bureaus by 15%. Then,
               the remaining reduction required by the entire department would be
               achieved by further reducing the resulting budget requests of Bureaus B
               and C by an equal dollar amount each.

21. Under Option I, the dollar amount request for Bureau E, after reduction by the department head, would be MOST NEARLY _____ millions.
   A. $1²/₃   B. $2¹/₃   C. $3¹/₆   D. $3½

22. Under Option II, the dollar amount of the request of Bureau B, after both reductions were made by the department head, would be MOST NEARLY _____ millions.
   A. $8   B. $9   C. $10   D. $11

23. The Summary of finding of a long management report intended for typical manager should generally appear _____ the report.
   A. at the very beginning of
   B. at the end of the report
   C. throughout
   D. in the middle of

24. Of the following, the BIGGEST disadvantage in allowing a free flow of communications in an agency is that such a free flow
   A. decreases creativity
   B. increases the use of the *grapevine*
   C. lengthens the chain of command
   D. reduces the executive's power to direct the flow of information

25. A downward flow of authority in an organization is one example of _____ communications.
   A. horizontal   B. informal   C. circular   D. vertical

26. Workers who belong to a cohesive group are generally thought to
   A. have more job-related anxieties than those who do not
   B. be less well-adjusted than those who do not
   C. derive little satisfaction from the group
   D. Conform to group norms more closely than those in noncohesive groups

27. The one of the following which BEST exemplifies negative motivation is
   A. a feeling on the part of the worker that the work is significant
   B. monetary rewards offered the worker for high levels of output
   C. reducing or withholding the worker's incentive rewards when performance is mediocre
   D. nonmonetary rewards given the worker, such as publicizing a good suggestion

28. Of the following, the one that would be MOST likely to block effective communication is
   A. concentration only on the issues at hand
   B. lack of interest or commitment
   C. use of written reports
   D. use of charts and graphs

29. Many functions formerly centralized in a department of personnel have been decentralized, in whole or in part, to operating agencies.
    The one of the following personnel functions which has been LEAST decentralized is
    A. positive evaluation
    B. investigation of non-competitive employees
    C. investigation of competitive employees
    D. jurisdictional classification

30. In making a position analysis for a duties classification, the one of the following factors which MUST be considered is the _____ the incumbent.
    A. capabilities of
    B. qualifications of
    C. efficiency attained by
    D. responsibility assigned to

KEY (CORRECT ANSWERS)

1.	A	11.	B	21.	C
2.	C	12.	C	22.	B
3.	B	13.	B	23.	A
4.	B	14.	A	24.	D
5.	C	15.	B	25.	D
6.	B	16.	A	26.	D
7.	D	17.	A	27.	C
8.	C	18.	C	28.	B
9.	C	19.	A	29.	D
10.	B	20.	C	30.	D

EXAMINATION SECTION
TEST 1

DIRECTIONS: Each question or incomplete statement is followed by several suggested answers or completions. Select the one that BEST answers the question or completes the statement. *PRINT THE LETTER OF THE CORRECT ANSWER IN THE SPACE AT THE RIGHT.*

1. Constitutional limitations on borrowing by local governments are less relevant today than 20 to 30 years ago PRIMARILY because of the

    A. continually rising rate of interest on mortgages
    B. growing importance of local non-property taxes
    C. growth in federal aid
    D. more rapid growth of the suburbs relative to central cities

2. Assume that the manager of an office or administrative activity has been cautioned to control the cost of peak load fluctuations and unforeseen emergencies in preparing his budget estimates.
   In conforming to these instructions, the manager should NOT budget for

    A. a reserve of trained employees
    B. *floating* or traveling trouble-shooting employees
    C. overtime work
    D. part-time help

3. A mail section consisted of incoming and outgoing units. By applying an hourly work count, a supervisor found that the peak load of the incoming unit occurred in the morning and almost equalled the peak load of the outgoing unit in the afternoon. As a result, the two units were combined. The former condition is BEST described as an example of

    A. decentralization   B. overspecialization
    C. overstaffing   D. reorganization

4. Of the following, the one whose yield would be MOST difficult to predict in preparing a budget is the _____ tax.

    A. commercial rent or occupancy   B. general corporation
    C. sales   D. transportation corporation

5. Of the following, the MOST useful data to use in predicting the yield of the sales tax normally are

    A. corporate profits
    B. personal incomes
    C. the deflated gross national product
    D. unemployment rates

6. Of the following, the criterion that is LEAST desirable for the selection of an output indicator for use in multi-year program analysis is

    A. cost effectiveness   B. data availability
    C. relevance   D. simplicity

7. The MOST valid generalization regarding the <u>attribute</u> as a form of data is that it is

   A. a source of contamination in the analysis of the basic problem
   B. distinguishable from other forms of data in varying amounts
   C. relatively impervious to scientific treatment because of its subjectivity
   D. a quality, trait, or function that is present or absent

8. The one of the following management techniques that would generally be LEAST useful in the work of a budget examiner is a _____ system.

   A. management information
   B. network type planning and scheduling
   C. paperwork simplification
   D. work measurement

9. A supervisor thought it necessary to maintain a double check for accuracy on the review of cases. A work count showed him that Reviewer A found a percentage of errors of 12 percent, whereas Reviewer B, spending the same amount of time, turned up an additional 0.1 percent of errors. Of the following, it would be MOST advisable for the supervisor to

   A. commend the first reviewer and discipline the second reviewer
   B. divide the percentage of errors equally between the two
   C. eliminate a second review in the future
   D. reclassify the first reviewer

10. Of the following, the one that BEST describes a well-defined economic criterion for assigning priorities to feasible projects is

    A. unit pricing theory
    B. diminishing marginal utility
    C. discounted cash flow rate of return
    D. economies of scale

11. The technical research term *stanine* refers to a(n)

    A. economical approximation for validity
    B. regressed form of the true score
    C. reliable measure of physical fitness
    D. special form of the standard score

12. A score NOT based upon the standard deviation is the

    A. scaled score
    B. T-score
    C. z-score
    D. percentile rank

13. PPBS is MOST difficult to apply to problems of

    A. fire   B. health   C. public works   D. welfare

14. Which of the following types of problems would be LEAST likely to lend itself to *operations research*?

    A. Determining program priorities
    B. Developing a controlled backlog
    C. Distribution of resources and jobs
    D. Sequence of work

15. The MOST valid of the following statements regarding measurement of government activities is:

    A. A viable program cannot be planned without work measurement
    B. Most government activities cannot be measured
    C. Some aspects of every activity can be measured
    D. Work measurement takes more time and effort than it is worth

16. In correlating results on reading and intelligence tests for a given set of population, the BEST data to utilize are

    A. intelligence quotient and reading quotient
    B. mental age and reading age
    C. mental age and reading grade
    D. raw scores on both tests

17. For the purpose of conducting a school survey, the practice of selecting a typical county on the basis of considerable known information about all of the counties in the United States is an example of _____ sampling.

    A. purposive   B. representative
    C. nested   D. cluster

18. Which one of the following problems is generally NOT encountered in cost analysis of multi-year plans for an ongoing program?

    A. Form in which costs should be summarized for decision-making
    B. Magnitude of uncertainty in cost estimates
    C. The obtaining of historical costs
    D. The question of price level changes

19. Select the statement which is MOST valid:

    A. Accounting object classes should be the categories of a program structure
    B. Each program should be related to the operations of a single agency
    C. The costs for each program should form the basis of the accounting system
    D. The costs for each program should include the costs of all relevant object classes

20. Assume that the number of buses (U_t) required for a given line-haul system serving the Central Business District depends upon roundtrip time (t), capacity of bus (c), and the total number of people to be moved in a peak hour (P) in the major direction, i.e., in the morning and out in the evening.
    The formula for the number of buses required is: $U_t =$

    A. Ptc   B. $\frac{tp}{c}$ C. $\frac{cp}{t}$ D. $\frac{ct}{p}$

21. The area, in blocks, that can be served by a single stop for any maximum walking distance is given by the following formula: $a = 2w^2$. In this formula, a = the area served by a stop, and w = maximum walking distance.
    If people will tolerate a walk of up to three blocks, how many stops would be needed to service an area of 288 square blocks?

    A. 9   B. 16   C. 18   D. 27

22. Among the following, the MOST appropriate technique for ascertaining the content of educational achievement is

    A. the analysis of textbooks and courses of study
    B. the reliance on the judgment of experts
    C. differential achievement by varied grades
    D. statistical correlations with class marks

23. Which of the following is a network chart? _____ chart.

    A. Critical path method   B. Gantt
    C. Multi-column process   D. Single-column process

24. Such measures as cost of square foot per road are MOST useful for

    A. evaluating goal attainment
    B. evaluation of current operations
    C. manning tables
    D. output plans

Questions 25-28.

DIRECTIONS: Questions 25 through 28 are to be answered on the basis of the following paragraph.

Under institutional training program 1, two-thirds of the recipients are poor, 40 percent are under 21 years of age, and the average net earnings gained by the participants are almost three times the per trainee cost. A competing program 2 increases the average earnings by only 120 percent of the per trainee cost but all participants are poor and under 21.

25. If the sole objective of the governmental agency is the greatest return to national income per dollar invested, the PREFERABLE alternative is

    A. 1   B. either 1 or 2
    C. 2   D. a combination of 1 and 2

26. If the basic objective is to assist youth, the PREFERABLE alternative is

    A. 1   B. either 1 or 2
    C. 2   D. a combination of 1 and 2

27. If the basic objective is to assist the poor, the PREFERABLE alternative is

    A. 1   B. either 1 or 2
    C. 2   D. a combination of 1 and 2

28. If the objectives are multiple: assist youth, assist the poor, and the greatest return to national income per dollar invested, the choice of the PREFERABLE program

    A. cannot be made
    B. is 1
    C. is 2
    D. depends on an appropriate weighting of objectives

29. ACIR refers to Advisory Commission on

    A. Industrial Resources
    B. Intergovernmental Relations
    C. Internal Revenue
    D. Institutional Research

30. The Constitution of the United States

    A. does not mention the budget process
    B. provides for an executive budget
    C. mandates a national budget, but does not specify procedure
    D. specifies the basic steps of budget preparation and authorization

31. The following four steps represent an analysis of an experimental procedure:
    I. Collection of evidence
    II. Appraisal of the tentative generalization
    III. Adoption of the operational hypotheses
    IV. Definition of problem
    The steps should be taken in the following order:

    A. III, IV, I, II
    B. I, II, III, IV
    C. IV, III, I, II
    D. II, I, IV, III

Questions 32-34.

DIRECTIONS: Questions 32 through 34 are to be answered on the basis of the following data.

A series of cost-benefit studies of various alternative health programs yields the following results:

Program	Benefit	Cost
K	30	15
L	60	60
M	300	150
N	600	500

In answering Questions 32 through 34, assume that all programs can be increased or decreased in scale without affecting their individual benefit-to-cost ratios.

32. The benefit-to-cost ratio of Program M is

    A. 10:1   B. 5:1   C. 2:1   D. 1:2

33. The budget ceiling for one or more of the programs included in the study is set at 75 units.
    It may MOST logically be concluded that

    A. Programs K and L should be chosen to fit within the budget ceiling
    B. Program K would be the most desirable one that could be afforded
    C. Program M should be chosen rather than Program K
    D. the choice should be between Program M and K

34. If no assumptions can be made regarding the effects of change of scale, the MOST logical conclusion, on the basis of the data available, is that

   A. more data are needed for a budget choice of program
   B. Program K is the most preferable because of its low cost and good benefit-to-cost ratio
   C. Program M is the most preferable because of its high benefits and good benefit-to-cost ratio
   D. there is no difference between Programs K and M, and either can be chosen for any purpose

35. The PRIMARY obstacle to the interpretation of educational experiments in which two or more groups of students have been matched on chronological age or intelligence is:

   A. Significance tests are not adequate to handle the data
   B. The matching process frequently inflates group differences
   C. Chronological age and intelligence are usually the wrong variables on which to equate students
   D. Populations of matched students do not exist to which to generalize

36. The LARGEST item of expenditure in the typical office or administrative organization is usually for

   A. charges for office machine usage
   B. office supplies, forms, and other materials
   C. rent of space occupied
   D. salaries and wages

37. Of the following, the MOST appropriate indicator of quality of service in a health program is usually

   A. average daily in-patient load in a general hospital
   B. number of children served in a disease-screening clinic
   C. number of patients treated in an alcoholic clinic
   D. number of therapy hours of care provided in a mental hospital

Questions 38-47.

DIRECTIONS: Questions 38 through 47 consists of a quotation which contains one word that is incorrectly used because it is not in keeping with the meaning that the quotation is evidently intended to convey. Determine which word is INCORRECTLY used. Then, select from the words lettered A, B, C, or D the word which, when substituted for the incorrectly used word, would BEST help to convey the meaning of the quotation.

38. A measure must be developed of all direct and indirect benefits, recognizing the non-quantifiable nature of many of the latter, yet guarding against the tendency to use the quantifiable as a justification for any difference between costs and benefits.

   A. cannot   B. non-quantifiable
   C. effects   D. ability

39. A persistent problem in the rationalization of public expenditures in the natural resources field stems from the varied objectives of different interests. A primary reason for this is that the cost and gains of contemplated actions are perceived clearly.

   A. differently
   B. minor
   C. potential
   D. programs

40. It is not imperative that the agency's table of organization follow the program structure rigidly, but a general parallelism is helpful, both in placing legislative responsibility for goal attainment and in program evaluation.

   A. executive
   B. harmful
   C. ineffective
   D. initiative

41. Some of the impediments to developing appropriate data systems stem from the fact that organization lines and program structures do not expand. The requirement for accounting on a program basis is superimposed across organizational requirements.

   A. coincide
   B. conflict
   C. inducements
   D. planning

42. Examples of a public good may be found also in domestic programs, although national income is probably the purest and most extreme example of a public good.

   A. international
   B. least
   C. private
   D. security

43. To avoid distortions in cost-benefit calculations, an appropriate discount interest rate should be calculated on the basis of the marginal cost principle.

   A. analysis
   B. estimated
   C. opportunity
   D. time horizon

44. Where budget deficits are developed at the agency level for use by operating bureaus, they must be harmonious with the directives that have come from the central budget office.

   A. assumptions
   B. consistent
   C. departmental
   D. large

45. A possible source of budgetary waste could be eliminated if estimates were prepared in no greater detail than was justified by their magnitude.

   A. accuracy
   B. budgets
   C. complexity
   D. mechanical

46. A capital budget may provide information useful in estimating national income. This is a very different type of consideration from budgetary and policy-formulation purposes.

   A. contain   B. economic   C. program   D. wealth

47. In some governments, the failure to bring budgeting and policy-making together at the operating level is often unfortunately attributable to the presence of a strong budget office attached to the chief executive, which is too concerned with threats to its authority.

   A. departmental
   B. effectiveness
   C. involved
   D. planning

48. The MOST important function served by a line-item budget is to

   A. control appropriations and expenditures in detail
   B. give the Budget Bureau information on each operating agency's financial plans
   C. measure cost-effectiveness
   D. provide a basis for management analysis

49. Assume that work to be distributed varies in difficulty and complexity. The workers are at junior and senior levels and differ in competence within each level.
Of the following, the BEST policy for the supervisor to follow in this case when distributing work is usually to

   A. divide the work among workers based on the individual speed and competence of each worker, regardless of worker level
   B. give the more difficult work to the seniors, and base the number of work units given to each level on the estimated time needed to complete each different work unit
   C. give the more difficult work to the seniors and the less difficult to the juniors, but give more units of work to the juniors
   D. give the work which will require the longest time to complete to the seniors

50. Generally, authority and responsibility for an activity should NOT be delegated until

   A. all authorized positions have been filled
   B. an organization is mature
   C. personnel have been trained in the staff functions
   D. policies can be spelled out so as to insure uniform administration

KEY (CORRECT ANSWERS)

1. B	11. D	21. B	31. C	41. A
2. A	12. D	22. A	32. C	42. D
3. B	13. D	23. A	33. D	43. C
4. B	14. A	24. B	34. A	44. A
5. B	15. C	25. A	35. D	45. A
6. A	16. D	26. C	36. D	46. D
7. D	17. A	27. C	37. D	47. A
8. C	18. C	28. D	38. B	48. A
9. C	19. D	29. B	39. A	49. B
10. C	20. B	30. A	40. A	50. D

TEST 2

DIRECTIONS: Each question or incomplete statement is followed by several suggested answers or completions. Select the one that BEST answers the question or completes the statement. *PRINT THE LETTER OF THE CORRECT ANSWER IN THE SPACE AT THE RIGHT.*

Questions 1-7.

DIRECTIONS: Questions 1 through 7 are to be answered on the basis of the following paragraphs. Indicate the correct answer for these questions as follows: If the paragraphs indicate it is true, mark answer A. If the paragraphs indicate it is probably true, mark answer B. If the paragraphs indicate it is probably false, mark answer C. If the paragraphs indicate it is false, mark answer D.

The fallacy underlying what some might call the eighteenth and nineteenth century misconceptions of the nature of scientific investigations seems to lie in a mistaken analogy. Those who said they were investigating the structure of the universe imagined themselves as the equivalent of the early explorers and mapmakers. The explorers of the fifteenth and sixteenth centuries had opened up new worlds with the aid of imperfect maps; in their accounts of distant lands, there had been some false and many ambiguous statements. But by the time everyone came to believe the world was round, the maps of distant continents were beginning to assume a fairly consistent pattern. By the seventeenth century, methods of measuring space and time had laid the foundations for an accurate geography.

On this basic issue, there is far from complete agreement among philosophers of science today. You can, each of you, choose your side and find highly distinguished advocates for the point of view you have selected. However, in view of the revolution in physics, anyone who now asserts that science is an exploration of the universe must be prepared to shoulder a heavy burden of proof. To my mind, the analogy between the mapmaker and the scientist is false. A scientific theory is not even the first approximation to a map; it is not a need; it is a policy -- an economical and fruitful guide to action, by scientific investigators.

1. The author thinks that 18th and 19th century science followed the same technique as the 15th century geographers. 1.____

2. The author disagrees with the philosophers who are labelled realists. 2.____

3. The author believes there is a permanent structure to the universe. 3.____

4. A scientific theory is an economical guide to exploring what cannot be known absolutely. 4.____

5. Philosophers of science accept the relativity implications of recent research in physics. 5.____

6. It is a matter of time and effort before modern scientists will be as successful as the geographers. 6.____

7. The author believes in an indeterminate universe. 7.____

8. Total government expenditures, Federal, State, and local, are APPROXIMATELY the following proportion of Gross National Product: 8.____

   A. 1/10 B. 1/5 C. 1/3 D. 1/2

23

Questions 9-12.

DIRECTIONS: Questions 9 through 12 are to be answered on the basis of the following.

The income elasticity of demand for selected items of consumer demand in the United States are:

Item	Elasticity
Airline travel	5.66
Alcohol	.62
Dentist fees	1.00
Electric utilities	3.00
Gasoline	1.29
Intercity bus	1.89
Local bus	1.41
Restaurant meals	.75

9. The demand for the item listed below that would be MOST adversely affected by a decrease in income is

   A. alcohol
   B. electric utilities
   C. gasoline
   D. restaurant meals

10. The item whose relative change in demand would be the same as the relative change in income would be

    A. dentist fees
    B. gasoline
    C. restaurant meals
    D. none of the above

11. If income increases by 12 percent, the demand for restaurant meals may be expected to increase by

    A. 9 percent
    B. 12 percent
    C. 16 percent
    D. none of the above

12. On the basis of the above information, the item whose demand would be MOST adversely affected by an increase in the sales tax from 7 percent to 8 percent to be passed on to the consumer in the form of higher prices

    A. would be airline travel
    B. would be alcohol
    C. would be gasoline
    D. cannot be determined

13. The PRIMARY purpose of randomization principles in the design of experiments is to

    A. exclude a number of alternative interpretations
    B. objectify the experimental evidence
    C. validate the tests of significance
    D. equate the number of degrees of freedom in the cells

14. Of the following, the GREATEST advantage of state collection as against local collection of local sales taxes in the state is:

A. Payments by retailers to the tax agency may be made at less frequent intervals
B. The burden of the tax is decreased
C. The net yield of the tax is increased
D. The tax rate is uniform throughout the state

15. A criticism of a *pay-as-you-go* policy in financing capital outlay is that it 15.____

    A. is more costly
    B. is more difficult to administer
    C. may be difficult to determine priorities among projects
    D. may lead to the postponement of needed projects

16. Which of the following tends to be the LEAST constraint encountered in the preparation of a municipal budget? 16.____

    A. Legislative   B. Political
    C. Revenue   D. Personnel

17. In the last two decades, the ability of the legislature to review the budget has been improved in many governments PRINCIPALLY by providing 17.____

    A. a long-range planning system
    B. for public hearings on the budget
    C. more details in the executive budget
    D. professional staff for the legislature

18. Recent research shows that some lower-level professional employees feel that they accomplish little in their work that is worthwhile. 18.____
    Management experts usually say that the one of the following which BEST explains such feelings is

    A. dissatisfaction among employees provoked by the activities of labor unions
    B. frequent salary increases unmatched by any significant increases in productivity
    C. the almost total indifference of employees to the vital issues of the times
    D. the failure to properly develop in these employees an understanding of the significance of their work

19. One way to get maximum effort from employees is for management to give employees the maximum possible personal freedom in accomplishing agency objectives. 19.____
    This encourages a feeling of self-management which is MOST basic to

    A. an impartial approach to work
    B. tightly coordinated team effort
    C. high levels of motivation
    D. uniformity of action

20. Interactions among public programs are often complex. The situation that is NOT an example of such interactions is: 20.____

    A. A solid waste disposal program may increase air pollution
    B. Changes in transportation may improve or reduce retail trade
    C. Paving of more highway mileage may enlarge traffic congestion
    D. Traffic control systems may reduce or enlarge motor vehicle accidents

21. The following are given as the objectives of a department's mission:
    I. Economic efficiency
    II. Optimal use of environmental resources
    III. Safety
    IV. Support of other national interests
    Which one of the departments listed below is MOST likely to have all four of the above objectives?

    A. Correction
    B. Education
    C. Health
    D. Transportation

22. An agency is considering the hiring of a consultant for a given project.
    Of the following, the GREATEST danger of reliance on outside experts is:

    A. It delays the work program because of the necessity of processing bids
    B. It does not contribute to internal staff capacity
    C. It involves greater project costs
    D. The resulting work, though excellent, may not be assimilated in the governmental process

23. Of the following, the MOST pertinent argument given against *revenue-sharing* is:

    A. Local governments are incapable of planning expenditures properly
    B. The expenditure needs of state and local governments have not grown as rapidly as the needs of the federal government
    C. The federal government has the more lucrative sources of revenue at its disposal
    D. There would be no flow-through to cities

24. In fixing beneficiary charges, governments generally do NOT consider

    A. the cost of the service
    B. the rate of return
    C. the value of the service
    D. what the market will bear

25. The MAXIMUM amount of the real property tax levy does NOT usually depend upon the

    A. assessed valuation
    B. equalization rate
    C. size of the budget
    D. value of tax-exempt property

26. An argument against the use of a task force for budget analysis is:
    It could

    A. facilitate participation of the agencies concerned
    B. not help clarify problems of coordination
    C. not result in in-depth considerations
    D. overemphasize subject matter areas singled out for intensive effort

27. A standard cost system produces   27.____

    A. a ratio of cost of goods sold to net sales
    B. a ratio of current assets to current liabilities
    C. original actual costs which may be compared to inflated costs
    D. predetermined costs which can be compared with actual costs

28. Which of the following is NOT a desirable characteristic of a capital budget?   28.____

    A. A long-range capital improvements plan (6 years)
    B. A master plan for physical development of the city (10-25 years)
    C. Financial analysis of present and anticipated municipal revenue
    D. Omission of operating expenses and other recurrent costs

29. The earmarking of revenues is often defended since it   29.____

    A. improves tax administration
    B. is a non-political device
    C. provides a direct link between the cost and benefit of a service
    D. simplifies the budgetary process

30. Of the following, the BEST measure of relative taxable capacity among states is   30.____

    A. per capita personal income
    B. per capita yield of a stock transfer tax
    C. personal income
    D. the yield of a sales tax

31. In identifying fundamental government objectives under PPBS, the LEAST important of the following questions is   31.____

    A. By whom is it to be done?
    B. For whom is it to be done?
    C. What is to be done?
    D. Why is each activity currently performed being done?

32. Which one of the following measures is of LEAST use as an output measure for a PPBS system?   32.____

    A. Gallons of water per housing unit
    B. Number of days of hospital care per capita
    C. Number of traffic accidents by 1,000 vehicle miles
    D. Number of traffic tickets per officer

33. Estimates of costs can be MOST *rough* for which of the following purposes?   33.____

    A. Budget
    B. One-year program and financial plan
    C. Program analyses
    D. Quarterly allotment system

34. A city built a golf course on land that it owns. In this situation,   34.____

    A. no additional costs are involved
    B. the cost is the initial cost of the land

C. the cost is related to possible alternate uses of the land
D. the cost is the initial cost adjusted for price changes

35. Two ten-year programs are estimated to have the same cost. Alternative 1 involves high costs in the early years and lower costs later. Alternative 2 incurs lowest costs initially and higher costs later.
In this case,

   A. Alternative 1 has the higher present discounted cost
   B. Alternative 2 has the higher present discounted cost
   C. the alternative with the higher present discounted cost cannot be determined from the information given
   D. both alternatives have exactly the same present discounted cost

36. Governmental accounting should serve as a tool of management .
This statement refers to the design of an accounting system to do which one of the following?

   A. Maintain accounts that permit an independent audit extending to all records, funds, securities, and property.
   B. Make possible a determination of the adequacy of custodianship of government assets by responsible officials.
   C. Make possible the measurements of activities at the administrative unit level.
   D. Show compliance with legal provisions.

37. Budgetary reform in the United States during the first quarter of the twentieth century emphasized control over the administrative agencies and _____ budgeting.

   A. accrual
   B. executive
   C. legislative
   D. program

38. The one basis of budgetary appropriation that is almost universally used is

   A. capital
   B. economic character
   C. performance unit
   D. organizational unit

39. The LEAST useful of the following bases of budgetary classification for a municipality would generally be by

   A. economic character
   B. object-item of expetur
   C. organizational unit
   D. program or activity

40. A functional classification of municipal budgetary expenditures is USUALLY prepared because it

   A. helps remove the budget from the political arena
   B. is required by local law
   C. keeps the public informed about the nature of governmental operations
   D. minimizes unnecessary budgetary appropriations

41. The following equation is used to estimate operating expenditures of a city: $Y = 90.2 + 6.2X$, where Y = operating expenditures in millions of dollars and where X = years.
Origin: Fiscal year 1989-90.
The equation indicates that operating expenditures may be expected to

A. level off at $96.4 million
B. increase at a rate of 6.2 percent per year
C. increase by $6.2 million per year
D. increase by $90.2 million per year

42. Of the following concepts associated with PPBS, the one that MOST distinguishes it from the basic characteristics of all prior forms of budgeting is 42.____

    A. input
    B. output
    C. systems analysis
    D. time span of budget appropriation

43. Of the following categories, the one which ivould receive the GREATEST percentage of total funds in a city executive capital budget would MOST LIKELY be for 43.____

    A. education   B. environmental protection
    C. health services   D. public safety

44. Among the sub-programs of a Physical and Mental Well-Being Program, a sub-program, Unassignable Items, is indicated. Unassignable items MOST likely would include 44.____

    A. Drug Addiction Treatment
    B. Mental Illness Prevention
    C. Physical Health
    D. Research and Planning

45. Under a PPBS system, it is BEST to account for employee benefit costs 45.____

    A. by applying them to individual programs
    B. by omitting them from relevant costs
    C. in a separate category
    D. in a special overhead account

46. In preparing the budget of expenses for any office or administrative unit, some expenses originate in and are chargeable directly to the office or administrative unit. Others must be allocated on some basis.
    Of the following, the expense that is LEAST typical of a direct expense, and therefore should be charged on an allocated basis, is 46.____

    A. depreciation of machines and equipment
    B. employee fringe benefits and salaries
    C. printing expense
    D. rent

47. Justification materials generally found in conventional budgets have failings as analysis documents because they 47.____

    A. do not contain comparisons with prior year budgets
    B. seldom discuss alternatives sufficiently
    C. very rarely contain work-load data
    D. very rarely provide information

48. Post-completion audits of capital expense projects are made for a variety of purposes. Of the following, the LEAST appropriate purpose for such an audit is to

    A. aid in assessing future capital expenditures proposals
    B. assess the abilities and competence of the analyst who submitted the original project proposal
    C. reveal reasons for project failures
    D. verify the resulting savings

49. The one of the following kinds of problems for which administrative measuring techniques tend to be LEAST applicable is

    A. administrative planning
    B. decisions in the realm of human relations
    C. determining relative effectiveness of alternative procedures and methods
    D. work programming

50. The one of the following which is an example of transfer payments by government is

    A. intergovernmental aid
    B. late payments of encumbered balances
    C. social security payments
    D. transportation payments for government employees

KEY (CORRECT ANSWERS)

1. D	11. A	21. D	31. A	41. C
2. B	12. D	22. D	32. D	42. C
3. D	13. C	23. A	33. C	43. A
4. A	14. C	24. B	34. C	44. D
5. D	15. D	25. C	35. A	45. A
6. D	16. D	26. D	36. C	46. D
7. B	17. D	27. D	37. B	47. B
8. C	18. D	28. C	38. D	48. B
9. B	19. C	29. C	39. A	49. B
10. A	20. B	30. A	40. C	50. C

EXAMINATION SECTION
TEST 1

DIRECTIONS: Each question or incomplete statement is followed by several suggested answers or completions. Select the one that BEST answers the question or completes the statement. *PRINT THE LETTER OF THE CORRECT ANSWER IN THE SPACE AT THE RIGHT.*

1. Among the following, the MOST regressive tax is the _____ tax.

    A. sales B. gasoline C. entertainment D. hotel

2. When a suburban community has a high proportion of industrial/commercial property, its real estate tax rate is likely to be relatively

    A. *high,* primarily because of load put on community facilities by the added traffic
    B. *low,* primarily because its school taxes will be low
    C. *high,* primarily because business and industry demand special services
    D. *low,* primarily because business and especially industrial areas need little police and fire protection at night and such costs are less at that time

3. A fare increase in a public transport system usually produces a less than proportionate increase in revenues PRIMARILY because of

    A. wasteful operations
    B. reduced economy of scale
    C. price elasticity of demand
    D. dishonesty by operating personnel

4. A larger sewage disposal system costs less per unit of capacity than the same system in a smaller area.
   This characteristic is known as

    A. reduced cost-benefit ratio   B. economy of scale
    C. diseconomy of scale   D. vertical integration

5. Assume that inflation has caused an increase in the average income of residents of a city which has a progressive income tax system. Assume also that there is no change in the relevant laws.
   As a result, the effect on tax revenues

    A. is proportional to the increase in personal income
    B. is proportionately smaller than the increase in personal income
    C. is proportionately greater than the increase in personal income
    D. cannot be determined without further information

6. The timing and valuation of benefits is the distinguishing feature of which of the following?

    A. Job evaluation   B. Program budgeting
    C. Planning-programming-budgeting   D. Operations forecasting

7. The planning technique for complex projects which focuses on the scheduling, timing, and sequencing of their individual operations is MOST appropriately called

   A. PERT   B. PPBS   C. MIS   D. EOQ Model

8. Before a PPB system can function, there has to be a specification of

   A. procedures
   B. methods
   C. costs and benefits
   D. goals

9. In the budgeting process, the FIRST major aim of the planning portion is the

   A. estimate of total revenues
   B. detailed itemization of inputs
   C. detailed itemization of outputs
   D. quantification of the program's outputs

10. In addition to quantifying the desired results and costs of programs, PPB also considers as MOST important their

    A. political desirability
    B. timing
    C. management
    D. public image

11. In governmental budgeting, the area in which benefits can be measured MOST easily is

    A. education
    B. defense spending
    C. any area in which the same product or service is obtainable commercially
    D. any area in which the agency concerned has had really long experience

12. Among government services meant for ultimate consumption, the supply of city water as compared to its price

    A. has strong price elasticity with respect to demand
    B. is essentially inelastic in demand with respect to price
    C. has negative price elasticity of demand
    D. varies at random with respect to price elasticity

13. In economic analysis, the cost of time used for anything is

    A. the value of the best alternative use of the same time
    B. determined by wage costs in union contracts
    C. set arbitrarily
    D. determined by historical trends subjected to statistical analysis

14. In determining the amount of detail which should be included in a public announcement of a new budgetary program, it is generally CORRECT that

    A. all known details should be included
    B. there is an optimal amount of detail for the effect the announcement is designed to obtain
    C. the maximum amount of detail is given so as to reduce the program's vulnerability to criticism
    D. there are so many uncertainties that any standard should not even be established

15. In the process of approving a new budget, opportunities to explain questioned budget items are offered FIRST to the

    A. chief fiscal officer of the city
    B. mayor's office, for items other than its own budget
    C. agency head involved
    D. appropriate committee of the city council

16. The PRINCIPAL objective of budgetary control is to

    A. see that an agency carries out its authorized functions within the limits of funds available
    B. minimize the expenditures of money by specific agencies
    C. place limitations on money expended for specific activities
    D. exercise line supervision over purchasing and payroll functions

17. Computers are MOST useful in budgeting in

    A. providing the basic data
    B. making decisions
    C. doing analytical operations on the data
    D. quantifying qualitative data

18. As understood by the budgeter, a model of a program is a(the)

    A. survey of its feasibility
    B. description of the relationship between inputs and outputs
    C. survey related to performance evaluation
    D. first stage of its implementation

19. With respect to private and public facilities of the same kind, the CHIEF accounting differences between the two operations lie in the areas of taxes, profits, and

    A. depreciation
    B. internal auditing
    C. disbursements
    D. receipts

20. In the absence of other information, the value of government service output is measured in national income accounts

    A. at cost of inputs
    B. at cost of inputs plus an allowance for extra benefits
    C. at cost of inputs minus an allowance for excess cost
    D. by estimates independent of costs

21. Strong seasonal variation in local industry is MOST clearly reflected in receipts for _____ tax.

    A. city income
    B. sales
    C. franchise
    D. business property

22. A government agency decides to decentralize its functions. Assuming that this process can be accomplished without new construction, i.e., in existing offices, the agency's budget will

   A. *decrease,* chiefly because decentralization always cuts red tape
   B. *increase,* chiefly because decentralization usually means duplicating at least some activities
   C. *decrease,* chiefly because some functions become unnecessary
   D. *increase,* chiefly because there is greater chance for empire building

23. Performance budgeting is MOST closely related to which of the following techniques for describing an approach to management?

   A. The managerial grid
   B. Management by exception
   C. Management by objectives
   D. Operations research

24. In cost-benefit analysis, certain non-tangible factors are given implicit values. The MOST common implicit estimate, of the ones listed below, defines the value of

   A. political feasibility
   B. sunk costs
   C. a human life
   D. aesthetics

25. Labor productivity among non-supervising employees, in man-hours per unit of output, is MOST easily measured in a(n)

   A. municipal asphalt plant
   B. department of sanitation truck repair shop
   C. income tax audit section
   D. engineering design office

26. Of the following, the BEST definition of *full funding* of a budget item is

   A. arranging for the commitment of funds from state and federal agencies
   B. funding the total cost, including indirect charges
   C. preparing a special bond issue
   D. putting the whole cost into the first year's budget of the agency

27. As contrasted to the traditional line-item budget, PPBS

   A. makes long-range planning easier
   B. facilitates very detailed review by the legislative branch
   C. makes larger projects more difficult to control than others
   D. reduces cost overruns in capital projects

28. To provide funds to support a legally balanced budget, the city sometimes relies on

   A. general obligation bonds
   B. tax anticipation notes
   C. special agency obligations
   D. deferring bill payments

29. The KEY to any attempt to prevent setbacks in governmental programs is to

   A. provide an adequate budget
   B. give proper consideration to long-run and short-run needs

C. concentrate managerial attention on short-run problems
D. reduce environmental limitations

30. The one of the following options which gives the MOST complete accounting of the factors upon which expenditure estimates by budget analysts are usually based is administrative

   A. units
   B. units and work programs
   C. units, work programs, and physical units required
   D. units, work programs, physical inputs required, and an estimate of social costs

30.____

31. The one of the following areas in which past expenditures are usually NOT used as a basis for estimating future expenditures is in

   A. reordering supplies and operation of office machinery
   B. replacement of office machinery
   C. payment of telephone bills
   D. maintenance of roads

31.____

32. Historically, *performance budgeting* was

   A. synonymous with line-item budgeting
   B. synonymous with PPBS
   C. an intermediate stage before PPBS
   D. superseded by line-item budgeting

32.____

33. The development of performance budgets are characterized by the use of a particular technique called

   A. computer analysts
   B. time and motion study
   C. efficiency rating of personnel
   D. cost effectiveness analysis

33.____

34. Of the following, which is generally considered to be the PRINCIPAL advantage of lump-sum appropriations?

   A. Legislatures need be given little detail of expenditures.
   B. Public hearings on the budget are greatly simplified.
   C. Pressures toward efficiency in an agency are reduced.
   D. Agency heads have more flexibility in internal operations.

34.____

35. City expense and capital budgets are prepared separately because

   A. expense budgets can be prepared for a year at a time whereas capital budgets deal only with long-range expenses
   B. expense budgets must be met from current revenues whereas capital budgets are met from borrowings
   C. common elements make it convenient to do so
   D. the expense budget depends on internal auditing practices whereas the capital budget is not affected

35.____

36. The MOST difficult part of budget review is a decision about

   A. recruitment of staff
   B. the importance of the program under review
   C. possible cost savings through elimination of certain jobs in the program
   D. the size of the proposed appropriation

37. The RELATIVE worth of alternative budgetary items may be judged in terms of _____ cost(s).

   A. sunk
   B. opportunity
   C. unavoidable
   D. out-of-pocket

38. The creation of maximum efficiency within an agency without regard to costs incurred elsewhere is termed

   A. system optimization
   B. maximization
   C. micro-economic analysis
   D. suboptimization

39. The term *full system cost* in governmental programs is taken to mean all direct and indirect

   A. costs incurred by the city in the project
   B. government costs at all levels
   C. public and private costs
   D. public and private costs as well as opportunity

40. Budget control is concerned MAINLY with

   A. making sure agencies do their job
   B. the formulation of tax policy
   C. the enforcement of tax collections
   D. measures to ensure honesty in governmental disbursements

41. The standard of management performance which the comptroller is expected to enforce is essentially that of

   A. making sure all the money is spent
   B. adequate record keeping
   C. operational efficiency
   D. ensuring that legal authorization exists for agency expenditures

42. *Comprehensive budgeting* is synonymous with

   A. full-system budgeting
   B. zero-base budgeting
   C. incremental budgeting
   D. cost-benefit analysis

43. *Systems analysis* impinges on the budget process MAINLY by

   A. reducing the need for budgetary review
   B. setting up systems and procedures for doing the job
   C. increasing the need for budgetary review
   D. requiring a large computer installation

44. Programs of federal assistance to state and local governments are HARD for budgetary authorities to evaluate because

    A. *assisting* is hard to define in terms of results
    B. the level of such assistance is nearly always inadequate
    C. federal and state contributions are highly restrictive
    D. responsibility for results is not clearly delineated

45. In the PERT project planning method, slack time is the difference between

    A. the most likely estimated time and the maximum
    B. minimum and maximum estimated time along the critical path
    C. the critical time and the expected time
    D. time along the critical path and another path

46. The PERT planning method is MUCH facilitated by

    A. computer execution
    B. special peripheral equipment, notably x-y plotters
    C. the theory of waiting lines
    D. Monte Carlo methods

47. Management by exception is facilitated by which one of the following managerial methods?

    A. Theory X
    B. Theory Y
    C. Fixed systems and procedures
    D. The managerial grid

48. In the PERT project planning method, the critical path is the

    A. maximum elapsed time to completion
    B. maximum average elapsed time to completion
    C. maximum expected elapsed time to completion
    D. best method of doing the job

49. Zero-base budgeting cannot be used universally PRIMARILY because

    A. it is too time-consuming to do properly
    B. there are mandatory programs which must be funded
    C. it reduces the efficient functioning of the agency whose budget is concerned
    D. the information for doing it is not always available

50. In establishing standards for clerical or physical tasks, it is MOST appropriate to use a(the)

    A. theoretical value
    B. absolute value, based on current study
    C. expected value and an expression of variability
    D. expected value and a time trend pertaining to it

KEY (CORRECT ANSWERS)

1. A	11. C	21. B	31. B	41. D
2. B	12. B	22. B	32. C	42. B
3. C	13. A	23. C	33. D	43. B
4. B	14. B	24. C	34. D	44. D
5. C	15. C	25. A	35. B	45. D
6. C	16. A	26. D	36. B	46. A
7. A	17. C	27. A	37. B	47. C
8. D	18. B	28. B	38. D	48. C
9. A	19. A	29. B	39. D	49. B
10. B	20. A	30. C	40. A	50. C

TEST 2

DIRECTIONS: Each question or incomplete statement is followed by several suggested answers or completions. Select the one that BEST answers the question or completes the statement. *PRINT THE LETTER OF THE CORRECT ANSWER IN THE SPACE AT THE RIGHT.*

1. All modern governments have developed specific procedures to ensure accountability for the receipt and expenditure of public funds. The steps in one such procedure are given below, out of their logical order.
   Select the option which BEST presents these stages in their logical sequence.
   I. Disbursing officers provide for the payment of cash or check to satisfy the liability.
   II. The central financial authority (treasury) places money at the disposal of disbursing officers.
   III. The heads of agencies extend to designated officials within the agency the authorization to incur obligations. Designated officials award contracts for goods and services and incur obligations for the payment of salaries.
   IV. The legislature authorizes the chief executive to make expenditure authority available to administrative agencies. The executive authority responsible for the execution of the budget, in accordance with legislative action, extends to the agencies authorization to incur obligations.
   V. Fiscal officers within agencies prepare and certify vouchers to show that obligations are due and payable by disbursing officers. Orders for payment are prepared by fiscal officers and submitted to disbursing officers.

   The BEST logical sequence is:

   A. II, V, IV, I, III   B. III, II, V, I, IV
   C. IV, III, II, V, I   D. V, I, III, IV, II

2. In a complex organization, particularly one with field offices, where generally similar activities are conducted in more than one location and administered by different organizational units, agency budgeting can be MOST facilitated by the use of which one of the following techniques?

   A. Gantt charting   B. Factorial estimating
   C. Econometric models   D. Double budgeting

Questions 3-5.

DIRECTIONS: Each of Questions 3 through 5 consists of a paragraph which contains one word that is incorrectly used because it is NOT in keeping with the meaning that the paragraph is evidently intended to convey. Determine which word is incorrectly used. Select from the choices lettered A, B, C, and D the word which, when substituted for the incorrectly used word, would BEST help to convey the meaning of the paragraph.

3. More difficult to set are standards not expressed in either physical or monetary measurements. What standard can a budget examiner use for determining the competence of an attorney or a personnel officer? What can he use for determining whether the agency's recruiting program meets both short- and long-term objectives? Or whether the public relations program is successful? Are supervisors loyal to the agency's objectives? Such questions show how difficult it is to establish standards for goals that cannot be given clear quantitative or qualitative measurement. Many definite standards exist in agencies because thorough research into what constitutes desired performance has not been done above the level of the repair shop, the stockroom, or the accounting department. Perhaps a more important reason is that where human relationships count in performance, it is very hard to measure what is *good, effective,* or *efficient.*

   A. completely
   B. meaningless
   C. resist
   D. reinforcement

4. The fact that some programs are not subject to constant budgetary review and that government budgets thus come to be at least partially uncontrollable has been viewed with great concern by some authorities. There is no doubt that strongly entrenched programs sustain the overall effectiveness of budgetary review. But in these circumstances, *uncontrollable* is probably a misnomer. These outlays can be controlled, but they may be irreducible. In many cases, programs are so well established, so strongly supported by interest groups, and so much a part of accepted public policy that frequent and searching budgetary review, extending to annual examination of substantive legislation, would be somewhat pointless. If there is widespread agreement, inside and outside the legislature, that veterans should receive pensions for service-connected disabilities, there is no need for extensive hearings before appropriations committees on the merits of funds for veterans' pensions.
   A change in policy toward veterans is not likely to come from appropriations committees.

   A. premature
   B. overriding
   C. misdirected
   D. limit

5. Promptness is a great virtue in control reports. Unfortunately, it is often difficult to be both prompt and accurate. An accurate evaluation may require a certain amount of investigation and double-checking. The person making an evaluation naturally wants to be sure he can justify his conclusions. In addition, delay is likely to be compounded if a report is prepared by someone who is trained to balance accounts to the last penny. A hospital administrator, for example, was having great difficulty in keeping down expenses partly because expense reports did not become available until six to eight weeks following the events presumably being controlled. Executives who use control reports should be fully aware of what kind of information they are getting. If they insist on prompt reports, they must learn to disregard substantial variations and to expect some false alarms. On the other hand, if they are interested in having the full facts and being deliberate in taking action, then they need a different kind of report. Because most organizations need both accurate and timely reports, managerial skill is required to ensure that the control reports are really suited to their purposes.

   A. annul
   B. insignificant
   C. monitoring
   D. unequivocal

6. Historically, those who favor *legislative* rather than executive budgeting assert that legislative budgeting would

   A. result in a better separation of powers
   B. cut down government spending
   C. be less susceptible to special pressure groups
   D. produce balanced budgets

7. In 2012, a department bought a piece of a certain supply item for a total of $x. In 2013, the department bought k percent fewer of the item but had to pay a total of g percent more for it.
   Which of the following formulae is CORRECT for determining the average price per item in 2013?

   A. $100\dfrac{xg}{nk}$
   B. $\dfrac{x(100+g)}{n(100-k)}$
   C. $\dfrac{x(100-g)}{n(100+k)}$
   D. $\dfrac{x}{n} - 100\dfrac{g}{k}$

8. A sample of 18 income tax returns, each with 4 personal exemptions, is taken for 2011 and for 2012. The breakdown is as follows in terms of income:

Average gross income (in thousands)	Number of returns 2011	Number of returns 2012
4	6	2
8	10	11
12	2	5

   There is a personal deduction per exemption of $500. There are no other expense deductions. In addition, there is an exclusion of $3000 for incomes less than $5000 and $2000 for incomes from $5000 to $9999.99. From $10,000 upward, there is no exclusion. Total net taxable income for the samples (in thousands) for 2011 is MOST NEARLY

   A. $60   B. $85   C. $10   D. $128

9. In the preceding question, the increase in total net taxable income for the sample (in thousands) between 2011 and 2012 is

   A. 18   B. 20   C. 24   D. 34

Questions 10-12.

DIRECTIONS: Answer Questions 10 through 12 on the basis of the following information.

Four batches of lightbulbs purchased by the city from four different suppliers contained defective units in the following percentages:

Supplier	Number	Percent Defective
A	3,000	1.2
B	5,000	1.4
C	4,000	1.6
D	8,000	0.8

10. The COMBINED percent defective is

    A. 1.25   B. 1.21   C. 1.17   D. 1.10

11. A further 13,000 bulbs split proportionately among the suppliers would have a number defective of about

    A. 152   B. 162   C. 175   D. 330

12. A systematic comparison of the quality of the four suppliers' products is called

    A. operations research
    B. cost-effectiveness analysis
    C. cost-benefit analysis
    D. value analysis

Questions 13-15.

DIRECTIONS: Answer Questions 13 through 15 on the basis of the following information.

In 2014, a police precinct records 456 oases of car thefts which is 22.6 percent of all grand larcenies. In 2015, there were 560 such cases, which constituted 35% of the broader category.

13. The number of crimes in the broader category in 2015 was MOST NEARLY

    A. 1600   B. 1700   C. 1960   D. 2800

14. The change from 2014 to 2015 in the number of crimes in the broader category represented MOST NEARLY a

    A. 2.5% decrease   B. 10.1% increase
    C. 12.5% increase   D. 20% decrease

15. In 2015, one out of every 6 of these crimes was solved. This represents MOST NEARLY what percentage of the total number of crimes in the broader category that year?

    A. 5.8   B. 6   C. 9.3   D. 12

16. Assume that a maintenance shop does 5 brake jobs to every 3 front-end jobs. It does 8000 jobs altogether in a 240-day year. In one day, one worker can do 3 front-end jobs or 4 brake jobs.
    About how many workers will be needed in the shop?

    A. 3   B. 5   C. 10   D. 18

17. Assume that the price of a certain item declines by 6 percent one year and then increases by 5 and 10 percent, respectively, during the next two years.
    What is the OVERALL increase in price over the three-year period?

    A. 4.2   B. 6   C. 8.6   D. 10.1

18. After finding the total percent change in a price (TC) over a three-year period, as in the preceding question, one could compute the average annual percent change in the price by using the formula:

A. $(1+TC)^{1/3}$
B. $\dfrac{(1+TC)}{3}$

C. $(1+TC)^{1/3}-1$
D. $\dfrac{1}{(1+TC)\sqrt[3]{3}-1}$

Questions 19-21.

DIRECTIONS: Answer Questions 19 through 21 on the basis of the following information.

The number of applications processed per day by a group of clerks can be expressed as follows:

Characteristic	No. Processed Per Day
mean	34.6
median	29.6
minimum	18.3
maximum	47.7

19. On the basis of the information given, it would be WRONG to conclude that

   A. the data are normally distributed
   B. the data are skewed to the right
   C. a suitable histogram could have a lower limit of 15 and an upper limit of 49.9
   D. employees processed more than 29.6 applications each per day

20. The range is

   A. 14.7   B. 29.4   C. 33.0   D. 66.0

21. The mid-range is

   A. 14.7   B. 29.4   C. 33.0   D. 66.0

Questions 22-25.

DIRECTIONS: Questions 22 through 25 are to be answered on the basis of the following information.

Assume that the Department of Industrial Waste and Combustibles of the City of Silver Keys is trying to decide what fee it will oharge private engineering organizations for a specific type of laboratory analysis that it performs for them. The Department's laboratory is equipped to process as many as 250 waste and soot samples per day. The Commissioner of Industrial Waste and Combustibles knows that at $5 per analysis, the laboratory will operate to capacity. He is convinced that raising the price will cause the private engineering organizations to perform the analyses themselves rather than submit their samples to the laboratory. On the average, he expects to lose one sample for each 2.5 cent increase in the fee (Chart A). The Commissioner's cost data indicate that there is a fixed expense of $275 to run the laboratory for one day. Extra technicians, supplies, and so forth, add a variable cost of $3 per sample for each sample analyzed.

CHART A

Fee	Number of Analyses	Income
$5.00	250	$1250.00
5.25	240	1260.00
5.50	230	1265.00
5.75	220	1265.00
6.00	210	1260.00
6.25	200	1250.00
6.50	190	1235.00
6.75	180	1215.00
7.00	170	1190.00
7.25	160	1160.00
7.50	150	1125.00
7.75	140	1085.00

22. Each five-cent rise in the fee will

   A. *decrease* expenses by $60
   B. *decrease* expenses by $30
   C. *increase* expenses by $12
   D. *decrease* expenses by $6

23. According to Chart A, if the Department sets its fee at a level that brings in the maximum net income, the number of samples it would receive will be MOST NEARLY

   A. 165   B. 188   C. 205   D. 215

24. Which of the following conclusions can LOGICALLY be drawn from the above information?

   A. Eventually, the decrease in the number of samples submitted for analysis will not be offset by the increase in the fee.
   B. Each time the fee is raised, net income will increase.
   C. Net income will increase until the total expense equals the fixed expense plus the variable expense; thereafter, net income will remain constant.
   D. Maximum gross returns will be reached each time the fee is raised.

25. For the Department to obtain maximum net income, the fee should be set between

   A. $7.50 and $7.75   B. $7.00 and $7.25
   C. $6.25 and $6.50   D. $5.25 and $5.75

26. Assume that supervisor S has four subordinates - A, B, C, and D. The MAXIMUM number of relationships, assuming that all combinations are included, that can exist between S and his subordinates is

   A. 28   B. 15   C. 7   D. 4

7 (#2)

27. If the workmen's compensation insurance rate for clerical workers is 93 cents per $100 of wages, the total premium paid by a city whose clerical staff earns $8,765,000 is MOST NEARLY

    A. $8,150   B. $81,515   C. $87,650   D. $93,765

27._____

28. Assume that a city council has approved a budget of $3,240,000,000 for the fiscal year beginning July 1, 2013. A city sales tax is expected to provide $1,100,000,000; licenses, fees, and sundry revenues are expected to yield $121,600,000; the balance is to be raised from property taxes. A tax equalization board has appraised all property in the city at a fair value of $42,500,000,000. The council wishes to assess property at 60% of its fair value.
    The tax rate would need to be MOST NEARLY_____ per $100 of assessed value.

    A. $12.70   B. $10.65   C. $7.90   D. $4.00

28._____

29. The basic approach to a choice of alternatives is a method called

    A. linear programming
    C. total cost analysis
    B. incremental analysis
    D. general systems analysis

29._____

Questions 30-33.

DIRECTIONS: Answer Questions 30 through 33 on the basis of the following information.

Consider the following costs of a fire prevention program which can be funded at five different levels:

Funding Level	Annual Cost $(000)	Estimated Annual Property Loss $(000)	Lives Lost Per Year
A	0	2,000	5
B	100	1,000	3
C	500	500	1
D	1,000	250	3/4*
E	1,800	150	1/2

*I,e., three lives every four years.

30. If Choice C is made as against B, the payoff (excluding value of a life) is

    A. $0
    C. $300,000
    B. $100,000
    D. $500,000

30._____

31. If Choice D is made as against C, the IMPLICIT value of a human life is

    A. $250,000
    C. $1,000,000
    B. $750,000
    D. $1,333,333

31._____

32. The annual rate of return (exclusive of lives saved) on alternative C is MOST NEARLY

    A. 0%   B. 20%   C. 33%   D. 40%

32._____

33. Among the properties to be protected is a special high-risk group, such that 65% of the costs would be needed to avoid 25% of the loss.
The return on that part of Alternative B applicable to this high-risk property class (exclusive of lives) would be MOST NEARLY

   A. 3.8 B. 16.25 C. 26 D. 90

34. The following chart shows the number of persons employed in a certain industry for each year from 2007 through 2012.

	Thousands of employees
2007	5.7
2008	6.8
2009	7.0
2010	7.1
2011	7.4
2012	6.4

   In making a forecast of future trends, the one of the following steps which should be taken FIRST is to

   A. take the six-year average
   B. fit a curvilinear trend to the data
   C. fit a straight line, omitting 1982 as an *outlier*, i.e., as an unusually low reading
   D. check on what happened to the industry in 1982

35. Of the following, the factor which is generally considered to be LEAST characteristic of a good control report is that it

   A. stresses performance that adheres to standard rather than emphasizing the exception
   B. supplies information intended to serve as the basis for corrective action
   C. provides feedback for the planning process
   D. includes data that reflect trends as well as current status

36. Of the following concepts, the one which CANNOT be represented suitably by a pie chart is

   A. percent shares
   B. shares in absolute units
   C. time trends
   D. successive totals over time, with their shares

37. A pictogram is ESSENTIALLY another version of a(n) _____ chart.

   A. plain bar   B. component bar
   C. pie   D. area

38. A time series for a certain cost is presented in a graph. It is drawn so that the vertical (cost) axis starts at a point well above zero.
This is a legitimate method of presentation for some purposes, but it may have the effect of

A. hiding fixed components of the cost
B. exaggerating changes which, in actual amounts, may be insignificant
C. magnifying fixed components of the cost
D. impairing correlation analysis

39. Certain budgetary data may be represented by bar, area, or volume charts. Which one of the following BEST expresses the most appropriate order of usefulness?

    A. Descends from bar to volume and area charts, the last two being about the same
    B. Descends from volume to area to bar charts
    C. Depends on the nature of the data presented
    D. Descends from bar to area to volume charts

40. Among the original purposes of the governmental budgeting process, one hoped-for improvement which was LARGELY realized was

    A. better managerial control over operations
    B. legislative consideration of proposed expenditures in close correlation with revenue receipts
    C. a budget balanced by a precise equivalence of taxes and expenditures
    D. keeping government spending down

41. As used in systems analysis, the term *scenario* denotes a

    A. policy
    B. procedure
    C. set of rules
    D. primitive model

42. In budgeting, the quantification of tangible and intangible benefits

    A. is legally required
    B. has been done regularly since governmental budgeting was instituted
    C. is difficult in most cases
    D. requires only the setting of goals

43. When a time series is plotted on a ratio scale and comes out as an ascending straight line, it means that the dependent variable is increasing

    A. by equal increments
    B. at an increasing percentage rate
    C. at a constant percentage rate
    D. at a declining percentage rate

44. The one of the following ingredients of the scientific method which CANNOT be used in program analysis is that of

    A. a complex hypothesis
    B. a provable theory
    C. computer simulation
    D. repeated controlled experiments

45. When government budgeting was first introduced, it was attacked PRIMARILY as a(n)
    A. generator of excessive red tape
    B. power play by the legislative branch
    C. power play by the judicial branch
    D. example of creeping socialism

Questions 46-50.

DIRECTIONS: Answer Questions 46 through 50 on the basis of the information below.

Department XYZ
Size Distribution of Purchasing Orders

Amount of Order (dollars)	Number of Orders
1 - 9.99	91
10 - 19.99	135
20 - 49.99	320
50 - 99.99	712
100 - 199.99	1,050
200 - 499.99	735
500 - 999.99	305
1,000 - 1,999.99	94
2,000 - 4,999.99	36
5,000 - 9,999.99	18
10,000 - 19,999.99	3
20,000 - 49,000.99	1

46. The mode of this distribution of purchase orders is APPROXIMATELY
    A. $100   B. $150   C. $200   D. $1050

47. The median value is APPROXIMATELY
    A. $100   B. $150   C. $200   D. $1050

48. The value which falls at the tenth percentile is MOST NEARLY
    A. $21   B. $39   C. $45   D. $107

49. Suppose ten orders are added to each class interval below $1,000, but only one order is added in each interval $1,000 and above.
    Lacking more detailed information about them, we can estimate the total cost of these additional orders to be APPROXIMATELY
    A. $23,800   B. $76,100   C. $81,000   D. $123,800

50. Suppose that, in the original date, the first class interval given were specified as *less than $10* and the last two as *$10,000 and over.*
    In that case, we would

    A. not be able to compute the mode
    B. not be able to compute the median
    C. not be able to compute the mean
    D. still be able to compute the mean, median, and mode

50.____

KEY (CORRECT ANSWERS)

1. C	11. A	21. C	31. C	41. D
2. B	12. D	22. D	32. B	42. C
3. B	13. A	23. A	33. B	43. C
4. D	14. D	24. A	34. D	44. D
5. B	15. A	25. B	35. A	45. A
6. D	16. C	26. B	36. C	46. B
7. B	17. C	27. B	37. A	47. B
8. A	18. C	28. C	38. B	48. B
9. D	19. A	29. B	39. D	49. B
10. C	20. B	30. B	40. A	50. C

EXAMINATION SECTION
TEST 1

DIRECTIONS: Each question or incomplete statement is followed by several suggested answers or completions. Select the one that BEST answers the question or completes the statement. *PRINT THE LETTER OF THE CORRECT ANSWER IN THE SPACE AT THE RIGHT.*

1. Assume that a manager is preparing a list of reasons to justify making a major change in methods and procedures in his agency.
   Which of the following reasons would be LEAST appropriate on such a list?
   A. Improve the means for satisfying needs and wants of agency personnel
   B. Increase efficiency
   C. Intensify competition and stimulate loyalty to separate work groups
   D. Contribute to the individual and group satisfaction of agency personnel

2. Many managers recognize the benefits of decentralization but are concerned about the danger of over-relaxation of control as a result of increased delegation.
   Of the following, the MOST appropriate means of establishing proper control under decentralization is for the manager to
   A. establish detailed standards for all phases of operation
   B. shift his attention from operating details to appraisal of results
   C. keep himself informed by decreasing the time span covered by reports
   D. make unilateral decisions on difficult situations that arise in decentralized locations

3. In some agencies, the counsel to the agency head is given the right to bypass the chain of command and issue orders directly to the staff concerning matters that involve certain specific processes and practices.
   This situation MOST NEARLY illustrates the principle of _____ authority.
   A. the acceptance theory of   B. multiple-linear
   C. splintered   D. functional

4. Assume that a manager is writing a brief report to his superior outlining the advantages of matrix organization.
   Of the following, it would be INCORRECT to state that
   A. in matrix organization, a project is emphasized by designating one individual as the focal point for all matters pertaining to it
   B. utilization of manpower can be flexible in matrix organization because a reservoir of specialists is maintained in the line operations
   C. the usual line staff arrangement is generally reversed in matrix organization
   D. in matrix organization, responsiveness to project needs is generally faster due to establishing needed communication lines and decision points

5. It is commonly understood that communication is an important part of the administrative process.
Which of the following is NOT a valid principle of the communication process in administration?
   A. The channels of communication should be spontaneous.
   B. The lines of communication should be as direct and as short as possible.
   C. Communications should be authenticated.
   D. The persons serving in communications centers should be competent.

6. The PRIMARY purpose of the quantitative approach in management is to
   A. identify better alternatives for management decision-making
   B. substitute data for judgment
   C. match opinions to data
   D. match data to opinions

7. If an executive wants to make a strong case for running his agency as a flat type of structure, he should point out that the PRIMARY advantage of doing so is to
   A. provide less experience in decision-making for agency personnel
   B. facilitate frequent contact between each superior and his immediate subordinates
   C. improve communication and unify attitudes
   D. improve communication and diversify attitudes

8. In deciding how detailed his delegation of authority to a subordinate should be, a manager should follow the general principle that
   A. delegation of authority is more detailed at the top of the organizational structure
   B. detailed delegation of authority is associated with detailed work assignments
   C. delegation of authority should be in sufficient detail to prevent overlapping assignments
   D. detailed delegation of authority is associated with broad work assignments

9. In recent years, newer and more fluid types of organizational forms have been developed. One of these is a type of free-form organization.
Another name for this type of organization is the
   A. project organization   B. semimix organization
   C. naturalistic structure   D. semipermanent structure

10. Which of the following is the MAJOR objective of operational or management systems audits?
    A. Determining the number of personnel needed
    B. Recommending opportunities for improving operating and management practices
    C. Detecting fraud
    D. Determining organization problems

11. Assume that a manager observes that conflict exists between his agency and another operating agency of government.
Which of the following statements is the LEAST probable cause of this conflict?
    A. Incompatibility between the agencies' goals but similarity in their resource allocations
    B. Compatibility between agencies' goals and resources
    C. Status differences between agency personnel
    D. Differences in perceptions of each other's policies

12. Of the following, a MAJOR purpose of brainstorming as a problem-solving technique is to
    A. develop the ability to concentrate
    B. encourage creative thinking
    C. evaluate employees' ideas
    D. develop critical ability

13. The one of the following requirements which is LEAST likely to accompany regular delegation of work from a manager to a subordinate is a(n)
    A. need to review the organization's workload
    B. indication of what work the subordinate is to do
    C. need to grant authority to the subordinate
    D. obligation for the subordinate who accepts the work to try to complete it

14. Of the following, the one factor which is generally considered LEAST essential to successful committee operation is
    A. stating a clear definition of the authority and scope of the committee
    B. selecting the committee chairman carefully
    C. limiting the size of the committee to four persons
    D. limiting the subject matter to that which can be handled in group discussion

15. In using the program evaluation and review technique, the *critical path* is the path that
    A. requires the shortest time
    B. requires the longest time
    C. focuses most attention on social constraints
    D. focuses most attention to repetitious jobs

16. Which one of the following is LEAST characteristic of the management-by-objectives approach?
    A. The scope within which the employee may exercise decision-making is broadened.
    B. The employee starts with a self-appraisal of his performances, abilities, and potential.
    C. Emphasis is placed on activities performed; activities orientation is maximized.
    D. Each employee participates in determining his own objectives.

17. The function of management which puts into effect the decisions, plans, and programs that have previously been worked out for achieving the goals of the group is MOST appropriately called
    A. scheduling   B. classifying   C. budgeting   D. directing

18. In the establishment of a plan to improve office productive efficiency, which of the following guidelines is LEAST helpful in setting sound work standards?
    A. Employees must accept the plan's objectives.
    B. Current production averages must be promulgated as work standards for a group.
    C. The work flow must generally be fairly constant.
    D. The operation of the plan must be expressed in terms understandable to the worker.

19. The one of the following activities which, generally speaking, is of *relatively* MAJOR importance at the lower-management level and of *somewhat* LESSER importance at higher-management levels is
    A. actuating   B. forecasting   C. organizing   D. planning

20. Three styles of leadership exist: democratic, authoritarian, and laissez-faire. Of the following work situations, the one in which a democratic approach would normally be the MOST effective is when the work is
    A. routine and moderately complex   B. repetitious and simple
    C. complex and not routine   D. simple and not routine

21. Governmental and business organizations *generally* encounter the GREATEST difficulties in developing tangible measures of which one of the following?
    A. The level of expenditures   B. Contributions to social welfare
    C. Retention rates   D. Causes of labor unrest

22. Of the following, a *management-by-objectives* program is BEST described as
    A. a new comprehensive plan of organization
    B. introduction of budgets and financial controls
    C. introduction of long-range planning
    D. development of future goals with supporting and related progress reviews

23. Research and analysis is probably the most widely used technique for selecting alternatives when major planning decisions are involved.
    Of the following, a VALUABLE characteristic of research and analysis is that this technique
    A. places the problem in a meaningful conceptual framework
    B. involves practical application of the various alternatives
    C. accurately analyzes all important tangibles
    D. is much less expensive than other problem-solving methods

24. If a manager were assigned the task of using a systems approach to designing a new work unit, which of the following should he consider FIRST in carrying out his design?
    A. Networks
    B. Work flows and information processes
    C. Linkages and relationships
    D. Decision points and control loops

25. The MAIN distinction between Theory X and Theory Y approaches to organization, in accordance with Douglas McGregor's view, is that Theory Y
    A. considers that work is natural to people; Theory X assumes that people are lazy and avoid work
    B. leads to a tall, narrow organization structure, while Theory X leads to one that is flat
    C. organizations motivate people with money; Theory X organizations motivate people with good working conditions
    D. represents authoritarian management, while Theory X management is participative

KEY (CORRECT ANSWERS)

1.	C	11.	B
2.	B	12.	B
3.	D	13.	A
4.	C	14.	C
5.	A	15.	B
6.	A	16.	C
7.	C	17.	D
8.	B	18.	B
9.	A	19.	A
10.	B	20.	C

21.	B
22.	D
23.	A
24.	B
25.	A

TEST 2

DIRECTIONS: Each question or incomplete statement is followed by several suggested answers or completions. Select the one that BEST answers the question or completes the statement. *PRINT THE LETTER OF THE CORRECT ANSWER IN THE SPACE AT THE RIGHT.*

1. Of the following, the stage in decision-making which is usually MOST difficult is
   A. stating the alternatives
   B. predicting the possible outcome of each alternative
   C. evaluating the relative merits of each alternative
   D. minimizing the undesirable aspects of the alternative selected

   1.____

2. In a department where a clerk is reporting both to a senior clerk in charge of the mail room and also to a supervising clerk in charge of the duplicating section, there may be a breakdown of the management principle called
   A. horizontal specialization   B. job enrichment
   C. unity of command   D. Graicunas' Law

   2.____

3. Of the following, the failure by line managers to accept and appreciate the benefits and limitations of a new program or system VERY frequently can be traced to the
   A. budgetary problems involved
   B. resultant need to reduce staff
   C. lack of controls it engenders
   D. failure of top management to support its implementation

   3.____

4. Although there is general agreement that *management-by-objectives* has made a major contribution to modern management of large organizations, criticisms of the system during the past few years have resulted in
   A. mounting pressure for relaxation of management goals
   B. renewed concern with human values and the manager's personal needs
   C. over-mechanistic application of the perceptions of the behavioral scientists
   D. disillusionment with *management-by-objectives* on the part of a majority of managers

   4.____

5. Of the following, which is usually considered to be a MAJOR obstacle to the systematic analysis of potential problems by managers?
   A. Managers have a tendency to think that all the implications of some proposed step cannot be fully understood.
   B. Rewards rarely go to those managers who are most successful at resolving current problems in management.
   C. There is a common conviction of manages that their goals are difficult to achieve.
   D. Managers are far more concerned about correcting today's problems than with preventing tomorrow's.

   5.____

6. Which of the following should generally have the MOST influence on the selection of supervisors?
   A. Experience within the work unit where the vacancies exist
   B. Amount of money needed to effect the promotion
   C. Personal preferences of the administration
   D. Evaluation of capacity to exercise supervisory responsibilities

7. In questioning a potential administrator for selection purposes, the one of the following practices which is MOST desirable is to
   A. encourage the job applicant to give primarily *yes* or *no* replies
   B. get the applicant to talk freely and in detail about his background
   C. let the job applicant speak most of the time
   D. probe the applicant's attitudes, motivation, and willingness to accept responsibility

8. In implementing the managerial function of training subordinates, it is USEFUL to know that a widely agreed-upon definition of human learning is that learning
   A. is a relatively permanent change in behavior that results from reinforced practice or experience
   B. involves an improvement, but not necessarily a change in behavior
   C. involves a change in behavior, but not necessarily an improvement
   D. is a temporary change in behavior which must be subject to practice or experience

9. If a manager were thinking about using a committee of subordinates to solve an operating problem, which of the following would generally NOT be an advantage of such use of the committee approach?
   A. Improved coordination   B. Low cost
   C. Increased motivation   D. Integrated judgment

10. Which one of the following management approaches MOST often uses model-building techniques to solve management problems? _____ approach.
    A. Behavioral   B. Fiscal   C. Quantitative   D. Process

11. Of the following, the MOST serious risk in using budgets as a tool for management control is the
    A. probable neglect of other good management practices
    B. likelihood of guesswork because of the need to plan far in advance
    C. possibility of undue emphasis on factors that are easiest to measure
    D. danger of making qualitative rather than quantitative assessments of performance

12. In government budgeting, the problem of relating financial transactions to the fiscal year in which they are budgeted is BEST met by
    A. determining the cash balance by comparing how much money has been received and how much has been paid out
    B. applying net revenue to the fiscal year in which they are collected as offset by relevant expenses

C. adopting a system whereby appropriations are entered when they are received and expenditures are entered when they are paid out
D. entering expenditures on the books when the obligation to make the expenditure is made

13. If the agency's bookkeeping system records income when it is received and expenditures when the money is paid out this system is USUALLY known as a _____ system.
    A. cash
    B. flow-payment
    C. deferred
    D. fiscal year income

14. An audit, as the term applies to budget execution, is MOST NEARLY a
    A. procedure based on the budget estimates
    B. control exercised by the executive on the legislature in the establishment of program priorities
    C. check on the legality of expenditures and is based on the appropriations act
    D. requirement which must be met before funds can be spent

15. In government budgeting, there is a procedure known as *allotment*.
    Of the following statements which relate to allotment, select the one that is MOST generally considered to be correct.
    Allotment
    A. increases the practice of budget units coming back to the legislature branch for supplemental appropriations
    B. is simply an example of red tape
    C. eliminates the requirement of timing of expenditures
    D. is designed to prevent waste

16. In government budgeting, the establishment of the schedules of allotments is MOST generally the responsibility of the
    A. budget unit and the legislature
    B. budget unit and the executive
    C. budget unit only
    D. executive and the legislature

17. Of the following statements relating to preparation of an organization's budget request, which is the MOST generally valid precaution?
    A. Give specific instructions on the format or budget requests and required supporting data
    B. Because of the complexity of preparing a budget request, avoid argumentation to support the requests
    C. Put requests in whatever format is desirable
    D. Consider that final approval will be given to initial estimates

18. Of the following statements which relate to the budget process in a well-organized government, select the one that is MOST NEARLY correct.
    A. The budget cycle is the step-by-step process which is repeated each and every fiscal year.
    B. Securing approval of the budget does not take place within the budget cycle.

C. The development of a new budget and putting it into effect is a two-step process known as the budget cycle.
D. The fiscal period, usually a fiscal year, has no relation to the budget cycle.

19. If a manager were asked what PPBS stands for, he would be RIGHT if he said _____ budgeting system.
    A. public planning
    B. planning programming
    C. planning projections
    D. programming procedures

19._____

Questions 20-21.

DIRECTIONS: Questions 20 and 21 are to be answered on the basis of the following information.

Sample Budget

Refuse Collection	Amount
Personal Services	$30,000
Contractual Services	5,000
Supplies and Materials	5,000
Capital Outlay	10,000
	$50,000

Residential Collections	
Dwellings – 1 pickup per week	1,000
Tons of refuse collected per year	375
Cost of collections per ton	$ 8
Cost per dwelling pickup per year	$ 3
Total annual cost	$3,000

20. The sample budget shown is a simplified example of a _____ budget.
    A. factorial   B. performance   C. qualitative   D. rational

20._____

21. The budget shown in the sample differs CHIEFLY from line-item and program budgets in that it includes
    A. objects of expenditure but not activities or functions
    B. only activities, functions, and control
    C. activities and functions but not objects of expenditures
    D. levels of service

21._____

Question 22.

DIRECTIONS: Question 22 is to be answered on the basis of the following information.

Sample Budget

Environmental Safety
  Air Pollution Protection
    Personal Services $20,000,000
    Contractual Services   4,000,000
    Supplies and Materials   4,000,000
    Capital Outlay   2,000,000
      Total Air Pollution Protection $30,000,000

  Water Pollution Protection
    Personal Services $23,000,000
    Supplies and Materials   4,500,000
    Capital Outlay   20,500,000
      Total Water Pollution Protection $48,000,000

Total Environmental Safety $78,000,000

22. Based on the above budget, which is the MOST valid statement?
    A. Environmental Safety, Air Pollution Protection, and Water Pollution Protection could all be considered program elements.
    B. The object listings included water pollution protection and capital outlay.
    C. Examples of the program element listings in the above are personal services and supplies and materials
    D. Contractual Services and Environmental Safety were the program element listings.

22.____

23. Which of the following is NOT an advantage of a program budget over a line-item budget?
    A program budget
    A. allows us to set up priority lists in deciding what activities we will spend our money on
    B. gives us more control over expenditures than a line-item budget
    C. is more informative in that we know the broad purposes of spending money
    D. enables us to see if one program is getting much less money than the others

23.____

24. If a manager were trying to explain the fundamental difference between traditional accounting theory and practice and the newer practice of managerial accounting, he would be MOST accurate if he said that
    A. traditional accounting practice focused on providing information for persons outside organizations, while managerial accounting focuses on providing information for people inside organizations
    B. traditional accounting practice focused on providing information for persons inside organizations while managerial accounting focuses on providing information for persons outside organizations

24.____

C. managerial accounting is exclusively concerned with historical facts while traditional accounting stresses future projections exclusively
D. traditional accounting practice is more budget-focused than managerial accounting

25. Which of the following formulas is used to determine the number of days required to process work?
 _____ = Days to Process Work

A. $\dfrac{\text{Employees} \times \text{Daily Output}}{\text{Volume}}$

B. $\dfrac{\text{Volume} \times \text{Daily Output}}{\text{Volume}}$

C. $\dfrac{\text{Volume}}{\text{Employees} \times \text{Daily Output}}$

D. $\dfrac{\text{Employees} \times \text{Volume}}{\text{Daily Output}}$

25.____

KEY (CORRECT ANSWERS)

1.	C		11.	C
2.	C		12.	D
3.	D		13.	A
4.	B		14.	C
5.	D		15.	D
6.	D		16.	C
7.	D		17.	A
8.	A		18.	A
9.	B		19.	B
10.	C		20.	B

21. D
22. A
23. B
24. A
25. C

TEST 3

DIRECTIONS: Each question or incomplete statement is followed by several suggested answers or completions. Select the one that BEST answers the question or completes the statement. *PRINT THE LETTER OF THE CORRECT ANSWER IN THE SPACE AT THE RIGHT.*

1. Electronic data processing equipment can produce more information faster than can be generated by any other means.
   In view of this, the MOST important problem faced by management at present is to
   A. keep computers fully occupied
   B. find enough computer personnel
   C. assimilate and properly evaluate the information
   D. obtain funds to establish appropriate information systems

   1.____

2. A well-designed management information system ESSENTIALLY provides each executive and manager the information he needs for
   A. determining computer time requirements
   B. planning and measuring results
   C. drawing a new organization chart
   D. developing a new office layout

   2.____

3. It is generally agreed that management policies should be periodically reappraised and restated in accordance with current conditions.
   Of the following, the approach which would be MOST effective in determining whether a policy should be revised is to
   A. conduct interviews with staff members at all levels in order to ascertain the relationship between the policy and actual practice
   B. make proposed revisions in the policy and apply it to current problems
   C. make up hypothetical situations using both the old policy and a revised version in order to make comparisons
   D. call a meeting of top level staff in order to discuss ways of revising the policy

   3.____

4. Every manager has many occasions to lead a conference or participate in a conference of some sort.
   Of the following statements that pertain to conferences and conference leadership, which is generally considered to be MOST valid?
   A. Since World War II, the trend has been toward fewer shared decisions and more conferences.
   B. The most important part of a conference leader's job is to direct discussion.
   C. In providing opportunities for group interaction, management should avoid consideration of its past management philosophy.
   D. A good administrator cannot lead a good conference if he is a poor public speaker.

   4.____

5. Of the following, it is usually LEAST desirable for a conference leader to
   A. turn the question to the person who asked it
   B. summarize proceedings periodically
   C. make a practice of not repeating questions
   D. ask a question without indicating who is to reply

6. The behavioral school of management thought bases its beliefs on certain assumptions.
   Which of the following is NOT a belief of this school of thought?
   A. People tend to seek and accept responsibility.
   B. Most people can be creative in solving problems.
   C. People prefer security above all else.
   D. Commitment is the most important factor in motivating people.

7. The one of the following objectives which would be LEAST appropriate as a major goal of research in the field of human resources management is to
   A. predict future conditions, events, and manpower needs
   B. evaluate established policies, programs, and practices
   C. evaluate proposed policies, programs, and practices
   D. identify deficient organizational units and apply suitable penalties

8. Of the following general interviewing methods or techniques, the one that is USUALLY considered to be effective in counseling, grievances, and appraisal interviews is the _____ interview.
   A. directed   B. non-directed   C. panel   D. patterned

9. The ESSENTIAL first phase of decision-making is
   A. finding alternative solutions
   B. making a diagnosis of the problem
   C. selecting the plan to follow
   D. analyzing and comparing alternative solutions

10. Assume that, in a certain organization, a situation has developed in which there is little difference in status or authority between individuals.
    Which of the following would be the MOST likely result with regard to communication in this organization?
    A. Both the accuracy and flow of communication will be improved.
    B. Both the accuracy and flow of communication will substantially decrease.
    C. Employees will seek more formal lines of communication.
    D. Neither the flow nor the accuracy of communication will be improved over the former hierarchical structure.

11. The main function of many agency administrative offices is *information management*. Information that is received by an administrative officer may be classified as active or passive, depending upon whether or not it requires the recipient to take some action.

Of the following, the item received which is clearly the MOST active information is
- A. an appointment of a new staff member
- B. a payment voucher for a new desk
- C. a press release concerning a past city event
- D. the minutes of a staff meeting

12. Which one of the following sets BEST describes the general order in which to teach an operation to a new employee?
    - A. Prepare, present, tryout, follow-up
    - B. Prepare, test, tryout, re-test
    - C. Present, test, tryout, follow-up
    - D. Test, present, follow-up, re-test

13. Of the following, public employees may be separated from public service
    - A. for the same reasons which are generally acceptable for discharging employees in private industry
    - B. only under the most trying circumstances
    - C. under procedures that are neither formalized nor subject to review
    - D. solely in extreme cases involving offenses of gravest character

14. Of the following, the one LEAST considered to be a communication barrier is
    - A. group feedback
    - B. charged words
    - C. selective perception
    - D. symbolic meanings

15. Of the following ways for a manager to handle his appointments, the BEST way, according to experts in administration, generally is to
    - A. schedule his own appointments and inform his secretary not to reserve his time without his approval
    - B. encourage everyone to make appointments through his secretary and tell her when he makes his own appointments
    - C. see no one who has not made a previous appointment
    - D. permit anyone to see him without an appointment

16. Assume that a manager decides to examine closely one of five units under his supervision to uncover problems common to all five.
    His research technique is MOST closely related to the method called
    - A. experimentation
    - B. simulation
    - C. linear analysis
    - D. sampling

17. If one views the process of management as a dynamic process, which one of the following functions is NOT a legitimate part of that process?
    - A. Communication
    - B. Decision-making
    - C. Organizational slack
    - D. Motivation

18. Which of the following would be the BEST statement of a budget-oriented purpose for a government administrator? To
    A. provide 200 hours of instruction in basic reading for 3,500 adult illiterates at a cost of $1 million in the next fiscal year
    B. inform the public of adult educational programs
    C. facilitate the transfer to a city agency of certain functions of a federally-funded program which is being phased out
    D. improve the reading skills of the adult citizens in the city

19. Modern management philosophy and practices are changing to accommodate the expectations and motivations of organization personnel.
    Which of the following terms INCORRECTLY describes these newer managerial approaches?
    A. Rational management
    B. Participative management
    C. Decentralization
    D. Democratic supervision

20. Management studies support the hypothesis that, in spite of the tendency of employees to censor the information communicated to their supervisor, subordinates are MORE likely to communicate problem-oriented information upward when they have
    A. a long period of service in the organization
    B. a high degree of trust in the supervisor
    C. a high educational level
    D. low status on the organizational ladder

KEY (CORRECT ANSWERS)

1.	C	11.	A
2.	B	12.	A
3.	A	13.	A
4.	B	14.	A
5.	A	15.	B
6.	C	16.	D
7.	D	17.	C
8.	B	18.	A
9.	B	19.	A
10.	D	20.	B

EXAMINATION SECTION
TEST 1

DIRECTIONS: Each question or incomplete statement is followed by several suggested answers or completions. Select the one that BEST answers the question or completes the statement. *PRINT THE LETTER OF THE CORRECT ANSWER IN THE SPACE AT THE RIGHT.*

1. It is often desirable for an administrator to consult, during the planning process, the persons to be affected by those plans.
   Of the following, the MAJOR justification for such consultation is that it recognizes the
   A. fact that participating in horizontal planning is almost always more effective than participating in vertical planning
   B. principle of participation and the need for a sense of belonging as a means of decreasing resistance and developing support
   C. principle that lower-level administrators normally are more likely than higher-level administrators to emphasize longer-range goals
   D. fact that final responsibility for the approval of plans should be placed in committees not individuals

2. In evaluating performance and, if necessary, correcting what is being done to assure attainment of results according to plan, it is GENERALLY best for the administrator to do which one of the following?
   A. Make a continual effort to increase the number of written control reports prepared
   B. Thoroughly investigate in equal detail all possible deviations indicated by comparison of performance to expectation
   C. Decentralize, within an operating unit or division, the responsibility for correcting deviations
   D. Concentrate on the exceptions, or outstanding variations, from the expected results or standards

3. Generally, changes in the ways in which the supervisors and employees in an organization do things are MORE likely to be welcomed by them when the changes
   A. threaten the security of the supervisors than when they do not
   B. are inaugurated after prior change has been assimilated than when they are inaugurated before other major changes have been assimilated
   C. follow a series of failures in changes when they follow a series of successful changes
   D. are dictated by personal order rather than when they result from an application of previously established impersonal principles

4. For sound organization relationships, of the following, it is generally MOST desirable that
   A. authority and responsibility be segregated from each other, in order to facilitate control
   B. the authority of a manager should be commensurate with his responsibility, and vice versa
   C. authority be defined as the obligation of an individual to carry out assigned activities to the best of his or her ability
   D. clear recognition be given to the fact that delegation of authority benefits only the manager who delegates it

5. In utilizing a checklist of questions for general managerial planning, which one of the following generally is the FIRST question to be asked and answered?
   A. Where will it take place?
   B. How will it be done?
   C. Why must it be done?
   D. Who will do it?

6. Of the following, it is USUALLY best to set administrative objectives so that they are
   A. at a level that is unattainable, so that administrators will continually be strongly motivated
   B. at a level that is attainable, but requires some stretching and reaching by administrators trying to attain them
   C. stated in qualitative rather than quantitative terms whenever a choice between the two is possible
   D. stated in a general and unstructured manner, to permit each administrator maximum freedom in interpreting them

7. In selecting from among administrative alternatives, three general bases for decisions are open to the manager – experience, experimentation, and research and analysis. Of the following, the best argument AGAINST primary reliance upon experimentation as the method of evaluating administrative alternatives is that experimentation is
   A. generally the most expensive of the three techniques
   B. almost always legally prohibited in procedural matters
   C. possible only in areas where results may be easily duplicated by other experimenters at any time
   D. an approach that requires information on scientific method seldom available to administrators

8. The administrator who utilizes the techniques of operations research, linear programming and simulation in making an administrative decision should MOST appropriately be considered to be using the techniques of _____ analysis.
   A. intuitive
   B. quantitative
   C. nonmathematical
   D. qualitative

9. When an additional organizational level is added within a department, that department has MOST directly manifested
    A. horizontal growth
    B. horizontal shrinkage
    C. vertical growth
    D. vertical shrinkage

    9._____

10. Of the following, the one which GENERALLY is the most intangible planning factor is
    A. budget dollars allocated to a function
    B. square feet of space for office use
    C. number of personnel in various clerical titles
    D. emotional impact of a proposed personnel policy among employees

    10._____

11. Departmentation by function is the same as, or most similar to, departmentation by
    A. equipment
    B. clientele
    C. territory
    D. activity

    11._____

12. Such verifiable factors as turnover, absenteeism or volume of grievances would generally BEST assist in measuring the effectiveness of a program to improve
    A. forms control
    B. employee morale
    C. linear programming
    D. executive creativity

    12._____

13. An organization increases the number of subordinates reporting to a manager up to the point where incremental savings in costs, better communication and morale, and other factors equal incremental losses in effectiveness of control, direction and similar factors. This action MOST specifically employs the technique of
    A. role playing
    B. queuing theory
    C. marginal analysis
    D. capital standards analysis

    13._____

14. The term *computer hardware* is MOST likely to refer to
    A. machines and equipment
    B. Ethernet and USB cables
    C. training manuals
    D. word processing and spreadsheet programs

    14._____

15. Determining what is being accomplished, that is, evaluating the performance and, if necessary, applying corrective measures so that performance takes place according to plans is MOST appropriately called management
    A. actuating
    B. planning
    C. controlling
    D. motivating

    15._____

16. Of the following, the BEST overall technique for choosing from among several alternative public programs proposed to try to achieve the same broad objective generally is _____ analysis.
    A. random-sample
    B. input
    C. cost-effectiveness
    D. output

17. When the success of a plan in achieving specific program objectives is measured against that plan's costs, the measure obtained is most directly that of the plan's
    A. pervasiveness
    B. control potential
    C. primacy
    D. efficiency

18. Generally, the degree to which an organization's planning will be coordinated varies MOST directly with the degree to which
    A. the individuals charged with executing plans are better compensated than those charged with developing and evaluating plans
    B. the individuals charged with planning understand and agree to utilize consistent planning premises
    C. a large number of position classification titles have been established for those individuals charged with organizational planning functions
    D. subordinate unit objectives are allowed to control the overall objectives of the departments of which such subordinate units are a part

19. The responsibility for specific types of decisions generally is BEST delegated to
    A. the highest organizational level at which there is an individual possessing the ability, desire, impartiality and access to relevant information needed to make these decisions
    B. the lowest organizational level at which there is an individual possessing the ability, desire, impartiality and access to relevant information needed to make these decisions
    C. a group of executives, rather than a single executive, if these decisions deal with an emergency
    D. the organizational level midway between that which will have to carry out these decisions and that which will have to authorize the resources for their implementation

20. The process of managing by objectives is MOST likely to lead to a situation in which the
    A. goal accomplishment objectives of managers tend to have a longer timespan as one goes lower down the line in an organization
    B. establishment of quantitative goals for staff positions is generally easier than the establishment of quantitative goals for line positions
    C. development of objectives requires the manager to think of the way he will accomplish given results, and of the organization, personnel and resources that he will need
    D. superiors normally develop and finally approve detailed goals for subordinates without any prior consultation with either those subordinates or with the top-level executives responsible for the longer-run objectives of the organization

21. As used with respect to decision making, the application of scientific method to the study of alternatives in a problem situation, with a view to providing a quantitative basis for arriving at an optimum solution in terms of the goals sought is MOST appropriately called
    A. simple number departmentation
    B. geographic decentralization
    C. operations research
    D. trait rating

21.____

22. Assume that a bureau head proposes that final responsibility and authority for all planning within the bureau is to be delegated to one employee who is to be paid at the level of an assistant division head in that bureau.
    Of the following, the MOST appropriate comment about this proposal is that it's
    A. *improper*, mainly because planning does not call for someone at such a high level
    B. *improper*, mainly because responsibility for a basic management function such as planning may not properly be delegated as proposed
    C. *proper*, mainly because ultimate responsibility for all bureau planning is best placed as proposed
    D. *proper*, mainly because every well-managed bureau should have a full-time planning officer

22.____

23. Of the following, the MOST important reason that participation has motivating effects is generally that it gives to the individual participating
    A. a recognition of his or her desire to feel important and to contribute to achievement of worthwhile goals
    B. an opportunity to participate in work that is beyond the scope of the class specification for his or her title
    C. a secure knowledge that his or her organization's top leadership is as efficient as possible considering all major circumstances
    D. the additional information likely to be crucial to his or her promotion

23.____

24. Of the following, the MOST essential characteristic of an effective employee suggestion system is that
    A. suggestions be submitted upward through the chain of command
    B. suggestions be acted upon promptly so that employees may be promptly informed of what happens to their submitted suggestions
    C. suggesters be required to sign their names on the material sent to the actual evaluators for evaluation
    D. suggesters receive at least 25% of the agency's savings during the first two years after their suggestions have been accepted and put into effect by the agency

24.____

25. Two organizations have the same basic objectives and the same total number of employees. The span of authority of each intermediate manager is narrower in one organization than it is in the other. It is MOST likely that the organization in which each intermediate manager has a narrower span of authority will have
   A. fewer intermediate managers
   B. more organizational levels
   C. more managers reporting to a larger number of intermediate supervisors
   D. more characteristics of a *flat* organizational structure

25.____

KEY (CORRECT ANSWERS)

1.	B	11.	D
2.	D	12.	B
3.	B	13.	C
4.	B	14.	A
5.	C	15.	C
6.	B	16.	C
7.	A	17.	D
8.	B	18.	B
9.	C	19.	B
10.	D	20.	C

21.	C
22.	B
23.	A
24.	B
25.	B

TEST 2

DIRECTIONS: Each question or incomplete statement is followed by several suggested answers or completions. Select the one that BEST answers the question or completes the statement. *PRINT THE LETTER OF THE CORRECT ANSWER IN THE SPACE AT THE RIGHT.*

1. Which one of the following BEST expresses the essence of the merit idea or system in public employment?
    A. A person's worth to the organization—the merit of his or her attributes and capacities—is the governing factor in his or her selection, assignment, pay, recognition, advancement and retention
    B. Written tests of the objective type are the only fair way to select on a merit basis from among candidates for open-competitive appointment to positions within the merit system
    C. Employees who have qualified for civil service positions shall have lifetime tenure during good behavior in those positions regardless of changes in public programs
    D. Periodic examinations with set date limits within which all persons desiring to demonstrate their merit may apply, shall be publicly advertised and held for all promotional titles

1.____

2. Of the following, the promotion selection policy generally considered MOST antithetical to the merit concept is the promotion selection policy which
    A. is based solely on objective tests of competence
    B. is based solely on seniority
    C. may require a manager to lose his or her best employee to another part of the organization
    D. permits operating managers collectively to play a significant role in promotion decisions

2.____

3. Of the following, the problems encountered by government establishments which are MOST likely to make extensive delegation of authority difficult to effectuate tend to be problems of
    A. accountability and ensuring uniform administration
    B. line and staff relationships within field offices
    C. generally employee opposition to such delegation of authority and to the subsequent record-keeping activities
    D. use of the management-by-objectives approach

3.____

4. The major decisions as to which jobs shall be created and who shall carry which responsibilities should GENERALLY be made by
    A. budgetary advisers
    B. line managers
    C. classification specialists
    D. peer-level rating committees

4.____

5. The ultimate controlling factor in structuring positions in the public service, MOST generally, should be the
   A. possibility of providing upgrading for highly productive employees
   B. collective bargaining demands initially made by established public employee unions
   C. positive motivational effects upon productivity resulting from an inverted pyramid job structure
   D. effectiveness of the structuring in serving the mission of the organization

6. Of the following, the most usual reason for unsatisfactory line-staff relationships is
   A. inept use of the abilities of staff personnel by line management
   B. the higher salaries paid to line officials
   C. excessive consultation between line officials and staff officials at the same organizational level
   D. a feeling among the staff members that only lower-level line members appreciate their work

7. Generally, an employee receiving new information from a fellow employee is MOST likely to
   A. forget the new information if it is consistent with his or her existing beliefs much more easily than he or she forgets the new information if it is inconsistent with existing beliefs
   B. accept the validity of the new information if it is consistent with his or her existing beliefs more readily than he or she accepts the validity of the new information if it is inconsistent with existing beliefs
   C. have a less accurate memory of the new information if it is consistent with his or her existing beliefs than he or she has of the new information if it is inconsistent with existing beliefs
   D. ignore the new information if it is consistent with his or her existing beliefs more often than he or she ignores the new information if it is inconsistent with existing beliefs

8. Virtually all of us use this principle in our human communications – perhaps without realizing it. In casual conversations, we are alert for cues to whether we are understood (e.g., attentive nods from the other person). Similarly, an instructor is always interested in reactions among those to whom he is giving instruction. The effective administrator is equally conscious of the need to determine his or her subordinates' reactions to what he or she is trying to communicate.
   The principle referred to in the above selection is MOST appropriately called
   A. cognitive dissonance   B. feedback
   C. negative reinforcement   D. noise transmission

9. Of the following, the PRINCIPAL function of an *ombudsman* generally is to
   A. review departmental requests for new data processing equipment so as to reduce duplication
   B. receive and investigate complaints from citizens who are displeased with the actions or non-actions of administrative officials and try to effectuate warranted remedies
   C. review proposed departmental reorganizations in order to advise the chief executive whether or not they are in accordance with the latest principles of proper management structuring
   D. presiding over courts of the judiciary convened to try *sitting* judges

10. Of the following, the MOST valid reason for recruiting an intermediate-level administrator from outside an agency, rather than from within the agency, normally is to
    A. improve the public image of the agency as a desirable place in which to be employed
    B. reduce the number of potential administrators who must be evaluated prior to filling the position
    C. minimize the morale problems arising from frequent internal staff upgradings
    D. obtain fresh ideas and a fresh viewpoint on agency problems

11. A MAJOR research finding regarding employee absenteeism is that
    A. absenteeism is likely to be higher on hot days
    B. male employees tend to be absent more than female employees
    C. the way an employee is treated as a definite bearing on absenteeism
    D. the distance employees have to travel is one of the most important factors in absenteeism

12. Of the following, the supervisory behavior that is of GREATEST benefit to the organization is exhibited by supervisors who
    A. are strict with subordinates about following rules and regulations
    B. encourage subordinates to be interested in the work
    C. are willing to assist with subordinates' work on most occasions
    D. get the most done with available staff and resources

13. The management of time is one of the critical aspects of any supervisor's performance.
    Therefore, in evaluating a subordinate from the viewpoint of how he manages time, a supervisor should rate HIGHEST the subordinate who
    A. concentrates on each task as he undertakes it
    B. performs at a standard and predictable pace under all circumstances
    C. takes shortened lunch periods when he is busy
    D. tries to do two things simultaneously

14. A MAJOR research finding regarding employee absenteeism is that
    A. absenteeism is likely to be higher on hot days
    B. male employees tend to be absent more than female employees
    C. the way an employee is treated as a definite bearing on absenteeism
    D. the distance employees have to travel is one of the most important factors in absenteeism

15. Of the following, the supervisory behavior that is of GREATEST benefit to the organization is exhibited by supervisors who
    A. are strict with subordinates about following rules and regulations
    B. encourage subordinates to be interested in the work
    C. are willing to assist with subordinates' work on most occasions
    D. get the most done with available staff and resources

16. In order to maintain a proper relationship with a worker who is assigned to staff rather than line functions, a line supervisor should
    A. accept all recommendations of the staff worker
    B. include the staff worker in the conferences called by the supervisor for his subordinates
    C. keep the staff worker informed of developments in the area of his staff assignment
    D. require that the staff worker's recommendations be communicated to the supervisor through the supervisor's own superior

17. Of the following, the GREATEST disadvantage of placing a worker in a staff position under the direct supervision of the supervisor whom he advises is the possibility that the
    A. staff worker will tend to be insubordinate because of a feeling of superiority over the supervisor
    B. staff worker will tend to give advice of the type which the supervisor wants to hear or finds acceptable
    C. supervisor will tend to be mistrustful of the advice of a worker of subordinate rank
    D. supervisor will tend to derive little benefit from the advice because to supervise properly he should know at least as much as his subordinate

5 (#2)

18. One factor which might be given consideration in deciding upon the optimum span of control of a supervisor over his immediate subordinates is the position of the supervisor in the hierarchy of the organization.
It is generally considered proper that the number of subordinates immediately supervised by a higher, upper echelon, supervisor
    A. is unrelated to and tends to form no pattern with the number of supervised by lower level supervisors
    B. should be about the same as the number supervised by a lower level supervisor
    C. should be larger than the number supervised by a lower level supervisor
    D. should be smaller than the number supervised by a lower level supervisor

18.____

19. Assume that you are a supervisor and have been assigned to assist the head of a large agency unit. He asks you to prepare a simple, functional organization chart of the unit.
Such a chart would be USEFUL for
    A. favorably impressing members of the public with the important nature of the agency's work
    B. graphically presenting staff relationships which may indicate previously unknown duplications, overlaps, and gaps in job duties
    C. motivating all employees toward better performance because they will have a better understanding of job procedures
    D. subtly and inoffensively making known to the staff in the unit that you are now in a position of responsibility

19.____

20. In some large organizations, management's traditional means of learning about employee dissatisfaction has been in the *open door policy*.
This policy USUALLY means that
    A. management lets it be known that a management representative is generally available to discuss employees' questions, suggestions, and complaints
    B. management sets up an informal employee organization to establish a democratic procedure for orderly representation of employees
    C. employees are encouraged to attempt to resolve dissatisfactions at the lowest possible level of authority
    D. employees are provided with an address or box so that they may safely and anonymously register complaints

20.____

KEY (CORRECT ANSWERS)

1.	B	11.	A
2.	A	12.	D
3.	D	13.	A
4.	B	14.	C
5.	A	15.	D
6.	A	16.	C
7.	B	17.	B
8.	B	18.	D
9.	D	19.	B
10.	C	20.	A

EXAMINATION SECTION
TEST 1

DIRECTIONS: Each question or incomplete statement is followed by several suggested answers or completions. Select the one that BEST answers the question or completes the statement. *PRINT THE LETTER OF THE CORRECT ANSWER IN THE SPACE AT THE RIGHT.*

1. In many instances, managers deliberately set up procedures and routines that more than one department or more than one employee is required to complete and verify an entire operation or transaction.
   The MAIN reason for establishing such routines is generally to
   A. minimize the chances of gaps and deficiencies in feedback of information to management
   B. expand the individual employee's vision and concern for broader organizational objectives
   C. provide satisfaction of employees' social and egoistic needs through teamwork and horizontal communications
   D. facilitate internal control designed to prevent errors, whether intentional or accidental

   1.____

2. Committees—sometimes referred to as boards, commissions, or task forces—are widely used in government to investigate certain problems or to manage certain agencies.
   Of the following, the MOST serious limitation of the committee approach to management in government is that
   A. it reflects government's inability to delegate authority effectively to individual executives
   B. committee members do not usually have similar backgrounds, experience, and abilities
   C. it promotes horizontal communication at the expense of vertical communication
   D. the spreading out of responsibility to a committee often results in a willingness to settle for weak, compromise solutions

   2.____

3. Of the following, the BEST reason for replacing methods of committees on a staggered or partial basis rather than replacing all members simultaneously is that this practice
   A. gives representatives of different interest groups a chance to contribute their ideas
   B. encourages continuity of policy since retained members are familiar with previous actions
   C. prevents the interpersonal frictions from building up and hindering the work of the group
   D. improves the quality of the group's recommendations and decisions by stimulating development of new ideas

   3.____

4. Assume that in considering a variety of actions to take to solve a given problem, a manager decides to take no action at all.
   According to generally accepted management practice, such a decision would be
   A. *proper*, because under normal circumstances it is better to make no decision
   B. *improper*, because inaction would be rightly construed as shunning one's responsibilities
   C. *proper*, since this would be a decision which might produce more positive results than the other alternatives
   D. *improper*, since such a solution would delay corrective action and exacerbate the problem

4._____

5. Some writers in the field of management assume that when a newly promoted manager has been informed by his superior about the subordinates he is to direct and the extent of his authority, that is all that is necessary.
   However, thereafter, this new manager should realize that, for practical purposes, his authority will be effective ONLY when
   A. he accepts full responsibility for the actions of his subordinates
   B. his subordinates are motivated to carry out their assignments
   C. it derives from acceptable personal attributes rather than from his official position
   D. he exercises it in an authoritarian manner

5._____

6. A newly appointed manager is assigned to assist the head of a small developing agency handling innovative programs. Although this manager is a diligent worker, he does not delegate authority to middle- and lower-echelon supervisors.
   The MOST important reason why it would be desirable to change this attitude toward delegation is because otherwise
   A. he may have to assume more responsibility for the actions of his subordinates than is implied in the authority delegated to him
   B. his subordinates will tend to produce innovative solutions on their own
   C. the agency will become a decentralized type of organization in which he cannot maintain adequate controls
   D. he may not have time to perform other essential tasks

6._____

7. All types of organizations and all functions within them are to varying degrees affected today by the need to understand the application of computer systems to management practices.
   The one of the following purposes for which such systems would be MOST useful is to
   A. lower the costs of problem-solving by utilizing data that is already in the agency's control system correlated with new data
   B. stabilize basic patterns of the organization into long-term structures and relationships
   C. give instant solutions to complex problems
   D. affect savings in labor costs for office tasks involving non-routine complex problems

7._____

8. Compared to individual decision-making, group decision-making is burdened with the DISADVANTAGE of
   A. making snap judgments
   B. pressure to examine all relevant elements of the problem
   C. greater motivation needed to implement the decision
   D. the need to clarify problems for the group participants

9. Assume that a manager in an agency, faced with a major administrative problem, has developed a number of alternative solutions to the problem. Which of the following would be MOST effective in helping the manager make the best decision?
   A. *Experience*, because a manager can distill from the past the fundamental reasons for success or failure since the future generally duplicates the past
   B. *Experimentation*, because it is the method used in scientific inquiry and can be tried out economically in limited areas
   C. *Research analysis*, because it is generally less costly than most other methods and involves the interrelationships among the more critical factors that bear upon the goal sought
   D. *Value forecasting*, because it assigns numerical significance to the values of alternative tangible and intangible choices and indicates the degree of risk involved in each choice

10. Management information systems operate more effectively for managers than mere data tabulating systems because information systems
    A. eliminate the need for managers to tell information processors what is required
    B. are used primarily for staff rather than line functions
    C. are less expensive to operate than manual methods of data collection
    D. present and utilize data in a meaningful form

11. Project-type organizations are in widespread use today because they offer a number of advantages.
    The MOST important purpose of the project organization is to
    A. secure a higher degree of coordination than could be obtained in a conventional line structure
    B. provide an orderly way of phrasing projects in and out of organizations
    C. expedite routine administrative processes
    D. allow for rapid assessment of the status of any given project and its effect on agency productivity

12. A manager adjusts his plans for future activity by reviewing information about the performance of his subordinates.
    This is an application of the process of
    A. human factor impact   B. coordinated response
    C. feedback communication   D. reaction control

13. From the viewpoint of the manager in an agency, the one of the following which is the MOST constructive function of a status system or a rank system based on employee performance is that the system
    A. makes possible effective communication, thereby lessening social distances between organizational levels
    B. is helpful to employees of lesser ability because it provides them with an incentive to exceed their capacities
    C. encourages the employees to attain or exceed the goals set for them by the organization
    D. diminishes friction in assignment and work relationships of personnel

14. Some managers ask employees who have been newly hired by their agency and then assigned to their divisions or units such questions as: *What are your personal goals? What do you expect from your job? Why do you want to work for this organization?*
    For a manager to ask these questions is GENERALLY considered
    A. *inadvisable*; these questions should have been asked prior to hiring the employee
    B. *inadvisable*; the answers will arouse subjective prejudices in the manager before he sees what kind of work the employee can do
    C. *advisable*; this approach indicates to the employee that the manager is interested in him as an individual
    D. *advisable*; the manager can judge how much of a disparity exists between the employee's goals and the agency's goals

15. Assume that you have prepared a report to your superior recommending a reorganization of your staff to eliminate two levels of supervision. The total number of employees would remain the same, with the supervisors of the two eliminated levels taking on staff assignments.
    In your report, which one of the following should NOT be listed as an expected result of such a reorganization?
    A. Fewer breakdowns and distortions in communications to staff
    B. Greater need for training
    C. Broader opportunities for development of employee skills
    D. Fewer employee errors due to exercise of closer supervision and control

16. *Administration* has often been criticized as being unproductive in the sense that it seems far removed from the end products of an organization.
    According to modern management thought, this criticism, for the most part, is
    A. *invalid*, because administrators make it possible for subordinates to produce goods or services by directing coordination, and controlling their activities
    B. *valid*, because most subordinates usually do the work required to produce goods and services with only general direction from their immediate superiors
    C. *invalid*, because administrators must see to all of the details associated with the production of services
    D. *valid*, because administrators generally work behind the scenes and are mainly concerned with long-range planning

17. A manager must be able to evaluate the relative importance of his decisions and establish priorities for carrying them out.
Which one of the following factors bearing on the relative importance of making a decision would indicate to a manager that he can delegate that decision to a subordinate or give it low priority? The
    A. decision concerns a matter on which strict confidentiality must be maintained
    B. community impact of the decision is great
    C. decision can be easily changed
    D. decision commits the agency to heavy expenditure of funds

17.____

18. Suppose that you are responsible for reviewing and submitting to your superior the monthly reports from ten field auditors. Despite your repeated warnings to these auditors, most of them hand in their reports close to or after the deadline dates, so that you have no time to return them for revision and find yourself working overtime to make the necessary corrections yourself. The deadline dates for the auditors' reports and your report cannot be changed.
Of the following, the MOST probable cause for this continuing situation is that
    A. these auditors need retraining in the writing of this type of report
    B. possible disciplinary action as a result of the delay by the auditors has not been impressed upon them
    C. the auditors have had an opportunity to provide you with feedback to explain the reasons for the delays
    D. you, as the manager, have not used disciplinary measures of sufficient severity to change their behavior

18.____

19. Assume that an agency desiring to try out a *management-by-objectives* program has set down the guidelines listed below to implement this activity. Which one of these guidelines is MOST likely to present obstacles to the success of this type of program?
    A. Specific work objectives should be determined by top management for employees at all levels.
    B. Objectives should be specific, attainable, and preferably measurable as to units, costs, ratios, time, etc.
    C. Standards of performance should be either qualitative or quantitative, preferably quantitative.
    D. There should be recognition and rewards for successful achievement or objectives.

19.____

20. Of the following, the MOST meaningful way to express productivity where employees work a standard number of hours each day is in terms of the relationship between man-
    A. hours expended and number of work-units needed to produce the final product
    B. days expended and goods and services produced
    C. days and energy expended
    D. days expended and number of workers

20.____

21. Agencies often develop productivity indices for many of their activities. Of the following, the MOST important use for such indices is generally to
    A. measure the agency's output against its own performance
    B. improve quality standards while letting productivity remain unchanged
    C. compare outputs of the agency with outputs in private industry
    D. determine manpower requirements

22. The MOST outstanding characteristic of staff authority, such as that of a public relations officer in an agency, as compared with line authority, is generally accepted to be
    A. reliance upon personal attributes
    B. direct relationship to the primary objectives of the organization
    C. absence of the right to direct or command
    D. responsibility for attention to technical details

23. In the traditional organization structure, there are often more barriers to upward communication than to downward communication.
    From the viewpoint of a manager whose goal is to overcome obstacles to communication, this situation should be
    A. *accepted*; the downward system is the more important since it is highly directive, giving necessary orders, instructions, and procedures
    B. *changed*; the upward system should receive more emphasis than the downward system, which represents stifling bureaucratic authority
    C. *accepted*; it is generally conceded that upward systems supply enough feedback for control purposes necessary to the organization's survival
    D. *changed*; research has generally verified the need for an increase in upward communications to supply more information about employees' ideas, attitudes, and performance

24. A principal difficulty in productivity measurement for local government services is in defining and measuring output, a problem familiar to managers. A measurement that merely looks good, but which may be against the public interest, is another serious problem. Managers should avoid encouraging employees to take actions that lead to such measurements.
    In accordance with the foregoing statement, it would be MOST desirable for a manager to develop a productivity measure that
    A. correlates the actual productivity measure with impact on benefit to the citizenry
    B. does not allow for a mandated annual increase in productivity
    C. firmly fixes priorities for resource allocations
    D. uses numerical output, by itself, in productivity incentive plans

25. For a manager, the MOST significant finding of the Hawthorne studies and experiments is that an employee's productivity is affected MOST favorably when the
    A. importance of tasks is emphasized and there is a logical arrangement of work functions

B. physical surroundings and work conditions are improved
C. organization has a good public relations program
D. employee is given recognition and allowed to participate in decision-making

---

KEY (CORRECT ANSWERS)

1.	D		11.	A
2.	D		12.	C
3.	B		13.	C
4.	C		14.	A
5.	B		15.	D
6.	D		16.	A
7.	A		17.	C
8.	D		18.	D
9.	C		19.	A
10.	D		20.	B

21. A
22. C
23. D
24. A
25. D

TEST 2

DIRECTIONS: Each question or incomplete statement is followed by several suggested answers or completions. Select the one that BEST answers the question or completes the statement. *PRINT THE LETTER OF THE CORRECT ANSWER IN THE SPACE AT THE RIGHT.*

1. Which one of the following is generally accepted by managers as the MOST difficult aspect of a training program in staff supervision?   1.____
   A. Determining training needs of the staff
   B. Evaluating the effectiveness of the courses
   C. Locating capable instructors to teach the courses
   D. Finding adequate space and scheduling acceptable times for all participants

2. Assume that, as a manager, you have decided to start a job enrichment program with the purpose of making jobs more varied and interesting in an effort to increase the motivation of a certain group of workers in your division.   2.____
   Which one of the following should generally NOT be part of this program?
   A. Increasing the accountability of these individuals for their own work
   B. Granting additional authority or job freedom to these employees in their job activities
   C. Mandating increased monthly production goals for this group of employees
   D. Giving each of these employees a complete unit of work

3. Both employer and employee have an important stake in effective preparation for retirement.   3.____
   According to modern management thinking, the one of the following which is probably the MOST important aspect of a sound pre-retirement program is to
   A. make assignments that utilize the employee's abilities fully
   B. reassign the employee to a less demanding position in the organization for the last year or two he is on the job
   C. provide the employee with financial data and other facts that would be pertinent to his retirement planning
   D. encourage the employee to develop interests and hobbies which are connected with the job

4. The civil service system generally emphasizes a policy of *promotion-from-within*. Employees in the direct line of promotion in a given occupational group are eligible for promotion to the next higher title in that occupational group. Which one of the following is LEAST likely to occur as a result of this policy and practice?   4.____
   A. Training time will be saved since employees in higher-level positions are already familiar with many agency rules, regulations, and procedures.
   B. The recruitment section will be able to show prospective employees that there are distinct promotional opportunities.

C. Employees will be provided with a clear-cut picture as to their possible career ladder.
D. Employees will be encouraged to seek broad-based training and education to enhance their promotability.

5. From a management point of view, the MAIAN drawback of seniority as opposed to merit as a basis for granting pay increases to workers is that a pay increase system based on seniority
   A. is favored by unions
   B. upsets organizational status relationships
   C. may encourage mediocre performance by employees
   D. is more difficult to administer than a merit plan

6. One of the actions that is often taken against employees in the non-uniformed forces who are accused of misconduct on the job is suspension without pay. The MOST justifiable reason for taking such action is to
   A. ease an employee out of the agency
   B. enable an investigation to be conducted into the circumstances of the offense
   C. improve the performance of the employee when he returns to the job
   D. punish the employee by imposing a hardship on him

7. A manager has had difficulty in getting good clerical employees to staff a filing section under his supervision. To add to his problems, one of his most competent senior clerks requests a transfer to the accounting division so that he can utilize his new accounting skill, which he is acquiring by going to college at night. The manager attempts to keep the senior clerk in his filing section by calling the director of personnel and getting him to promise not to authorize any transfer.
   GENERALLY, this manager's action is
   A. *desirable*; he should not help his staff to develop themselves if it means losing good people
   B. *undesirable*; he should recommend that the senior clerk get a raise in the hope of preventing him from transferring to another section
   C. *desirable*; it shows that the manager is concerned about the senior clerk's future performance
   D. *undesirable*; it is good policy to transfer employees to the type of work they are interested in and for which they are acquiring training

8. One of your subordinates, a unit supervisor, comes to you, the division chief, because he feels that he is working out of title, and he suggests that his competitive class position should be reclassified to a higher title.
   Which one of the following statements that the subordinate has made is generally LEAST likely to be a valid support for his suggestion?
   A. The work he is doing conforms to the general statement of duties and responsibilities as described in the class specification for the next higher title in his occupational group.
   B. Most of the typical tasks he performs are listed in the class specification for a title with a higher salary range and are not listed for his current title.

C. His education and experience qualifications far exceed the minimum requirements for the position he holds.
D. His duties and responsibilities have changed recently and are now similar to those of his supervisor.

9. Assume that a class specification for a competitive title used exclusively by your agency is outdated, and that no examination for the title has been given since the specification was issued.
Of the following, the MOST appropriate action for your agency to take is to
   A. make the necessary changes and submit the revised class specification to the city civil service commission
   B. write the personnel director to recommend that the class specification be updated, giving the reasons and suggested revisions
   C. prepare a revised class specification and submit it to the office of management and budget for their approval
   D. secure approval of the state civil service commission to update the class specification, and then submit the revised specification to the city civil service commission

10. Assume that an appropriate eligible list has been established and certified to your agency for a title in which a large number of provisionals are serving in your agency.
In order to obtain permission from the personnel director to retain some of them beyond the usual time limit set by rules (two months) following certification of the list, which one of the following conditions MUST apply?
   A. The positions are sensitive and require investigation of eligibles prior to appointment.
   B. Replacement of all provisionals within two months would impair essential public service.
   C. Employees are required to work rotating shifts, including nights and weekends.
   D. The duties of the positions require unusual physical effort and endurance.

11. Under the federally-funded Comprehensive Employment and Training Act (CETA), the hiring by the city of non-civil servants for CETA jobs is PROHIBITED when the
   A. applicants are unemployed because of seasonal lay-offs in private industry
   B. applicants do not meet U.S. citizenship and city residence requirements
   C. jobs have minimum requirements of specialized professional or technical training and experience
   D. jobs are comparable to those performed by laid-off civil servants

12. Assume you are in charge of the duplicating service in your agency. Since employees assigned to this operation lack a sense of accomplishment because the work is highly specialized and repetitive, your superior proposes to enlarge the jobs of these workers and asks you about your reaction to this strategy.

The MOST appropriate response for you to make is that job enlargement would be
- A. *undesirable*, primarily because it would increase production costs
- B. *undesirable*, primarily because it would diminish the quality of the output
- C. *desirable*, primarily because it might make it possible to add an entire level of management to the organizational structure of your agency
- D. *desirable*, primarily because it might make it possible to decrease the amount of supervision the workers will require

13. According to civil service law, layoff or demotion must be made in inverse order of seniority among employees permanently serving in the same title and layoff unit.
    Which one of the following is now the CORRECT formula for computing seniority?
    Total continuous service in the
    - A. competitive class only
    - B. competitive, non-competitive, or labor class
    - C. classified or unclassified services
    - D. competitive, non-competitive, exempt, and labor classes

14. Under which of the following conditions would an appointing officer be permitted to consider the sex of a candidate in making an employment decision?
    When
    - A. the duties of the position require considerable physical effort or strength
    - B. the duties of the position are considered inherently dangerous
    - C. separate toilet facilities and dressing rooms for the sexes are unavailable and/or cannot be provided in any event
    - D. the public has indicated a preference to be served by persons of a specified sex

15. Assume that an accountant under your supervision signs out to the field to make an agency audit. It is later discovered that, although he had reported himself at work until 5 P.M. that day, he had actually left for home at 3:30 P.M. Although this accountant has worked for the city for ten years and has had an excellent performance record, he is demoted to a lower title in punishment for this breach of duty.
    According to generally accepted thinking on personnel management, the disciplinary action taken in this case should be considered
    - A. *appropriate*; a lesser penalty might encourage repetition of the offense
    - B. *inappropriate*; the correct penalty for such a breach of duty should be dismissal
    - C. *appropriate*; the accountant's abilities may be utilized better in the new assignment
    - D. *inappropriate*; the impact of a continuing stigma and loss of salary is not commensurate with the offense committed

16. Line managers often request more funds for their units than are actually required to attain their current objectives.
    Which one of the following is the MOST important reason for such inflated budget requests?
    The
    A. expectation that budget examiners will exercise their prerogative of budget cutting
    B. line manager's interest in improving the performance of his unit is thereby indicated to top management
    C. expectation that such requests will make it easier to obtain additional funds in future years
    D. opinion that it makes sense to obtain additional funds and decide later how to use them

17. Integrating budgeting with program planning and evaluation in a city agency is GENERALLY considered to be
    A. *undesirable*; budgeting must focus on the fiscal year at hand, whereas planning must concern itself with developments over a period of years
    B. *desirable*; budgeting facilitates the choice-making process by evaluating the financial implications of agency programs and forcing cost comparisons among them
    C. *undesirable*; accountants and statisticians with the required budgetary skills have little familiarity with the substantive programs that the agency is conducting
    D. *desirable*; such a partnership increases the budgetary skills of planners, thus promoting more effective use of public resources

18. An aspect of the managerial function, a budget is described BEST as a
    A. set of qualitative management controls over productivity
    B. tool based on historical accounting reports
    C. type of management plan expressed in quantitative terms
    D. precise estimate of future quantitative and qualitative contingencies

19. Which one of the following is generally accepted as the MAJOR immediate advantage of installing a system of program budgeting?
    It
    A. encourages managers to relate their decisions to the agency's long-range goals
    B. is a replacement for the financial or fiscal budget
    C. decreases the need for managers to make trade-offs in the decision-making process
    D. helps to adjust budget figures to provide for unexpected developments

20. Of the following, the BEST means for assuring necessary responsiveness of a budgetary program to changing conditions is by
    A. overestimating budgetary expenditures by 15% and assigning the excess to unforeseen problem areas
    B. underestimating budgetary expenditures by at least 20% and setting aside a reserve account in the same amount

C. reviewing and revising the budget at regular intervals so that it retains its character as a current document
D. establishing *budget-by-exception* policies for each division in the agency

21. According to expert thought in the area of budgeting, participation in the preparation of a government agency's budget should GENERALLY involve
    A. only top management
    B. only lower levels of management
    C. all levels of the organization
    D. only a central budget office or bureau

22. Of the following, the MOST useful guide to analysis of budget estimates for the coming fiscal year is a comparison with
    A. appropriations as amended for the current fiscal year
    B. manpower requirements for the previous two years
    C. initial appropriations for the current fiscal year
    D. budget estimates for the preceding five years

23. A manager assigned to analyze the costs and benefits associated with a program which the agency head proposes to undertake may encounter certain factors which cannot be measured in dollar terms.
    In such a case, the manager should GENERALLY
    A. ignore the factors which cannot be quantified
    B. evaluate the factors in accordance with their degree of importance to the overall agency goals
    C. give the factors weight equal to the weight given to measurable costs and benefits
    D. assume that non-measurable costs and benefits will balance out against one another

24. If city employees believe that they are receiving adverse treatment in terms of training and disciplinary actions because of their national origin, they may file charges of discrimination with the Federal government's
    A. Human Rights Commission
    B. Public Employee Relations Board
    C. Equal Employment Opportunity Commission
    D. United States Department of Commerce

25. Under existing employment statutes, the city is obligated, as an employer, to take *affirmative action* in certain instances.
    This requirement has been imposed to ensure that
    A. employees who are members of minority groups, or women, be given special opportunities for training and promotion even though they are not available to other employees
    B. employees or applicants for employment are treated without regard to race, color, religion, sex, or national origin

C. proof exists to show that the city has acted with good intentions in any case where it has disregarded this requirement
D. men and women are treated alike except where State law provides special hour or working conditions for women

KEY (CORRECT ANSWERS)

1.	B	11.	D
2.	C	12.	D
3.	C	13.	D
4.	D	14.	C
5.	C	15.	D
6.	B	16.	A
7.	D	17.	B
8.	C	18.	C
9.	B	19.	A
10.	B	20.	D

21.	C
22.	A
23.	B
24.	C
25.	B

EXAMINATION SECTION
TEST 1

DIRECTIONS: Each question or incomplete statement is followed by several suggested answers or completions. Select the one that BEST answers the question or completes the statement. *PRINT THE LETTER OF THE CORRECT ANSWER IN THE SPACE AT THE RIGHT.*

1. The one of the following which has had GREATEST effect upon size of the budget of large cities in the last twenty years is
    A. change in the organization of the city resulting from new charters
    B. increase in services rendered by the city
    C. development of independent authorities
    D. increase in the city's ability to borrow money
    E. increase in the size of the city

1.____

2. The one of the following services for which cities receive the LEAST amount of direct financial assistance from state governments is
    A. education   B. welfare   C. housing
    D. roads   E. museums

2.____

3. Major problems which face most large cities, including New York, arise from the vertical sandwiching of governments in a single area and from the many independent governments that crowd the boundaries of the central city.
    Of the following methods of solving these problems, the one which has been MOST successful in the past has been to
    A. decentralize the administration of the central city
    B. create various supra-municipal authorities which tend to integrate the activities of the metropolitan area
    C. bring the metropolitan population under a single local government
    D. set up intermunicipal coordinating agencies to solve area administrative and economic problems
    E. allow each government element in the metropolitan area to work out its own solution

3.____

4. By means of the *debt limit*, the states regulate many facets of the debt of the cities.
    The one of the following factors which is NOT regulated in this manner is the
    A. purpose for which the debt is incurred
    B. amount of debt which may be incurred
    C. terms of the notes or bonds issued by the city
    D. forms of debts which may be incurred
    E. source from which the money may be borrowed

4.____

5. The one of the following which is a characteristic of NEITHER the state nor the federal governments, but which is a characteristic of the government of cities is that the latter 5._____
   A. is not sovereign but an agent
   B. does not have the power to raise taxes
   C. cannot enter into contracts
   D. may not make treaties with foreign countries
   E. may not coin money

Questions 6-8.

DIRECTIONS: Questions 6 through 8 are to be answered on the basis of the following paragraph.

The regressive uses of discipline is ubiquitous. Administrative architects who seek the optimum balance between structure and morale must accordingly look toward the identification and isolation of disciplinary elements. The whole range of disciplinary sanctions, from the reprimand to the dismissal presents opportunities for reciprocity and accommodation of institutional interests. When rightly seized upon, these opportunities may provide the moment and the means for fruitful exercise of leadership and collaboration.

6. The one of the following ways of reworking the ideas presented in this paragraph in order to be BEST suited for presentation in an in-service training course in supervision is: 6._____
   A. When one of your men does something wrong, talk it over with him. Tell him what he should have done. This is a chance for you to show the man that you are on his side and that you would welcome him on your side.
   B. It is not necessary to reprimand or to dismiss an employee because he needs disciplining. The alert foreman will lead and collaborate with his subordinates making discipline unnecessary.
   C. A good way to lead the men you supervise is to take those opportunities which present themselves to use the whole range of disciplinary sanctions from reprimand to dismissal as a means for enforcing collaboration.
   D. Chances to punish a man in your squad should be welcomed as opportunities to show that you are a "*good guy*" who does not bear a grudge.
   E. Before you talk to a man or have him report to the office for something he has done wrong, attempt to lead him and get him to work with you. Tell him that his actions were wrong, that you expect him not to repeat the same wrong act, and that you will take a firmer stand if the act is repeated.

7. Of the following, the PRINCIPAL point made in the paragraph is that 7._____
   A. discipline is frequently used improperly
   B. it is possible to isolate the factors entering into a disciplinary situation
   C. identification of the disciplinary elements is desirable

D. disciplinary situations may be used to the advantage of the organization
E. obtaining the best relationship between organizational form and spirit, depend upon the ability to label disciplinary elements

8. The MOST novel idea presented in the paragraph is that 8._____
   A. discipline is rarely necessary
   B. discipline may be a joint action of man and supervisor
   C. there are disciplinary elements which may be identified
   D. a range of disciplinary sanctions exist
   E. it is desirable to seek for balance between structure and morale

9. When, in the process of developing a classification plan, it has been decided that 9._____
   certain positions all have distinguishing characteristics sufficiently similar to justify treating them alike in the process of selecting appointees and establishing pay rates or scales, then the kind of employment represented by such positions will be called a "class."
   According to this paragraph, a group of positions is called a class if they
   A. have distinguishing characteristics
   B. represent a kind of employment
   C. can be treated in the same manner for some functions
   D. all have the same pay rates
   E. are treated in the same manner in the development of a classification plan

Questions 10-12.

DIRECTIONS: Questions 10 through 12 are to be answered on the basis of the following paragraph.

   The fundamental characteristic of the type of remote control which management needs to bridge the gap between itself and actual operations is the more effective use of records and reports—more specifically, the gathering and interpretation of the facts contained in records and reports. Facts, for management purposes, are those data (narrative and quantitative) which express in simple terms the current standing of the agency's program, work and resources in relation to the plans and policies formulated by management. They are those facts or measures (1) which permit management to compare current status with past performance and with its forecasts for the immediate future, and (2) which provide management with a reliable basis for long-range forecasting.

10. According to the above statement, a characteristic of a type of management 10._____
    control
    A. is the kind of facts contained in records and reports
    B. is narrative and quantitative data
    C. is its remoteness from actual operations
    D. is the use of records
    E. which expresses in simple terms the current standing of the agency's program, provides management with a reliable basis for long-range forecasting

11. For management purposes, facts are, according to the paragraph, 11.____
    A. forecasts which can be compared to current status
    B. data which can be used for certain control purposes
    C. a fundamental characteristic of a type of remote control
    D. the data contained in records and reports
    E. data (narrative and quantitative) which describe the plans and policies formulated by management

12. An inference which can be drawn from this statement is that 12.____
    A. management which has a reliable basis for long-range forecasting has at its disposal a type of remote control which is needed to bridge the gap between itself and actual operations
    B. data which do not express in simple terms the current standing of the agency's program, work and resources in relationship to the plans and policies formulated by management, may still be facts for management purposes
    C. data which express relationships among the agency's program, work, and resources are management facts
    D. the gap between management and actual operations can only be bridged by characteristics which are fundamentally a type of remote control
    E. management compares current status with past performance in order to obtain a reliable basis for long-range forecasting

Questions 13-14.

DIRECTIONS: Questions 13 and 14 are to be answered on the basis of the following paragraph.

People must be selected to do the tasks involved and must be placed on a payroll in jobs fairly priced. Each of these people must be assigned those tasks which he can perform best: the work of each must be appraised, and good and poor work singled out appropriately. Skill in performing assigned tasks must be developed, and the total work situation must be conducive to sustained high performance. Finally, employees must be separated from the work force either voluntarily or involuntarily because of inefficient or unsatisfactory performance or because of curtailment of organizational activities.

13. A personnel function which is NOT included in the above description is 13.____
    A. classification   B. training   C. placement
    D. severance   E. service rating

14. The underlying implied purpose of the policy enunciated in the above paragraph is 14.____
    A. to plan for the curtailment of the organizational program when it becomes necessary
    B. to single out appropriate skill in performing assigned tasks
    C. to develop and maintain a high level of performance by employees

D. that training employees in relation to the total work situation is essential if good and poor work are to be singled out
E. that equal money for equal work results in a total work situation which insures proper appraisal

15. Changes in program must be quickly and effectively translated into organizational adjustments if the administrative machinery is to be fully adapted to current operating needs. Continuous administrative planning is indispensable to the successful and expeditious accomplishment of such organization changes.
According to this statement,
   A. the absence of continuous administrative planning must result in out-moded administrative machinery
   B. continuous administrative planning is necessary for changes in program
   C. if changes in program are quickly and effectively translated into organizational adjustments, the administrative machinery is fully adapted to current operating needs
   D. continuous administrative planning results in successful and expeditious accomplishment of organization changes
   E. if administrative machinery is not fully adapted to current operating needs, then continuous administrative planning is absent

16. The first-line supervisor executes policy as elsewhere formulated. He does not make policy. He is the element of the administrative structure closest to the employee group.
From this point of view, it follows that a MAJOR function of the first-line supervisor is to
   A. suggest desirable changes in procedure to top management
   B. prepare time schedules showing when his unit will complete a piece of work so that it will dovetail with the requirements of other units
   C. humanize policy so as to respect employee needs and interests
   D. report danger points to top management in order to forestall possible bottlenecks
   E. discipline employees who continuously break departmental rules

17. During a supervisory staff meeting, the department head said to the first-line supervisors, "*The most important job you have is to get across to the employees in your units the desirability of achieving our department's aims and the importance of the jobs they are performing toward reaching our goals.*"
In general, adoption of this point of view would tend to result in an organization
   A. in which supervisors would be faced by many disciplinary problems caused by employee reaction to the program
   B. in which less supervision is required of the work of the average employee
   C. having more clearly defined avenues of communication
   D. lacking definition; supervisors would tend to forget their primary mission of getting the assigned work completed as efficiently as possible
   E. in which most employees would be capable of taking over a supervisory position when necessary

18. A supervisor, in assigning a man to a job, generally followed the policy of fitting the man to the job.
This procedure is
    A. *undesirable*; the job should be fitted to the man
    B. *desirable*; primary emphasis should be on the work to be accomplished
    C. *undesirable*; the policy does not consider human values
    D. *desirable*; setting up a definite policy and following it permits careful analysis
    E. *undesirable*; it is not always possible to fit the available man to the job

18.____

19. Assume that one of the units under your jurisdiction has 40 typists. Their skill range from 15 to 80 words a minute.
The MOST feasible of the following methods to increase the typing output of this unit is to
    A. study the various typing jobs to determine the skill requirements for each type of work and assign to each typist tasks commensurate with her skill
    B. assign the slow typists to clerical work and hire new typists
    C. assign such tasks as typing straight copy to the slower typists
    D. reduce the skill requirements necessary to produce a satisfactory quantity of work
    E. simplify procedures and keep records, memoranda, and letters short and concise

19.____

20. In a division of a department, private secretaries were assigned to members of the technical staff since each required a secretary who was familiar with his particular field and who could handle various routine matters without referring to anyone. Other members of the staff depended for their dictation and typing work upon a small pool consisting of two stenographers and two typists. Because of turnover and the difficulty of recruiting new stenographers and typists, the pool had to be discontinued.
Of the following, the MOST satisfactory way to provide stenographic and typing service for the division is to
    A. organize the private secretaries into a decentralized pool under the direction of a supervisor to whom nontechnical staff members would send requests for stenographic and typing assistance
    B. organize the private secretaries into a central pool under the direction of a supervisor to whom all staff members would send requests for stenographic and typing assistance
    C. train clerks as typists and typists as stenographers
    D. relieve stenographers and typists of jobs that can be done by messengers or clerks
    E. conserve time by using such devices as indicating minor corrections on a final draft in such a way that they can be erased and by using duplicating machines to eliminate typing many copies

20.____

21. Even under perfect organizational conditions, the relationships between the line units and the units charged with budget planning and personnel management may be precarious at times.
 The one of the following which is a MAJOR reason for this is that
    A. service units assist the head of the agency in formulating and executing policies
    B. line units frequently find lines of communication to the agency head blocked by service units
    C. there is a natural antagonism between planners and doers
    D. service units tend to become line in attitude and emphasis, and to conflict with operating units
    E. service units tend to function apart from the operating units

22. The one of the following which is the CHIEF reason for training supervisors is that
    A. untrained supervisors find it difficult to train their subordinates
    B. most persons do not start as supervisors and consequently are in need of supervisory training
    C. training permits a higher degree of decentralization of the decision-making process
    D. training permits a higher degree of centralization of the decision-making process
    E. coordinated actions on the part of many persons pre-supposes familiarity with the procedures to be employed

23. The problem of determining the type of organization which should exist is inextricably interwoven with the problem of recruitment.
 In general, this statement is
    A. *correct*; since organizations are man-made, they can be changed
    B. *incorrect*; the organizational form which is most desirable is independent of the persons involved
    C. *correct*; the problem of organization cannot be considered apart from employee qualifications
    D. *incorrect*; organizational problems can be separated into many parts and recruitment is important in only few of these
    E. *correct*; a good recruitment program will reduce the problems of organization

24. The conference as an administrative tool is MOST valuable for solving problems which
    A. are simple and within a familiar frame of reference
    B. are of long standing
    C. are novel and complex
    D. are not solvable
    E. require immediate solution

25. Of the following, a recognized procedure for avoiding conflicts in the delegation of authority is to 25.____
    A. delegate authority so as to preserve control by top management
    B. provide for a workable span of control
    C. preview all assignments periodically
    D. assign all related work to the same control
    E. use the linear method of assignment

KEY (CORRECT ANSWERS)

1.	B	11.	B
2.	E	12.	A
3.	C	13.	A
4.	E	14.	C
5.	A	15.	A
6.	A	16.	C
7.	D	17.	B
8.	B	18.	B
9.	C	19.	A
10.	D	20.	A

21. D
22. C
23. C
24. C
25. D

TEST 2

DIRECTIONS: Each question or incomplete statement is followed by several suggested answers or completions. Select the one that BEST answers the question or completes the statement. *PRINT THE LETTER OF THE CORRECT ANSWER IN THE SPACE AT THE RIGHT.*

1. A danger which exists in any organization as complex as that required for administration of a large city is that each department comes to believe that it exists for its own sake.
   The one of the following which has been attempted in some organizations as a cure for this condition is to
   A. build up the departmental esprit de corps
   B. expand the functions and jurisdictions of the various departments so that better integration is possible
   C. develop a body of specialists in the various subject matter fields which cut across departmental lines
   D. delegate authority to the lowest possible echelon
   E. systematically transfer administrative personnel from one department to another

   1._____

2. At best, the organization chart is ordinarily and necessarily an idealized picture of the intent of top management, a reflection of hopes and aims rather than a photograph of the operating facts within an organization.
   The one of the following which is the BASIC reason for this is that the organization chart
   A. does not show the flow of work within the organization
   B. speaks in terms of positions rather than of live employees
   C. frequently contains unresolved internal ambiguities
   D. is a record of past organization or of proposed future organization and never a photograph of the living organization
   E. does not label the jurisdiction assigned to each component unit

   2._____

3. The drag of inadequacy is always downward. The need in administration is always for the reverse; for a department head to project his thinking to the city level, for the unit chief to try to see the problems of the department.
   The inability of a city administration to recruit administrators who can satisfy this need usually results in departments characterized by
   A. disorganization   B. poor supervision
   C. circumscribed viewpoints D. poor public relations
   E. a lack of programs

   3._____

4. When, as a result of a shift in public sentiment, the elective officers of a city are changed, is it desirable for career administrators to shift ground without performing any illegal or dishonest act in order to conform to the policies of the new elective officers?
   A. *No*; the opinions and beliefs of the career officials are the result of long experience in administration and are more reliable than those of politicians.

   4._____

101

B. *Yes*; only in this way can citizens, political officials, and career administrators alike have confidence in the performance of their respective functions.
C. *No*; a top career official who is so spineless as to change his views or procedures as a result of public opinion is of little value to the public service.
D. *Yes*; legal or illegal, it is necessary that a city employee carry out the orders of his superior officers
E. *No*; shifting ground with every change in administration will preclude the use of a constant overall policy.

5. Participation in developing plans which will affect levels in the organization in addition to his own, will contribute to an individual's understanding of the entire system. When possible, this should be encouraged.
   This policy is, in general,
   A. *desirable*; the maintenance of any organization depends upon individual understanding
   B. *undesirable*; employees should participate only in those activities which affect their own level, otherwise conflicts in authority may arise
   C. *desirable*; an employee's will to contribute to the maintenance of an organization depends to a great extent on the level which he occupies
   D. *undesirable*; employees can be trained more efficiently and economically in an organized training program than by participating in plan development
   E. *desirable*; it will enable the employee to make intelligent suggestions for adjustment of the plan in the future

5.____

6. Constant study should be made of the information contained in reports to isolate those elements of experience which are static, those which are variable and repetitive, and those which are variable and due to chance.
   Knowledge of those elements of experience in his organization which are static or constant will enable the operating official to
   A. fix responsibility for their supervision at a lower level
   B. revise the procedure in order to make the elements variable
   C. arrange for follow-up and periodic adjustment
   D. bring related data together
   E. provide a frame of reference within which detailed standards for measuremeant can be installed

6.____

7. A chief staff officer, serving as one of the immediate advisors to the department head, has demonstrated a special capacity for achieving internal agreements and for sound judgment. As a result he has been used more and more as a source of counsel and assistance by the department head. Other staff officers and line officials as well have discovered that it is wise for them to check with this colleague in advance on all problematical matters handed up to the department head.
   Developments such as this are
   A. *undesirable*; they disrupt the normal lines for flow of work in an organization

7.____

B. *desirable*; they allow an organization to make the most of its strength wherever such strength resides
C. *undesirable*; they tend to undermine the authority of the department head and put it in the hands of a staff officer who does not have the responsibility
D. *desirable*; they tend to resolve internal ambiguities in organization
E. *undesirable*; they make for bad morale by causing *cut throat* competition

8. A common difference among executives is that some are not content unless they are out in front of everything that concerns their organization, while others prefer to run things by pulling strings, by putting others out in front and by stepping into the breach only when necessary.
Generally speaking, an advantage this latter method of operation has over the former is that it
   A. results in a higher level of morale over a sustained period of time
   B. gets results by exhortation and direct stimulus
   C. makes it necessary to calculate integrated moves
   D. makes the personality of the executive felt further down the line
   E. results in the executive getting the reputation for being a good fellow

9. Administrators frequently have to get facts by interviewing people. Although the interview is a legitimate fact-gathering technique, it has definite limitations which should not be overlooked.
The one of the following which is an important limitation is that
   A. people who are interviewed frequently answer questions with guesses rather than admit their ignorance
   B. it is a poor way to discover the general attitude and thinking of supervisors interviewed
   C. people sometimes hesitate to give information during an interview which they will submit in written form
   D. it is a poor way to discover how well employees understand departmental policies
   E. the material obtained from the interview can usually be obtained at lower cost from existing records

10. It is desirable and advantageous to leave a maximum measure of planning responsibility to operating agencies or units, rather than to remove the responsibility to a central planning staff agency.
Adoption of the former policy (decentralized planning) would lead to
   A. *less effective* planning; operating personnel do not have the time to make long-term plans
   B. *more effective* planning; operating units are usually better equipped technically than any staff agency and consequently are in a better position to set up valid plans
   C. *less effective* planning; a central planning agency has a more objective point of view than any operating agency can achieve
   D. *more effective* planning; plans are conceived in terms of the existing situation and their execution is carried out with the will to succeed

E. *less effective* planning; there is little or no opportunity to check deviation from plans in the proposed set-up

Questions 11-15.

DIRECTIONS: The following sections appeared in a report on the work production of two bureaus of a department. Questions 10 through 12 are to be answered on the basis of the following information. Throughout the report, assume that each month has 4 weeks.

Each of the two bureaus maintains a chronological file. In Bureau A, every 9 months on the average, this material fills a standard legal size file cabinet sufficient for 12,000 work units. In Bureau B, the same type of cabinet is filled in 18 months. Each bureau maintains three complete years of information plus a current file. When the current file cabinet is filled, the cabinet containing the oldest material is emptied, the contents disposed of and the cabinet used for current material. The similarity of these operations makes it possible to consolidate these files with little effort.

Study of the practice of using typists as filing clerks for periods when there is no typing work showed (1) Bureau A has for the past 6 months completed a total of 1,500 filing work units a week using on the average 200 man-hours of trained file clerk time and 20 man-hours of typist time, (2) Bureau B has in the same period completed a total of 2,000 filing work units a week using on the average 125 man-hours of trained file clerk time and 60 hours of typist time. This includes all work in chronological files. Assuming that all clerks work at the same speed and that all typists work at the same speed, this indicates that work other than filing should be found for typists or that they should be given some training in the filing procedures used. It should be noted that Bureau A has not been producing the 1,600 units of technical (not filing) work per 30 day period required by Schedule K, but is at present 200 units behind. The Bureau should be allowed 3 working days to get on schedule.

11. What percentage (approximate) of the total number of filing work units completed in both units consists of the work involved in the maintenance of the chronological files?
A. 5%   B. 10%   C. 15%   D. 20%   E. 25%

11.____

12. If the two chronological files are consolidated, the number of months which should be allowed for filling a cabinet is
A. 2   B. 4   C. 6   D. 8   E. 14

12.____

13. The MAXIMUM number of file cabinets which can be released for other uses as a result of the consolidation recommended is
A. 0
B. 1
C. 2
D. 3
E. not determinable on the basis of the data given

13.____

5 (#2)

14. If all the filing work for both units is consolidated without any diminution in the amount to be done and all filing work is done by trained file clerks, the number of clerks required (35-hour work week) is
    A. 4   B. 5   C. 6   D. 7   E. 8

    14.____

15. In order to comply with the recommendation with respect to Schedule K, the present work production of Bureau A must be increased by
    A. 50%
    B. 100%
    C. 150%
    D. 200%
    E. an amount which is not determinable on the basis of the data given

    15.____

16. A certain training program during World War II resulted in training of thousands of supervisors in industry. The methods of this program were later successfully applied in various governmental agencies. The program was based upon the assumption that there is an irreducible minimum of three supervisory skills. The one of these skills among the following is
    A. to know how to perform the job at hand well
    B. to be able to deal personally with workers, especially face-to-face
    C. to be able to imbue workers with the will to perform the job well
    D. to know the kind of work that is done by one's unit and the policies and procedures of one's agency
    E. the "know-how" of administrative and supervisory processes

    16.____

17. A comment made by an employee about a training course was, *We never have any idea how we are getting along in that course."*
    The fundamental error in training methods to which this criticism points is
    A. insufficient student participation
    B. failure to develop a feeling of need or active want for the material being presented
    C. the training sessions may be too long
    D. no attempt may have been made to connect the new material with what was already known
    E. no goals have been set for the students

    17.____

18. Assume that you are attending a departmental conference on efficiency ratings at which it is proposed that a man-to-man rating scale be introduced.
    You should point out that, of the following, the CHIEF weakness of the man-to-man rating scale is that
    A. it involves abstract numbers rather than concrete employee characteristics
    B. judges are unable to select their own standards for comparison
    C. the standard for comparison shifts from man to man for each person rated
    D. not every person rated is given the opportunity to serve as a standard for comparison
    E. standards for comparison will vary from judge to judge

    18.____

19. Assume that you are conferring with a supervisor who has assigned to his subordinates efficiency ratings which you believe to be generally too low. The supervisor argues that his ratings are generally low because his subordinates are generally inferior.
Of the following, the evidence MOST relevant to the point at issue can be secured by comparing efficiency ratings assigned by this supervisor
   A. with ratings assigned by other supervisors in the same agency
   B. this year with ratings assigned by him in previous years
   C. to men recently transferred to his unit with ratings previously earned by these men
   D. with the general city average of ratings assigned by all supervisors to all employees
   E. with the relative order of merit of his employees as determined independently by promotion test marks

19.____

20. The one of the following which is NOT among the most common of the compensable factors used in wage evaluation studies is
    A. initiative and ingenuity required
    B. physical demand
    C. responsibility for the safety of others
    D. working conditions
    E. presence of avoidable hazards

20.____

21. If independent functions are separated, there is an immediate gain in conserving special skills. If we are to make optimum use of the abilities of our employees, these skills must be conserved.
Assuming the correctness of this statement, it follows that
    A. if we are not making optimum use of employee abilities, independent functions have not been separated
    B. we are making optimum use of employee abilities if we conserve special skills
    C. we are making optimum use of employee abilities if independent functions have been separated
    D. we are not making optimum use of employee abilities if we do not conserve special skills
    E. if special skills are being conserved, independent functions need not be separated

21.____

22. A reorganization of the bureau to provide for a stenographic pool instead of individual unit stenographer will result in more stenographic help being available too each unit when it is required, and consequently will result in greater productivity for each unit. An analysis of the space requirements shows that setting up a stenographic pool will require a minimum of 400 square feet of good space. In order to obtain this space, it will be necessary to reduce the space available for technical personnel, resulting in lesser productivity for each unit.
On the basis of the above discussion, it can be stated that in order to obtain greater productivity for each unit,

22.____

A. a stenographic pool should be set up
B. further analysis of the space requirement should be made
C. it is not certain as to whether or not a stenographic pool should be set up
D. the space available for each technician should be increased in order to compensate for the absence of a stenographic pool
E. a stenographic pool should not be set up

23. The adoption of a single consolidated form will mean that most of the form will not be used in any one operation. This would create waste and confusion. This conclusion is based upon the unstated hypothesis that
    A. if waste and confusion are to be avoided, a single consolidated form should be used
    B. if a single consolidated form is constructed, most of it can be used in each operation
    C. if waste and confusion are to be avoided, most of the form employed should be used
    D. most of a single consolidated form is not used
    E. a single consolidated form should not be used

23.____

24. Assume that you are studying the results of mechanizing several hand operations.
    The type of data which would be MOST useful in proving that an increase in mechanization is followed by a lower cost of operation is data which show that in
    A. some cases a lower cost of operation was not preceded by an increase in mechanization
    B. no case was a higher cost of operation preceded by a decrease in mechanization
    C. some cases a lower cost of operation was preceded by a decrease in mechanization
    D no case was a higher cost of operation preceded by an increase in mechanization
    E. some cases an increase in mechanization was followed by a decrease in cost of operation

24.____

25. The type of data which would be MOST useful in determining if an increase in the length of rest periods is followed by an increased rate of production is data which would indicate that _____ in the length of the rest period.

    A. *decrease* in the total production never follows an increase in
    B. *increase* in the total production never follows an increase
    C. *increase* in the rate of production never follows a decrease
    D. *decrease* in the total production may follow a decrease
    E. *increase* in the total production sometimes follows an increase

25.____

KEY (CORRECT ANSWERS)

1.	E		11.	C
2.	B		12.	C
3.	C		13.	B
4.	B		14.	D
5.	E		15.	E
6.	A		16.	B
7.	B		17.	E
8.	A		18.	E
9.	A		19.	C
10.	D		20.	E

21. D
22. C
23. C
24. D
25. A

TEST 3

DIRECTIONS: Each question or incomplete statement is followed by several suggested answers or completions. Select the one that BEST answers the question or completes the statement. *PRINT THE LETTER OF THE CORRECT ANSWER IN THE SPACE AT THE RIGHT.*

1. You have been asked to answer a request from a citizen of the city. After giving the request careful consideration, you find that it cannot be granted. In answering the letter, you should begin by
   A. saying that the request cannot be granted
   B. discussing in detail the consideration you have to the request
   C. quoting the laws relating to the request
   D. explaining in detail why the request cannot be granted
   E. indicating an alternative method of achieving the end desired

   1.____

2. Reports submitted to the department head should be complete to the last detail. A far as possible, summaries should be avoided.
   This statement is, in general,
   A. *correct*; only on the basis of complete information can a proper decision be reached
   B. *incorrect*; if all reports submitted were of this character, a department head would never complete his work
   C. *correct*; the decision as to what is important and what is not can only be made by the person who is responsible for the action
   D. *incorrect*; preliminary reports, obviously, cannot be complete to the last detail
   E. *correct*; summaries tend to conceal the actual state of affairs and to encourage generalizations which would not be made if the details were known; consequently, they should be avoided if possible

   2.____

3. The supervisor of a large bureau, who was required in the course of business to answer a large number of letters from the public, completely formalized his responses, that is, the form and vocabulary of every letter he prepared were the same as far as possible.
   This method of solving the problem of how to handle correspondence is, in general
   A. *good*; it reduces the time and thought necessary for a response
   B. *bad*; the time required to develop a satisfactory standard form and vocabulary is usually not available in an active organization
   C. *good*; the use of standard forms causes similar requests to be answered in a similar way
   D. *bad*; the use of standard forms and vocabulary to the extent indicated results in letters in *officialese* hindering unambiguous explanation and clear understanding
   E. *good*; if this method were applied to an entire department, the answering of letters could be left to clerks and the administrators would be free for more constructive work

   3.____

109

4. Of the following systems of designating the pages in a looseleaf manual subject to constant revision and addition, the MOST practicable one is to use _____ for main divisions and _____ for subdivisions.
   A. decimals; integers
   B. integers; letters
   C. integers; decimals
   D. letters; integers
   E. integers; integers

5. A subordinate submits a proposed draft of a form which is being revised to facilitate filling in the form on a typewriter. The draft shows that the captions for each space will be printed below the space to be filled in.
   This proposal is
   A. *undesirable*; it decreases visibility
   B. *desirable*; it makes the form easy to understand
   C. *undesirable*; it makes the form more difficult to understand
   D. *desirable*; it increases visibility
   E. *undesirable*; it is less compact than other layouts

6. The one of the following which is NOT an essential element of an integrated reporting system for work-measurement is a
   A. uniform record form for accumulating data and instructions for its maintenance
   B. procedure for routing reports upward through the organization and routing summaries downward
   C. standard report form for summarizing basic records and instructions for its preparation
   D. method for summarizing, analyzing and presenting data from several reports
   E. looseleaf revisable manual which contains all procedural materials that are reasonably permanent and have a substantial reference value

7. Forms control only accomplishes the elimination, consolidation, and simplification of forms. It contributes little to the elimination, consolidation, and simplification of procedures.
   This statement is
   A. *correct*; the form is static while the procedure is dynamic; consequently, control of one does not necessarily result in control of the other
   B. *incorrect*; forms frequently dictate the way work is laid out; consequently, control of one frequently results in control of the other
   C. *correct*; the procedure is primary and the form secondary; consequently, control of procedure will also control form
   D. *incorrect*; the form and procedure are identical from the viewpoint of work control; consequently, control of one means control of the other
   E. *correct*; the assurance that forms are produced and distributed economically has little relationship to the consolidation and simplification of procedures

8. Governmental agencies frequently attempt to avoid special interest group pressures by referring them to the predetermined legislative policy, or to the necessity for rules and regulations applying generally to all groups and situations.
Of the following, the MOST important weakness of this formally correct position is that
   A. it is not tenable in the face of determined opposition
   B. it tends to legalize and formalize the informal relationships between citizen groups and the government
   C. the achievement of an agency's aims is in large measure dependent upon its ability to secure the cooperation and support of special interest groups
   D. independent groups which participate in the formulation of policy in their sphere of interest tend to criticize openly and to press for changes in the direction of their policy
   E. agencies following this policy find it difficult to decentralize their public relation activities as subdivisions can only refer to the agency's overall policy

8.____

9. One of the primary purposes of the performance budget is to improve the ability to examine budgetary requirement by groups who have not been engaged in the construction of the budget.
This is accomplished by
   A. making line by line appropriations
   B. making lump sum appropriations by department
   C. enumerating authorization for all expenditures
   D. standardizing the language used and the kinds of authorizations permitted
   E. permitting examination on the level of accomplishment

9.____

10. When engaged in budget construction or budget analysis, there is no point in trying to determine the total or average benefits to be obtained from total expenditures for a particular commodity or function.
The validity of this argument is USUALLY based upon the
   A. viewpoint that it is not possible to construct a functional budget
   B. theory (or phenomenon) of diminishing utility
   C. hypothesis that as governmental budgets provide in theory for minimum requirements, there is no need to determine total benefits
   D. assumption that such determinations are not possible
   E. false hypothesis that a comparison between expected and achieved results does not aid in budget construction

10.____

Questions 11-12.

DIRECTIONS: Questions 11 and 12 are to be answered on the basis of the following paragraph.

Production planning is mainly a process of synthesis. As a basis for the positive act of bringing complex production elements properly together, however, analysis is necessary, especially if improvement is to be made in an existing organization. The necessary analysis requires customary means of orientation and preliminary fact gathering with emphasis, however, on the recognition of administrative goals and of the relationship among work steps.

11. The entire process described is PRIMARILY one of
    A. taking apart, examining, and recombining
    B. deciding what changes are necessary, making the changes and checking on their value
    C. fact finding so as to provide the necessary orientation
    D. discovering just where the emphasis in production should be placed and then modifying the existing procedure so that it is placed properly
    E. recognizing administrative goals and the relationship among work steps

12. In production planning according to the above paragraph, analysis is used PRIMARILY as
    A. a means of making important changes in an organization
    B. the customary means of orientation and preliminary fact finding
    C. a development of the relationship among work steps
    D. a means for holding the entire process intact by providing a logical basis
    E. a method to obtain the facts upon which a theory can be built

Questions 13-15.

DIRECTIONS: Questions 13 through 15 are to be answered on the basis of the following paragraph.

Public administration is policy-making. But it is not autonomous, exclusive or isolated policy-making. It is policy-making on a field where mighty forces contend, forces engendered in and by society. It is policy-making subject to still other and various policy makers. Public administration is one of a number of basic political processes by which these people achieves and controls government.

13. From the point of view expressed in the above paragraph, public administration is
    A. becoming a technical field with completely objective processes
    B. the primary force in modern society
    C. a technical field which should be divorced from the actual decision-making function
    D. basically anti-democratic
    E. intimately related to politics

14. According to the above paragraph, public administration is NOT entirely
    A. a force generated in and by society
    B. subject at times to controlling influences
    C. a social process
    D. policy-making relating to administrative practices
    E. related to policy-making at lower levels

15. The above paragraph asserts that public administration 15.____
    A. develops the basic and controlling policies
    B. is the result of policies made by many different forces
    C. should attempt to break through its isolated policy-making and engage on a broader field
    D. is a means of directing government
    E. is subject to the political processes by which acts are controlled

Questions 16-18.

DIRECTIONS: Questions 16 through 18 are to be answered on the basis of the following chart.

In order to understand completely the source of an employee's insecurity on his job, it is necessary to understand how he came to be, who he is and what kind of person he is away from his job. This would necessitate an understanding of those personal assets and liabilities which the employee brings to the job situation. These arise from his individual characteristics and his past experiences and established patterns of interpersonal relations. This whole area is of tremendous scope, encompassing everything included within the study of psychiatry and interpersonal relations. Therefore, it has been impracticable to consider it in detail. Attention has been focused on the relatively circumscribed area of the actual occupational situation. The factors considered those which the employee brings to the job situation and which arise from his individual characteristics and his past experience and established patterns of interpersonal relations are: intellectual-level or capacity, specific aptitudes, education, work experience, health, social and economic background, patterns of interpersonal relations and resultant personality characteristics.

16. According to the above paragraph, the one of the following fields of study which would be of LEAST importance in the study of the problem is the 16.____
    A. relationships existing among employees
    B. causes of employee insecurity in the job situation
    C. conflict, if it exists, between intellectual level and work experience
    D. distribution of intellectual achievement
    E. relationship between employee characteristics and the established pattern of interpersonal relations in the work situation

17. According to the above paragraph, in order to make a thoroughgoing and comprehensive study of the sources of employee insecurity, the field of study should include 17.____
    A. only such circumscribed areas as are involved in extra-occupational situations
    B. a study of the dominant mores of the period
    C. all branches of the science of psychology
    D. a determination of the characteristics, such as intellectual capacity, which an employee should bring to the job situation
    E. employee personality characteristics arising from previous relationships with other people

18. It is implied by this paragraph that it would be of GREATEST advantage to bring 18.____
to this problem a comprehensive knowledge of
    A. all established patterns of interpersonal relations
    B. the milieu in which the employee group is located
    C. what assets and liabilities are presented in the job situation
    D. methods of focusing attention on relatively circumscribed regions
    E. the sources of an employee's insecurity on his job

Questions 19-20.

DIRECTIONS: Questions 19 and 20 are to be answered on the basis of the following paragraph.

If, during a study, some hundreds of values of a variable (such as annual number of latenesses for each employee in a department) have been noted merely in the arbitrary order in which they happen to occur, the mind cannot properly grasp the significance of the record, the observations must be ranked or classified in some way before the characteristics of the series can be comprehended, and those comparisons, on which arguments as to causation depend, can be made with other series. A dichotomous classification is too crude; if the values are merely classified according to whether they exceed or fall short of some fixed value, a large part of the information given by the original record is lost. Numerical measurements lend themselves with peculiar readiness to a manifold classification.

19. According to the above paragraph, if the values of a variable which are gathered 19.____
during a study are classified in a few subdivisions, the MOST likely result will be
    A. an inability to grasp the signification of the record
    B. an inability to relate the series with other series
    C. a loss of much of the information in the original data
    D. a loss of the readiness with which numerical measurements lend themselves to a manifold classification
    E. that the order in which they happen to occur will be arbitrary

20. The above paragraph advocates, with respect to numerical data, the use of 20.____
    A. arbitrary order   B. comparisons with other series
    C. a two-value classification   D. a many value classification
    E. all values of a variable

Questions 21-25.

DIRECTIONS: Questions 21 through 25 are to be answered on the basis of the following chart.

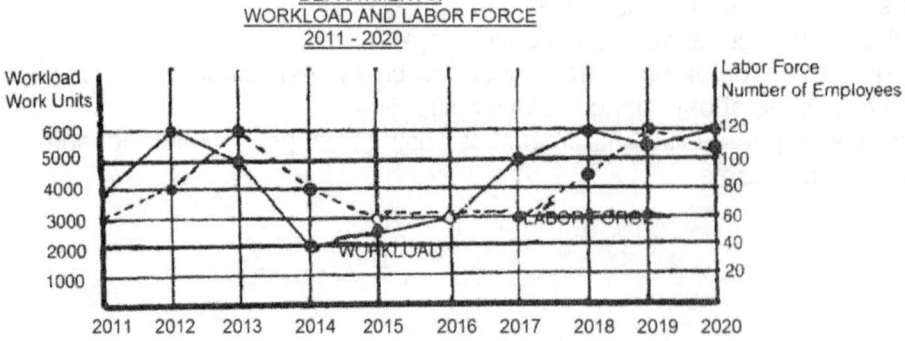

7 (#3)

21. The one of the following years for which average employee production was LOWEST was 21.____
    A. 2012   B. 2014   C. 2016   D. 2018   E. 2020

22. The average annual employee production for the ten-year period was, in terms of work units, MOST NEARLY 22.____
    A. 30   B. 50   C. 70   D. 80   E. 90

23. On the basis of the chart, it can be deduced that personnel needs for the coming year are budgeted on the basis of 23.____
    A. workload for the current year
    B. expected workload for the coming year
    C. no set plan
    D. average workload over the five years immediately preceding the period
    E. expected workload for the five coming years

24. The chart indicates that the operation is carefully programmed and that the labor force has been used properly. 24.____
    This opinion is
    A. *supported* by the chart; the organization has been able to meet emergency situations requiring much additional work without commensurate increase in staff
    B. *not supported* by the chart; the irregular workload shows a complete absence of planning
    C. *supported* by the chart; the similar shapes of the workload and labor force curves show that these important factors are closely related
    D. *not supported* by the chart; poor planning with respect to labor requirements is obvious from the chart
    E. *supported* by the chart; the average number of units of work performed in any 5-year period during the 10 years shows sufficient regularity to indicate a definite trend

25. The chart indicates that the department may be organized in such a way as to require a permanent minimum staff which is too large for the type of operation indicated. 25.____
    This opinion is
    A. *supported* by the chart; there is indication that the operation calls for an irreducible minimum number of employees and application of the most favorable work production records shows this to be too high for normal operation
    B. *not supported* by the chart; the absence of any sort of regularity makes it impossible to express any opinion with any degree of certainty
    C. *supported* by the chart; the expected close relationship between workload and labor force is displaced somewhat, a phenomenon which usually occurs as a result of a fixed minimum requirement
    D. *not supported* by the chart; the violent movement of the labor force curve makes it evident that no minimum requirements are in effect

8 (#3)

E. *supported* by the chart; calculation shows that the average number of employees was 84 with an average variation of 17.8, thus indicating that the minimum number of 60 persons was too high for efficient operation

KEY (CORRECT ANSWERS)

1.	A	11.	A
2.	B	12.	E
3.	D	13.	E
4.	C	14.	D
5.	A	15.	D
6.	E	16.	D
7.	B	17.	E
8.	C	18.	B
9.	E	19.	C
10.	B	20.	D

21. B
22. B
23. A
24. D
25. A

INTERPRETING STATISTICAL DATA
GRAPHS, CHARTS AND TABLES
EXAMINATION SECTION
TEST 1

DIRECTIONS: Each questioner incomplete statement is followed by several suggested answers or completions. Select the one that BEST answers the question or completes the statement. *PRINT THE LETTER OF THE CORRECT ANSWER IN THE SPACE AT THE RIGHT.*

Questions 1-3.

DIRECTIONS: Questions 1 through 3 are to be answered SOLELY on the basis of the following table.

QUARTERLY SALES REPORTED BY MAJOR INDUSTRY GROUPS

DECEMBER 2021 – FEBRUARY 2023
Reported Sales, Taxable & Non-Taxable (in Millions)

Industry Groups	12/21-2/22	3/22-5/22	6/22-8/22	9/22-11/22	12/22-2/23
Retailers	2,802	2,711	2,475	2,793	2,974
Wholesalers	2,404	2,237	2,269	2,485	2,974
Manufacturers	3,016	2,888	3,001	3,518	3,293
Services	1,034	1,065	984	1,132	1,092

1. The trend in total reported sales may be described as

   A. downward
   B. downward and upward
   C. horizontal
   D. upward

2. The two industry groups that reveal a similar seasonal pattern for the period December 2021 through November 2022 are

   A. retailers and manufacturers
   B. retailers and wholesalers
   C. wholesalers and manufacturers
   D. wholesalers and service

3. Reported sales were at a MINIMUM between

   A. December 2021 and February 2022
   B. March 2022 and May 2022
   C. June 2022 and August 2022
   D. September 2022 and November 2022

TEST 2

DIRECTIONS: Each question or incomplete statement is followed by several suggested answers or completions. Select the one that BEST answers the question or completes the statement. *PRINT THE LETTER OF THE CORRECT ANSWER IN THE SPACE AT THE RIGHT*

Questions 1-4.

DIRECTIONS: Questions 1 through 4 are to be answered SOLELY on the basis of the following information.

The income elasticity of demand for selected items of consumer demand in the United States are:

Item	Elasticity
Airline Travel	5.66
Alcohol	.62
Dentist Fees	1.00
Electric Utilities	3.00
Gasoline	1.29
Intercity Bus	1.89
Local Bus	1.41
Restaurant Meals	.75

1. The demand for the item listed below that would be MOST adversely affected by a decrease in income is

   A. alcohol
   B. electric utilities
   C. gasoline
   D. restaurant meals

2. The item whose relative change in demand would be the same as the relative change in income would be

   A. dentist fees
   B. gasoline
   C. restaurant meals
   D. none of the above

3. If income increases by 12 percent, the demand for restaurant meals may be expected to increase by

   A. 9 percent
   B. 12 percent
   C. 16 percent
   D. none of the above

4. On the basis of the above information, the item whose demand would be MOST adversely affected by an increase in the sales tax from 7 percent to 8 percent to be passed on to the consumer in the form of higher prices

   A. would be airline travel
   B. would be alcohol
   C. would be gasoline
   D. cannot be determined

TEST 3

DIRECTIONS: Each question or incomplete statement is followed by several suggested answers or completions. Select the one that BEST answers the question or completes the statement. *PRINT THE LETTER OF THE CORRECT ANSWER IN THE SPACE AT THE RIGHT.*

Questions 1-3.

DIRECTIONS: Questions 1 through 3 are to be answered SOLELY on the basis of the following graphs depicting various relationships in a single retail store.

GRAPH 1
RELATIONSHIP BETWEEN NUMBER OF CUSTOMERS STORE AND TIME OF DAY

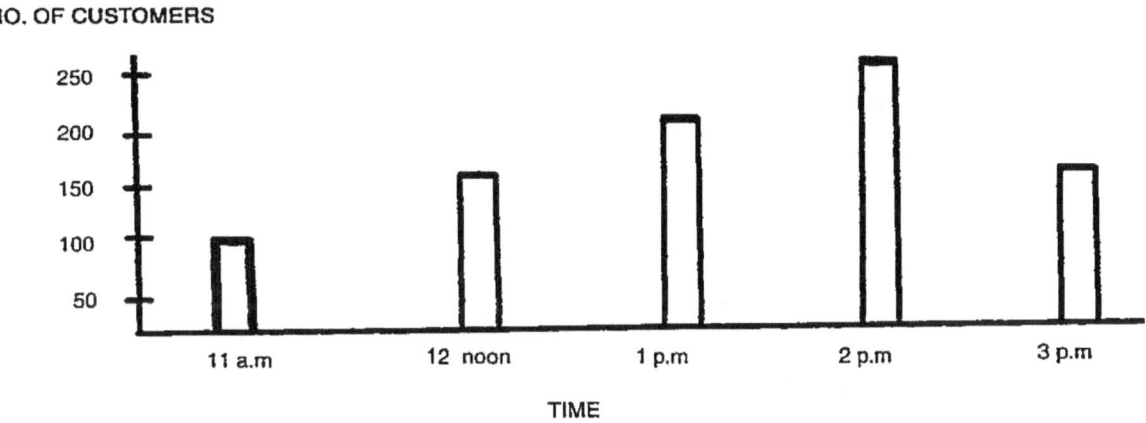

GRAPH II
RELATIONSHIP BETWEEN NUMBER OF CHECK-OUT LANES AVAILABLE IN STORE AND WAIT TIME FOR CHECK-OUT

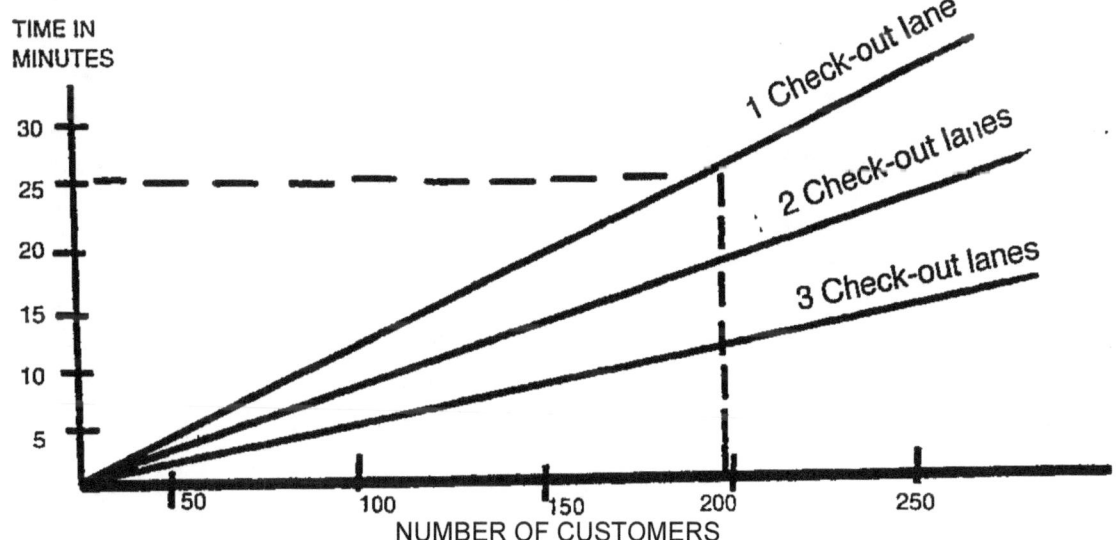

Note the dotted lines in Graph II. They demonstrate that, if there are 200 people in the store and only one check-out lane is open, the wait time will be 25 minutes.

1. At what time would a person be most likely NOT to have to wait more than 15 minutes if only one check-out lane is open?

   A. 11 A.M.　　　B. 12 Noon　　　C. 1 P.M.　　　D. 3 P.M.

2. At what time of day would a person have to wait the LONGEST to check out if three check-out lanes are available?

   A. 11 A.M.　　　B. 12 Noon　　　C. 1 P.M.　　　D. 2 P.M

3. The difference in wait times between 1 and 3 check-out lanes at 3 P.M. is MOST NEARLY

   A. 5　　　B. 10　　　C. 15　　　D. 20

———

TEST 4

DIRECTIONS: Each question or incomplete statement is followed by several suggested answers or completions. Select the one that BEST answers the question or completes the statement. *PRINT THE LETTER OF THE CORRECT ANSWER IN THE SPACE AT THE RIGHT.*

Questions 1-4.

DIRECTIONS: Questions 1 through 4 are to be answered SOLELY on the basis of the graph below.

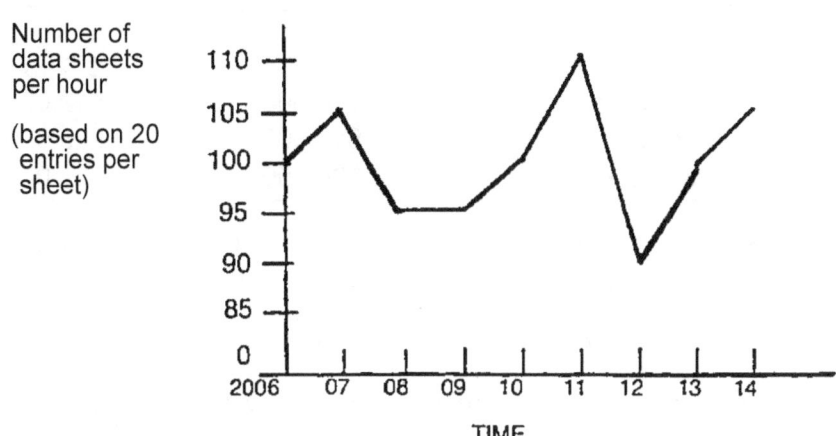

1. Of the following, during what four-year period did the average output of computer operators fall BELOW 100 sheets per hour?

   A. 2007-10 B. 2008-11 C. 2010-13 D. 2011-14

2. The average percentage change in output over the previous year's output for the years 2009 to 2012 is MOST NEARLY

   A. 2 B. 0 C. -5 D. -7

3. The difference between the actual output for 2012 and the projected figure based upon the average increase from 2006-2011 is MOST NEARLY

   A. 18 B. 20 C. 22 D. 24

4. Assume that after constructing the above graph you, an analyst, discovered that the average number of entries per sheet in 2012 was 25 (instead of 20) because of the complex nature of the work performed during that period.
   The average output in sheets per hour for the period 2010-13, expressed in terms of 20 items per sheet, would then be MOST NEARLY

   A. 95 B. 100 C. 105 D. 110

121

TEST 6

DIRECTIONS: Each question or incomplete statement is followed by several suggested answers or completions. Select the one that BEST answers the question or completes the statement. *PRINT THE LETTER OF THE CORRECT ANSWER IN THE SPACE AT THE RIGHT.*

Questions 1-3.

DIRECTIONS: Questions 1 through 3 are to be answered on the basis of the following data assembled for a cost-benefit analysis.

	Cost	Benefit
No program	0	0
Alternative W	$ 3,000	$ 6,000
Alternative X	$10,000	$17,000
Alternative Y	$17,000	$25,000
Alternative Z	$30,000	$32,000

1. From the point of view of selecting the alternative with the best cost benefit ratio, the BEST alternative is Alternative

   A. W   B. X   C. Y   D. Z

2. From the point of view of selecting the alternative with the best measure of net benefit, the BEST alternative is Alternative

   A. W   B. X   C. Y   D. Z

3. From the point of view of pushing public expenditure to the point where marginal benefit equals or exceeds marginal cost, the BEST alternative is Alternative

   A. W   B. X   C. Y   D. Z

TEST 6

DIRECTIONS: Each question or incomplete statement is followed by several suggested answers or completions. Select the one that BEST answers the question or completes the statement. *PRINT THE LETTER OF THE CORRECT ANSWER IN THE SPACE AT THE RIGHT.*

Questions 1-3.

DIRECTIONS: Questions 1 through 3 are to be answered SOLELY on the basis of the following data.

A series of cost-benefit studies of various alternative health programs yields the following results:

Program	Benefit	Cost
K	30	15
L	60	60
M	300	150
N	600	500

In answering Questions 1 and 2, assume that all programs can be increased or decreased in scale without affecting their individual benefit-to-cost ratios.

1. The benefit-to-cost ratio of Program M is

   A. 10:1   B. 5:1   C. 2:1   D. 1:2

2. The budget ceiling for one or more of the programs included in the study is set at 75 units. It may MOST logically be concluded that

   A. Programs K and L should be chosen to fit within the budget ceiling
   B. Program K would be the most desirable one that could be afforded
   C. Program M should be chosen rather than Program K
   D. the choice should be between Programs M and K

3. If no assumptions can be made regarding the effects of change of scale, the MOST logical conclusion, on the basis of the data available, is that

   A. more data are needed for a budget choice of program
   B. Program K is the most preferable because of its low cost and good benefit-to-cost ratio
   C. Program M is the most preferable because of its high benefits and good benefit-to-cost ratio
   D. there is no difference between Programs K and M, and either can be chosen for any purpose

TEST 7

DIRECTIONS: Each question or incomplete statement is followed by several suggested answers or completions. Select the one that BEST answers the question or completes the statement. *PRINT THE LETTER OF THE CORRECT ANSWER IN THE SPACE AT THE RIGHT.*

Questions 1-6.

DIRECTIONS: Questions 1 through 6 are to be answered SOLELY on the basis of the information contained in the charts below which relate to the budget allocations of City X, a small suburban community. The charts depict the annual budget allocations by Department and by expenditures over a five-year period.

CITY X BUDGET IN MILLIONS OF DOLLARS
TABLE I. Budget Allocations by Department

Department	2017	2018	2019	2020	2021
Public Safety	30	45	50	40	50
Health and Welfare	50	75	90	60	70
Engineering	5	8	10	5	8
Human Resources	10	12	20	10	22
Conservation & Environment	10	15	20	20	15
Education & Development	15	25	35	15	15
TOTAL BUDGET	120	180	225	150	180

TABLE II. Budget Allocations by Expenditures

Category	2017	2018	2019	2020	2021
Raw Materials & Machinery	36	63	68	30	98
Capital Outlay	12	27	56	15	18
Personal Services	72	90	101	105	64
TOTAL BUDGET	120	180	225	150	180

1. The year in which the SMALLEST percentage of the total annual budget was allocated to the Department of Education and Development is

   A. 2017   B. 2018   C. 2020   D. 2021

2. Assume that in 2020 the Department of Conservation and Environment divided its annual budget into the three categories of expenditures and in exactly the same proportion as the budget shown in Table II for the year 2020. The amount allocated for capital outlay in the Department of Conservation and Environment's 2020 budget was MOST NEARLY _____ million.

   A. $2   B. $4   C. $6   D. $10

2 (#9)

3. From the year 2018 to the year 2020, the sum of the annual budgets for the Departments of Public Safety and Engineering showed an overall _____ million.

   A. decline; $8
   B. increase; $7
   C. decline; $15
   D. increase; $22

4. The LARGEST dollar increase in departmental budget allocations from one year to the next was in _____ from _____.

   A. Public Safety; 2017 to 2018
   B. Health and Welfare; 2017 to 2018
   C. Education and Development; 2019 to 2020
   D. Human Resources; 2019 to 2020

5. During the five-year period, the annual budget of the Department of Human Resources was GREATER than the annual budget for the Department of Conservation and Environment in _____ of the years.

   A. none
   B. one
   C. two
   D. three

6. If the total City X budget increases at the same rate from 2021 to 2022 as it did from 2020 to 2021, the total City X budget for 2022 will be MOST NEARLY _____ million.

   A. $180
   B. $200
   C. $210
   D. $215

TEST 8

DIRECTIONS: Each question or incomplete statement is followed by several suggested answers or completions. Select the one that BEST answers the question or completes the statement. *PRINT THE LETTER OF THE CORRECT ANSWER IN THE SPACE AT THE RIGHT.*

Questions 1-3.

DIRECTIONS: Questions 1 through 3 are to be answered SOLELY on the basis of the following information.

Assume that in order to encourage Program A, the State and Federal governments have agreed to make the following reimbursements for money spent on Program A, provided the unreimbursed balance is paid from City funds.

During Fiscal Year 2021-2022 - For the first $2 million expended, 50% Federal reimbursement and 30% State reimbursement; for the next $3 million, 40% Federal reimbursement and 20% State reimbursement; for the next $5 million, 20% Federal reimbursement and 10% State reimbursement. Above $10 million expended, no Federal or State reimbursement.

During Fiscal Year 2022-2023 - For the first $1 million expended, 30% Federal reimbursement and 20% State reimbursement; for the next $4 million, 15% Federal reimbursement and 10% State reimbursement. Above $5 million expended, no Federal or State reimbursement.

1. Assume that the Program A expenditures are such that the State reimbursement for Fiscal Year 2021-2022 will be $1 million.
   Then, the Federal reimbursement for Fiscal Year 2021-2022 will be

   A. $1,600,000 B. $1,800,000
   C. $2,000,000 D. $2,600,000

2. Assume that $8 million were to be spent on Program A in Fiscal Year 2022-2023.
   The TOTAL amount of unreimbursed City funds required would be

   A. $3,500,000 B. $4,500,000
   C. $5,500,000 D. $6,500,000

3. Assume that the City desires to have a combined total of $6 million spent in Program A during both the Fiscal Year 2021-2022 and the Fiscal Year 2022-2023.
   Of the following expenditure combinations, the one which results in the GREATEST reimbursement of City funds is _____ in Fiscal Year 2021-2022 and _____ in Fiscal Year 2022-2023.

   A. $5 million; $1 million   B. $4 million; $2 million
   C. $3 million; $3 million   D. $2 million; $4 million

KEY (CORRECT ANSWERS)

TEST 1	TEST 2	TEST 3	TEST 4
1. D	1. B	1. A	1. A
2. C	2. A	2. D	2. B
3. C	3. A	3. B	3. C
	4. D		4. C

TEST 5	TEST 6	TEST 7	TEST 8
1. A	1. C	1. D	1. B
2. C	2. D	2. A	2. D
3. C	3. A	3. A	3. A
		4. B	
		5. B	
		6. D	

PREPARING WRITTEN MATERIAL

PARAGRAPH REARRANGEMENT
COMMENTARY

The sentences that follow are in scrambled order. You are to rearrange them in proper order and indicate the letter choice containing the correct answer at the space at the right.

Each group of sentences in this section is actually a paragraph presented in scrambled order. Each sentence in the group has a place in that paragraph; no sentence is to be left out. You are to read each group of sentences and decide upon the best order in which to put the sentences so as to form a well-organized paragraph.

The questions in this section measure the ability to solve a problem when all the facts relevant to its solution are not given.

More specifically, certain positions of responsibility and authority require the employee to discover connection between events sometimes, apparently, unrelated. In order to do this, the employee will find it necessary to correctly infer that unspecified events have probably occurred or are likely to occur. This ability becomes especially important when action must be taken on incomplete information.

Accordingly, these questions require competitors to choose among several suggested alternatives, each of which presents a different sequential arrangement of the events. Competitors must choose the MOST logical of the suggested sequences.

In order to do so, they may be required to draw on general knowledge to infer missing concepts or events that are essential to sequencing the given events. Competitors should be careful to infer only what is essential to the sequence. The plausibility of the wrong alternatives will always require the inclusion of unlikely events or of additional chains of events which are NOT essential to sequencing the given events.

It's very important to remember that you are looking for the best of the four possible choices, and that the best choice of all may not even be one of the answers you're given to choose from.

There is no one right way to solve these problems. Many people have found it helpful to first write out the order of the sentences, as they would have arranged them, on their scrap paper before looking at the possible answers. If their optimum answer is there, this can save them some time. If it isn't, this method can still give insight into solving the problem. Others find it most helpful to just go through each of the possible choices, contrasting each as they go along. You should use whatever method feels comfortable and works for you.

While most of these types of questions are not that difficult, we've added a higher percentage of the difficult type, just to give you more practice. Usually there are only one or two questions on this section that contain such subtle distinctions that you're unable to answer confidently. And you then may find yourself stuck deciding between two possible choices, neither of which you're sure about.

PREPARING WRITTEN MATERIAL
PARAGRAPH REARRANGEMENT
EXAMINATION SECTION
TEST 1

DIRECTIONS: The following groups of sentences need to be arranged in an order that makes sense. Select the letter preceding the sequence that represents the best sentence order. *PRINT THE LETTER OF THE CORRECT ANSWER IN THE SPACE AT THE RIGHT.*

1.
   I. The ostrich egg shell's legendary toughness makes it an excellent substitute for certain types of dishes or dinnerware, and in parts of Africa ostrich shells are cut and decorated for use as containers for water.
   II. Since prehistoric times, people have used the enormous egg of the ostrich as a part of their diet, a practice which has required much patience and hard work—to hard boil an ostrich egg takes about four hours.
   III. Opening the egg's shell, which is rock hard and nearly an inch thick, requires heavy tools, such as a saw or chisel; from inside, a baby ostrich must use a hornlike projection on its beak as a miniature pick-axe to escape from the egg.
   IV. The offspring of all higher-order animals originate from single egg cells that are carried by mothers, and most of these eggs are relatively small, often microscopic.
   V. The egg of the African ostrich, however, weighs a massive thirty pounds, making it the largest single cell on earth, and a common object of human curiosity and wonder.

   The BEST order is:
   A. V, IV, I, II, III   B. I, IV, V, III, II   C. IV, II, III, V, I   D. IV, V, II, III, I

   1.____

2.
   I. Typically only a few feet high on the open sea, individual tsunami have been known to circle the entire globe two or three times if their progress is not interrupted, but are not usually dangerous until they approach the shallow water that surrounds land masses.
   II. Some of the most terrifying and damaging hazards caused by earthquakes are tsunami, which were once called "tidal waves"—a poorly chosen name, since these waves have nothing to do with tides.
   III. Then a wave, slowed by the sudden drag on the lower part of its moving water column, will pile upon itself, sometimes reaching a height of over 100 feet.
   IV. Tsunami (Japanese for "great harbor wave") are seismic waves that are caused by earthquakes near oceanic trenches, and once triggered, can travel up to 600 miles an hour on the open ocean.
   V. A land-shoaling tsunami is capable of extraordinary destruction; some tsunami have deposited large boats miles inland, washed out two-foot-thick seawalls, and scattered locomotive trains over long distances.

   The BEST order is:
   A. IV, I, III, II, V   B. I, III, IV, II, V   C. V, I, III, II, IV   D. II, IV, I, III, V

   2.____

131

3.
   I. Soon, by the 1940s, jazz was the most popular type of music among American intellectuals and college students.
   II. In the early days of jazz, it was considered "lowdown" music, or music that was played only in rough, disreputable bars and taverns.
   III. However, jazz didn't take too long to develop from early ragtime melodies into more complex, sophisticated forms, such as Charlie Parker's "bebop" style of jazz.
   IV. After charismatic band leaders such as Duke Ellington and Count Basie brought jazz to a larger audience, and jazz continued to evolve into more complicated forms, white audiences began to accept and even to enjoy the new American art form.
   V. Many white Americans, who then dictated the tastes of society, were wary of music that was played almost exclusively in black clubs in the poorer sections of cities and towns.

   The BEST order is:
   A. V, IV, III, II, I   B. II, V, III, IV, I   C. IV, V, III, I, II   D. I, II, IV, III, V

4.
   I. Then, hanging in a windless place, the magnetized end of the needle would always point to the south.
   II. The needle could then be balanced on the rim of a cup, or the edge of a fingernail, but this balancing act was hard to maintain, and the needle often fell off.
   III. Other needles would point to the north, and it was important for any traveler finding his way with a compass to remember which kind of magnetized needle he was carrying.
   IV. To make some of the earliest compasses in recorded history, ancient Chinese "magicians" would rub a needle with a piece of magnetized iron called a lodestone.
   V. A more effective method of keeping the needle free to swing with its magnetic pull was to attach a strand of silk to the center of the needle with a tiny piece of wax.

   The BEST order is:
   A. IV, II, V, I, III   B. IV, III, V, II, I   C. IV, V, II, I, III   D. IV, I, III, V, II

5.
   I. The now-famous first mate of the *H.M.S. Bounty*, Fletcher Christian, founded one of the world's most peculiar civilizations in 1790.
   II. The men knew they had just committed a crime for which they could be hanged, so they set sail for Pitcairn, a remote, abandoned island in the far eastern region of the Polynesian archipelago, accompanied by twelve Polynesian women and six men.
   III. In a mutiny that has become legendary, Christian and the others forced Captain Bligh into a lifeboat and set him adrift off the coast of Tonga in April of 1789.
   IV. In early 1790, the *Bounty* landed at Pitcairn Island, where the men lived out the rest of their lives and founded an isolated community which to this day includes direct descendants of Christian and the other Crewmen.

V. The *Bounty*, commanded by Captain William Bligh, was in the middle of a global voyage, and Christian and his shipmates had come to the conclusion that Bligh was a reckless madman who would lead them to their deaths unless they took the ship from him.

The BEST order is:
   A. IV, V, III, II, I   B. I, III, V, II, IV   C. I, V, III, II, IV   D. III, I, V, IV, II

6.
   I. But once the vines had been led to make orchids, the flowers had to be carefully hand-pollinated, because unpollinated orchids usually lasted less than a day, wilting and dropping off the vine before it had even become dark.
   II. The Totonac farmers discovered that looping a vine back around once it reached a five-foot height on its host tree would cause the vine to flower.
   III. Though they knew how to process the fruit pods and extract vanilla's flavoring agent, the Totonacs also knew that a wild vanilla vine did not produce abundant flowers or fruit.
   IV. Wild vines climbed along the trunks and canopies of trees, and this constant upward growth diverted most of the vine's energy to making leaves instead of the orchid flowers that once pollinated, would produce the flavorful pods.
   V. Hundreds of years before vanilla became a prized food flavoring in Europe and the Western World, the Totonac Indians of the Mexican Gulf Coast were skilled cultivators of the vanilla vine, whose fruit they literally worshipped as a goddess.

The BEST order is:
   A. II, III, IV, I, V   B. II, IV, III, I, V   C. V, III, IV, II, I   D. III, IV, I, II, V

6.____

7.
   I. Once airborne, the spider is at the mercy of the air currents—usually the spider takes a brief journey, traveling close to the ground, but some have been found in air samples collected as high as 10,000 feet, or been reported landing on ships far out at sea.
   II. Once a young spider has hatched, it must leave the environment into which it was born as quickly as possible, in order to avoid competing with its hundreds of brothers and sisters for food.
   III. The silk rises into warm air currents, and as soon as the pull feels adequate the spider lets go and drifts up into the air, suspended from the silk strand in the same way that a person might parasail.
   IV. To help young spiders do this, many species have adapted a practice known as "aerial dispersal," or, in common speech, "ballooning."
   V. A spider that wants to leave its surroundings quickly will climb to the top of a grass system or twig, face into the wind, and aim its back end into the air, releasing a long stream of silk from the glands near the tip of its abdomen.

The BEST order is:
   A. V, IV, II, III, I   B. V, II, IV, I, III   C. II, V, IV, III, I   D. II, IV, V, III, I

7.____

8. I. For about a year, Tycho worked at a castle in Prague with a scientist named Johannes Kepler, but their association was cut short by another argument that drove Kepler out of the castle, to later develop, on his own, the theory of planetary orbits.
    II. Tycho found life without a nose embarrassing, so he made a new nose for himself out of silver, which reportedly remained glued to his face for the rest of his life.
    III. Tycho Brahe, the 17th-century Danish astronomer, is today more famous for his odd and arrogant personality than for any contribution he has made to our knowledge of the stars and planets.
    IV. Early in his career, as a student at Rostock University, Tycho got into an argument with another student about who was the better mathematician, and the two became so angry that the argument turned into a sword fight, during which Tycho's nose was sliced off.
    V. Later in his life, Tycho's arrogance may have kept him from playing a part in one of the greatest astronomical discoveries in history: the elliptical orbits of the solar system's planets.
    The BEST order is:
    A. I, IV, II, III, V   B. IV, II, III, V, I   C. IV, II, I, III, V   D. III, IV, II, V, I

8.____

9. I. The processionaries are so used to this routine that if a person picks up the end of a silk line and brings it back to the origin—creating a closed circle—the caterpillars may travel around and around for days, sometimes starving or freezing, without changing course.
    II. Rather than relying on sight or sound, the other caterpillars, who are lined up end-to-end behind the leader, travel to and from their nests by walking on this silk line, and each will reinforce it by laying down its own marking line as it passes over.
    III. In order to insure the safety of individuals, the processionary caterpillar nests in a tree with dozens of other caterpillars, and at night, when it is safest, they all leave together in search of food.
    IV. The processionary caterpillar of the European continent is a perfect illustration of how much some inspect species rely on instinct in their daily routines.
    V. As they leave their nests, the processionaries form a single-file line behind a leader who spins and lays out a silk line to mark the chosen path.
    The BEST order is:
    A. IV, III, V, II, I   B. III, V, IV, II, I   C. III, V, II, I, IV   D. IV, V, III, I, II

9.____

10. I. Often, the child is also given a handcrafted walker or push cart, to provide support for its first upright explorations.
    II. In traditional Indian families, a child's first steps are celebrated as a ceremonial event, rooted in ancient myth.
    III. These carts are often intricately designed to resemble the chariot of Krishna, an important figure in Indian mythology.
    IV. The sound of these anklet bells is intended to mimic the footsteps of the legendary child Rama, who is celebrated in devotional songs throughout India.

10.____

V. When the child's parents see that the child is ready to begin walking, they will fit it with specially designed ankle bracelets, adorned with gently ringing bells.

The BEST order is:
A. II, III, IV, I, V
B. II, V, III, I, IV
C. V, IV, I, III, II
D. V, III, II, I, IV

11.
I. The settlers planted Osage oranges all across Middle America, and today long lines and rectangles of Osage orange trees can still be seen on the prairies, running along the former boundaries of farms that no longer exist.
II. After trying sod walls and water-filled ditches with no success, American farmers began to look for a plant that was adaptable to prairie weather, and that could be trimmed into a hedge that was "pig-tight, horse-high, and bull-strong."
III. The tree, so named because it bore a large (but inedible) fruit the size of an orange, was among the sturdiest and hardiest of American trees, and was prized among Native Americans for the strength and flexibility of bows which were made from its wood.
IV. The first people to practice agriculture on the American flatlands were faced with an important problem: what would they use to fence their land in a place that was almost entirely without trees or rocks?
V. Finally, an Illinois farmer brought the settlers a tree that was native to the land between the Red and Arkansas rivers, a tree called the Osage orange.

The BEST order is:
A. II, I, V, III, IV
B. I, II, III, IV, V
C. IV, II, V, III, I
D. IV, II, I, III, V

12.
I. After about ten minutes of such spirited and complicated activity, the head dancer is free to make up his or her own movements while maintaining the interest of the New Year's crowd.
II. The dancer will then perform a series of leg kicks, while at the same time operating the lion's mouth with his own hand and moving the ears and eyes by means of a string which is attached to the dancer's own mouth.
III. The most difficult role of this dance belongs to the one who controls the lion's head; this person must lead all the other "parts" of the lion through the choreographed segments of the dance.
IV. The head dancer begins with a complex series of steps. alternately stepping forward with the head raised, and then retreating a few steps while lowering the head, a movement that is intended to create the impression that the lion is keeping a watchful eye for anything evil.
V. When performing a traditional Chinese New Year's lion dance, several performers must fit themselves inside a large lion costume and work together to enact different parts of the dance.

The BEST order is:
A. V, III, IV, II, I
B. III, IV, II, V, I
C. III, I, V, IV, II
D. IV, II, III, V, I

13. I. For many years the shell of the chambered nautilus was treasured in Europe for its beauty and intricacy, but collectors were unaware that they were in possession of the structure that marked a "missing link" in the evolution of marine mollusks.
   II. The nautilus, however, evolved a series of enclosed chambers in its shell, and invented a new use for the structure: the shell began to serve as a buoyancy device.
   III. Equipped with this new flotation device, the nautilus did not need the single, muscular foot of its predecessors, but instead developed flaps, tentacles, and a gentle form of jet propulsion that transformed it into the first mollusk able to take command of its own density and explore a three-dimensional world.
   IV. By pumping and adjusting air pressure into the chambers, the nautilus could spend the day resting on the bottom, and then rise toward the surface at night in search of food.
   V. The nautilus shell looks like a large snail shell, similar to those of its ancestors, who used their shells as protective coverings while they were anchored to the sea floor.

   The BEST order is:
   A. V, II, IV, I, III   B. V, I, II, III, IV   C. I, II, V, III, IV   D. I, V, II, IV, III

14. I. While France and England battled for control of the region, the Acadiens prospered on the fertile farmland, which was finally secured by England in 1713.
   II. Early in the 17th century, settlers from Western France founded a colony called Acadie in what is now the Canadian province of Nova Scotia.
   III. At this time, English officials feared the presence of spies among the Acadiens who might be loyal to their French homeland, and the Acadiens were deported to spots along the Atlantic and Caribbean shores of America.
   IV. The French settlers remained on this land, under English rule, for around forty years, until the beginning of the French and Indian War, another conflict between France and England.
   V. As the Acadien refugees drifted toward a final home in Southern Louisiana, neighbors shortened their name to "Cadien," and finally "Cajun," the name which the descendants of early Acadiens still call themselves.

   The BEST order is:
   A. I, IV, II, III, V   B. II, I, III, V, IV   C. II, I, IV, III, V   D. V, II, III, IV, I

15. I. Traditional households in the Eastern and Western regions of Africa serve two meals a day—one at around noon, and the other in the evening.
   II. The starch is then used in the way that Americans might use a spoon, to scoop up a portion of the main dish on the person's plate.
   III. The reason for the starch's inclusion in every meal has to do with taste as well as nutrition; African food can be very spicy, and the starch is known to cool the burning effect of the main dish.
   IV. When serving these meals, the main dish is usually served on individual plates, and the starch is served on a communal plate, from which diners break off a piece of bread or scoop rice or fufu in their fingers.

V. The typical meals usually consist of a thick stew or soup as the main course, and an accompanying starch—either bread, rice, or *fufu*, a starchy grain paste similar in consistency to mashed potatoes.
The BEST order is:
A. V, II, III, IV, I   B. V, I, IV, III, II   C. I, IV, V, III, II   D. I, V, IV, II, III

16. I. In the early days of the American Midwest, Indiana settlers sometimes came together to hold an event called an apple peeling, where neighboring settlers gathered at the homestead of a host family to help prepare the hosts' apple crop for cooking, canning, and making apple butter.
II. At the beginning of the event, each peeler sat down in front of a ten- or twenty-gallon stone jar and was given a crock of apples and a paring knife.
III. Once a peeler had finished with a crock, another was placed next to him; if the peeler was an unmarried man, he kept a strict count of the number of apples he had peeled, because the winner was allowed to kiss the girl of his choice.
IV. The peeling usually ended by 9:30 in the evening, when the neighbors gathered in the host family's parlor for a dance social.
V. The apples were peeled, cored, and quartered, and then placed into the jar.
The BEST order is:
A. I, V, III, IV, II   B. II, V, III, IV, I   C. I, II, V, III, IV   D. II, I, V, IV, III

16.____

17. I. If your pet turtle is a land turtle and is native to temperate climates, it will stop eating some time in October, which should be your cue to prepare the turtle for hibernation.
II. The box should then be covered with a wire screen, which will protect the turtle from any rodents or predators that might want to take advantage of a motionless and helpless animal.
III. When your turtle hasn't eaten for a while and appears ready to hibernate, it should be moved to its winter quarters, most likely a cellar or garage, where the temperature should range between 40° and 45°F.
IV. Instead of feeding the turtle, you should bathe it every day in warm water, to encourage the turtle to empty its intestines in preparation for its long winter sleep.
V. Here the turtle should be placed in a well-ventilated box whose bottom is covered with a moisture-absorbing layer of clay beads, and then filled three-fourths full with almost dry peat moss or wood chips, into which the turtle will burrow and sleep for several months.
The BEST order is:
A. I, IV, III, V, II   B. III, IV, II, V, I   C. III, II, IV, I, V   D. IV, V, II, III, I

17.____

18. I. Once he has reached the nest, the hunter uses two sturdy bamboo poles like huge chopsticks to pull the next away from the mountainside, into a large basket that will be lowered to people waiting below.
II. The world's largest honeybees colonize the Nealese mountainsides, building honeycombs as large as a person on sheer rock faces that are often hundreds of feet high.

18.____

III. In the remote mountain country of Nepal, a small band of "honey hunters" carry out a tradition so ancient that 10,000 year-old drawings of the practice have been found in the caves of Nepal.
IV. To harvest the honey and beeswax from these combs, a honey hunter climbs above the nests, lowers a long bamboo-fiber ladder over the cliff, and then climbs down.
V. Throughout this dangerous practice, the hunter is stung repeatedly, and only the veterans, with skin that has been toughened over the years, are able to return from a hunt without the painful swelling caused by stings.

The BEST order is:

A. II, IV, III, V, I   B. II, IV, I, V, III   C. V, III, II, IV, I   D. III, II, IV, I, V

19. I. After the Romans left Britain, there were relentless attacks on the islands from the barbarian tribes of northern Germany—the Angles, Saxons, and Jutes.
    II. As the empire weakened, Roman soldiers withdrew from Britain, leaving behind a country that continued to practice the Christian religion that had been introduced by the Romans.
    III. Early Latin writings tell of a Christian warrior named Arturius (Arthur, in English) who led the British citizens to defeat these barbarian invades, and brought an extended period of peace to the lands of Britain.
    IV. Long ago, the British Isles were part of the far-flung Roman Empire that extended across most of Europe and into Africa and Asia.
    V. The romantic legend of King Arthur and his knights of the Round Table, one of the most popular and widespread stories of all time, appears to have some foundation in history.

    The BEST order is:

    A. V, IV, III, II, I   B. V, IV, II, I, III   C. IV, V, II, III, I   D. IV, III, II, I, V

20. I. The cylinder was allowed to cool until it could stand on its own, and then it was cut from the tube and split down the side with a single straight cut.
    II. Nineteenth-century glassmakers, who had not yet discovered the glazier's modern techniques for making panes of glass, had to create a method for converting their blown gas into flat sheets.
    III. The bubble was then pierced at the end to make a hole that opened up while the glassmaker gently spun it, creating a cylinder of glass.
    IV. Turned on its side and laid on a conveyor belt, the cylinder was strengthened, or tempered, by being heated again and cooled very slowly, eventually flattening out into a single rectangular of glass.
    V. To do this, the glassmaker dipped the end of a long tube into melted glass and blew into the other end of the tube, creating an expanding bubble of glass.

    The BEST order is:

    A. II, V, III, IV, I   B. II, IV, V, III, I   C. III, V, II, IV, I   D. III, I, IV, V, II

21. I. The splints are almost always hidden, but horses are occasionally born whose splinted toes project from the leg on either side, just above the hoof.
II. The second and fourth toes remained, but shrank to thin splints of bone that fused invisibly to the horse's leg bone.
III. Horses are unique among mammals, having evolved feet that each end in what is essentially a single toe, capped by a large, sturdy hoof.
IV. Julius Caesar, an emperor of ancient Rome, was said to have owned one of these three-toed horses, and considered it so special that he would not permit anyone else to ride it.
V. Though the horse's earlier ancestors possessed the traditional mammalian set of five toes on each foot, the horse has retained only its third toe; its first and fifth toes disappeared completely as the horse evolved.
The BEST order is:
A. III, V, II, I, IV   B. V, III, II, IV, I   C. III, II, V, I, IV   D. V, II, III, I, IV

22. I. The new building materials—some of which are twenty feet long, and weigh nearly six tons—were transported to Pohnpei on rafts, and were brought into their present position by using hibiscus fiber ropes and leverage to move the stone columns upward along the inclined trunks of coconut palm trees.
II. The ancestors built great fires to heat the stone, and then poured cool seawater on the columns, which caused the stone to contract and split along natural fracture lines.
III. The now-abandoned enclave of Nan Madol, a group of 92 man-made islands off the shore of the Micronesian island of Pohnpei, is estimated to have been built around the year 500 A.D.
IV. The islanders say their ancestors quarried stone columns from a nearby island, where large basalt columns were formed by the cooling of molten lava.
V. The structures of Nan Madol are remarkable for the sheer size of some of the stone "longs" or columns that were used to create the walls of the offshore community, and today anthropologists can only rely on the information of existing local people for clues about how Nan Madol was built.
The BEST order is:
A. V, IV, III, II, I   B. V, III, I, IV, II   C. III, V, IV, II, I   D. III, I, IV, II, V

23. I. One of the most easily manipulated substances on earth, glass can be made into ceramic tiles that are composed of over 90% air.
II. NASA's space shuttles are the first spacecraft ever designed to leave and re-enter the earth's atmosphere while remaining intact.
III. These ceramic tiles are such effective insulators that when a tile emerges from the oven in which it was fired, it can be held safely in a person's hand by the edges while its interior still glows at a temperature well over 2000°F.
IV. Eventually, the engineers were led to a material that is as old as our most ancient civilization.
V. Because the temperature during atmospheric re-entry is so incredibly hot, it took NASA's engineers some time to find a substance capable of protecting the shuttles.

The BEST order is:
A. V, II, I, II, IV   B. II, V, IV, I, III   C. II, III, I, IV, V   D. V, IV, III, I, II

24. I.   The secret to teaching any parakeet to talk is patience, and the understanding that when a bird talks," it is simply imitating what it hears, rather than putting ideas into words.
     II. You should stay just out of sight of the bird and repeat the phrase you want it to learn, for at least fifteen minutes every morning and evening.
     III. It is important to leave the bird without any words of encouragement or farewell; otherwise it might combine stray remarks or phrases, such as "Good night," with the phrase you are trying to teach it.
     IV. For this reason, to train your bird to imitate your words you should keep it free of any distractions, especially other noises, while you are giving it "lesson."
     V.   After your repetition, you should quietly leave the bird alone for a while, to think over what it has just heard.

24.____

The BEST order is:
A. I, IV, II, V, III   B. I, II, IV, III, V   C. III, II, I, V, IV   D. III, I, V, IV, II

25. I.   As a school approaches, fishermen from neighboring communities join their fishing boats together as a fleet, and string their gill nets together to make a huge fence that is held up by cork floats.
     II. At a signal from the party leaders, or *nakura*, the family members pound the sides of the boats or beat the water with long poles, creating a sudden and deafening noise.
     III. The fishermen work together to drag the trap into a half-circle that may reach 300 yards in diameter, and then the families move their boats to form the other half of the circle around the school of fish.
     IV. The school of fish flee from the commotion into the awaiting trap, where a final wall of net is thrown over the open end of the half-circle, securing the day's haul.
     V.   Indonesian people from the area around the Sulu islands live on the sea, in floating villages made of lashed-together or stilted homes, and make much of their living by fishing their home waters for migrating schools of snapper, scad, and other fish.

25.____

The BEST order is:
A. I, V, III, IV, II   B. I, II, IV, III, V   C. V, I, II, III, IV   D. V, I, III, II, IV

KEY (CORRECT ANSWERS)

1. D
2. D
3. B
4. A
5. C

6. C
7. D
8. D
9. A
10. B

11. C
12. A
13. D
14. C
15. D

16. C
17. A
18. D
19. B
20. A

21. A
22. C
23. B
24. A
25. D

PREPARING WRITTEN MATERIAL
EXAMINATION SECTION
TEST 1

DIRECTIONS: Each of the sentences in this test may be classified under one of the following four categories:
- A. *Incorrect* because of faulty grammar or sentence structure
- B. *Incorrect* because of faulty punctuation
- C. *Incorrect* because of faulty capitalization
- D. *Correct*

Examine each sentence carefully to determine under which of the above four options it is best classified. Then, in the space at the right, print the capital letter preceding the option which is the BEST of the four suggested above.

(Each incorrect sentence contains but one type of error. Consider a sentence to be correct if it contains none of the types of errors mentioned, even though there may be other correct ways of expressing the same thought.)

1. This fact, together with those brought out at the previous meeting, prove that the schedule is satisfactory to the employees.   1.____

2. Like many employees in scientific fields, the work of bookkeepers and accountants requires accuracy and neatness.   2.____

3. "What can I do for you," the secretary asked as she motioned to the visitor to take a seat.   3.____

4. Our representative, Mr. Charles will call on you next week to determine whether or not your claim has merit.   4.____

5. We expect you to return in the spring; please do not disappoint us.   5.____

6. Any supervisor, who disregards the just complaints of his subordinates, is remiss in the performance of his duty.   6.____

7. Because she took less than an hour for lunch is no reason for permitting her to leave before five o'clock.   7.____

8. "Miss Smith," said the supervisor, "Please arrange a meeting of the staff for two o'clock on Monday."   8.____

9. A private company's vacation and sick leave allowance usually differs considerably from a public agency.   9.____

10. Therefore, in order to increase the efficiency of operations in the department, a report on the recommended changes in procedures was presented to the departmental committee in charge of the program.   10.____

11. We told him to assign the work to whoever was available. 11._____

12. Since John was the most efficient of any other employee in the bureau, he received the highest service rating. 12._____

13. Only those members of the national organization who resided in the middle West attended the conference in Chicago. 13._____

14. The question of whether the office manager has as yet attained, or indeed can ever hope to secure professional status is one which has been discussed for years. 14._____

15. No one knew who to blame for the error which, we later discovered, resulted in a considerable loss of time. 15._____

KEY (CORRECT ANSWERS)

1.	A	6.	B	11.	D
2.	A	7.	A	12.	A
3.	B	8.	C	13.	C
4.	B	9.	A	14.	B
5.	D	10.	D	15.	A

TEST 2

DIRECTIONS: Each of the sentences in this test may be classified under one of the following four categories:
   A. *Incorrect* because of faulty grammar or sentence structure
   B. *Incorrect* because of faulty punctuation
   C. *Incorrect* because of faulty capitalization
   D. *Correct*

1. The National alliance of Businessmen is trying to persuade private businesses to hire youth in the summertime. 1._____

2. The supervisor who is on vacation, is in charge of processing vouchers. 2._____

3. The activity of the committee at its conferences is always stimulating. 3._____

4. After checking the addresses again, the letters went to the mailroom. 4._____

5. The director, as well as the employees, are interested in sharing the dividends. 5._____

KEY (CORRECT ANSWERS)

1. C
2. B
3. D
4. A
5. A

TEST 3

DIRECTIONS: In each of the following groups of sentences, one of the four sentences is faulty in grammar, punctuation, or capitalization. Select the INCORRECT sentence in each case.

1. A. Sailing down the bay was a thrilling experience for me.
   B. He was not consulted about your joining the club.
   C. This story is different than the one I told you yesterday.
   D. There is no doubt about his being the best player.

2. A. He maintains there is but one road to world peace.
   B. It is common knowledge that a child sees much he is not supposed to see.
   C. Much of the bitterness might have been avoided if arbitration had been resorted to earlier in the meeting.
   D. The man decided it would be advisable to marry a girl somewhat younger than him.

3. A. In this book, the incident I liked least is where the hero tries to put out the forest fire.
   B. Learning a foreign language will undoubtedly give a person a better understanding of his mother tongue.
   C. His actions made us wonder what he planned to do next.
   D. Because of the war, we were unable to travel during the summer vacation.

4. A. The class had no sooner become interested in the lesson than the dismissal bell rang.
   B. There is little agreement about the kind of world to be planned at the peace conference.
   C. "Today," said the teacher, "we shall read 'The Wind in the Willows,' I am sure you'll like it.
   D. The terms of the legal settlement of the family quarrel handicapped both sides for many years.

5. A. I was so surprised that I was not able to say a word.
   B. She is taller than any other member of the class.
   C. It would be much more preferable if you were never seen in his company.
   D. We had no choice but to excuse her for being late.

KEY (CORRECT ANSWERS)

1. C
2. D
3. A
4. C
5. C

TEST 4

DIRECTIONS: In each of the following groups of sentences, one of the four sentences is faulty in grammar, punctuation, or capitalization. Select the INCORRECT sentence in each case.

1. A. Please send me these data at the earliest opportunity.
   B. The loss of their material proved to be a severe handicap.
   C. My principal objection to this plan is that it is impracticable.
   D. The doll had laid in the rain for an hour and was ruined.

1._____

2. A. The garden scissors, left out all night in the rain, were in a badly rusted condition.
   B. The girls felt bad about the misunderstanding which had arisen
   C. Sitting near the campfire, the old man told John and I about many exciting adventures he had had.
   D. Neither of us is in a position to undertake a task of that magnitude.

2._____

3. A. The general concluded that one of the three roads would lead to the besieged city.
   B. The children didn't, as a rule, do hardly anything beyond what they were told to do.
   C. The reason the girl gave for her negligence was that she had acted on the spur of the moment.
   D. The daffodils and tulips look beautiful in that blue vase.

3._____

4. A. If I was ten years older, I should be interested in this work.
   B. Give the prize to whoever has drawn the best picture.
   C. When you have finished reading the book, take it back to the library.
   D. My drawing is as good as or better than yours.

4._____

5. A. He asked me whether the substance was animal or vegetable.
   B. An apple which is unripe should not be eaten by a child.
   C. That was an insult to me who am your friend.
   D. Some spy must of reported the matter to the enemy.

5._____

6. A. Limited time makes quoting the entire message impossible.
   B. Who did she say was going?
   C. The girls in your class have dressed more dolls this year than we.
   D. There was such a large amount of books on the floor that I couldn't find a place for my rocking chair.

6._____

7. A. What with his sleeplessness and his ill health, he was unable to assume any responsibility for the success of the meeting.
   B. If I had been born in February, I should be celebrating my birthday soon.
   C. In order to prevent breakage, she placed a sheet of paper between each of the plates when she packed them.
   D. After the spring shower, the violets smelled very sweet.

7._____

2 (#4)

8. A. He had laid the book down very reluctantly before the end of the lesson. 8.____
   B. The dog, I am sorry to say, had lain on the bed all night.
   C. The cloth was first lain on a flat surface; then it was pressed with a hot iron.
   D. While we were in Florida, we lay in the sun until we were noticeably tanned.

9. A. If John was in New York during the recent holiday season, I have no doubt 9.____
      he spent most of the time with his parents.
   B. How could he enjoy the television program; the dog was barking and the
      baby was crying.
   C. When the problem was explained to the class, he must have been asleep.
   D. She wished that her new dress were finished so that she could go to the
      party.

10. A. The engine not only furnishes power but light and heat as well. 10.____
    B. You're aware that we've forgotten whose guilt was established, aren't you?
    C. Everybody knows that the woman made many sacrifices for her children.
    D. A man with his dog and gun is a familiar sight in this neighborhood.

KEY (CORRECT ANSWERS)

1. D   6. D
2. C   7. B
3. B   8. C
4. A   9. B
5. D   10. A

TEST 5

DIRECTIONS: Each of Questions 1 through 5 consists of a sentence which may be classified appropriately under one of the following four categories:
A. *Incorrect* because of faulty grammar
B. *Incorrect* because of faulty punctuation
C. *Incorrect* because of faulty spelling
D. *Correct*

Examine each sentence carefully. Then, print in the space at the right the letter preceding the category which is the BEST of the four suggested above
(Note: Each incorrect sentence contains only one type of error. Consider a sentence correct if it contains no errors, although there may be other correct ways of writing the sentence.)

1. Of the two employees, the one in our office is the most efficient. 1.____

2. No one can apply or even understand, the new rules and regulations. 2.____

3. A large amount of supplies were stored in the empty office. 3.____

4. If an employee is occassionally asked to work overtime, he should do so willingly. 4.____

5. It is true that the new procedures are difficult to use but, we are certain that you will learn them quickly. 5.____

6. The office manager said that he did not know who would be given a large allotment under the new plan. 6.____

7. It was at the supervisor's request that the clerk agreed to postpone his vacation. 7.____

8. We do not believe that it is necessary for both he and the clerk to attend the conference. 8.____

9. All employees, who display perseverance, will be given adequate recognition. 9.____

10. He regrets that some of us employees are dissatisfied with our new assignments. 10.____

11. "Do you think that the raise was merited," asked the supervisor? 11.____

12. The new manual of procedure is a valuable supplament to our rules and regulations. 12.____

13. The typist admitted that she had attempted to pursuade the other employees to assist her in her work. 13.____

2 (#5)

14. The supervisor asked that all amendments to the regulations be handled by you and I. 14.____

15. The custodian seen the boy who broke the window. 15.____

KEY (CORRECT ANSWERS)

1.	A	6.	D	11.	B
2.	B	7.	D	12.	C
3.	A	8.	A	13.	C
4.	C	9.	B	14.	A
5.	B	10.	D	15.	A

152

PRINCIPLES AND PRACTICES, OF ADMINISTRATION, SUPERVISION AND MANAGEMENT

TABLE OF CONTENTS

	Page
GENERAL ADMINISTRATION	1
SEVEN BASIC FUNCTIONS OF THE SUPERVISOR	2
I. Planning	2
II. Organizing	3
III. Staffing	3
IV. Directing	3
V. Coordinating	3
VI. Reporting	3
VII. Budgeting	3
PLANNING TO MEET MANAGEMENT GOALS	4
I. What is Planning	4
II. Who Should Make Plans	4
III. What are the Results of Poor Planning	4
IV. Principles of Planning	4
MANAGEMENT PRINCIPLES	5
I. Management	5
II. Management Principles	5
III. Organization Structure	6
ORGANIZATION	8
I. Unity of Command	8
II. Span of Control	8
III. Uniformity of Assignment	9
IV. Assignment of Responsibility and Delegation of Authority	9
PRINCIPLES OF ORGANIZATION	9
I. Definition	9
II. Purpose of Organization	9
III. Basic Considerations in Organizational Planning	9
IV. Bases for Organization	10
V. Assignment of Functions	10
VI. Delegation of Authority and Responsibility	10
VII. Employee Relationships	11

DELEGATING		11
I.	WHAT IS DELEGATING:	11
II.	TO WHOM TO DELEGATE	11
REPORTS		12
I.	DEFINITION	12
II.	PURPOSE	12
III.	TYPES	12
IV.	FACTORS TO CONSIDER BEFORE WRITING REPORT	12
V.	PREPARATORY STEPS	12
VI.	OUTLINE FOR A RECOMMENDATION REPORT	12
MANAGEMENT CONTROLS		13
I.	Control	13
II.	Basis for Control	13
III.	Policy	13
IV.	Procedure	14
V.	Basis of Control	14
FRAMEWORK OF MANAGEMENT		14
I.	Elements	14
II.	Manager's Responsibility	15
III.	Control Techniques	16
IV.	Where Forecasts Fit	16
PROBLEM SOLVING		16
I.	Identify the Problem	16
II.	Gather Data	17
III.	List Possible Solutions	17
IV.	Test Possible Solutions	18
V.	Select the Best Solution	18
VI.	Put the Solution into Actual Practice	19
COMMUNICATION		19
I.	What is Communication?	19
II.	Why is Communication Needed?	19
III.	How is Communication Achieved?	20
IV.	Why Does Communication Fail?	21
V.	How to Improve Communication	21
VI.	How to Determine If You Are Getting Across	21
VII.	The Key Attitude	22
HOW ORDERS AND INSTRUCTIONS SHOULD BE GIVEN		22
I.	Characteristics of Good Orders and Instructions	22
FUNCTIONS OF A DEPARTMENT PERSONNEL OFFICE		23

SUPERVISION		23
I.	Leadership	23
	A. The Authoritarian Approach	23
	B. The Laissez-Faire Approach	24
	C. The Democratic Approach	24
II.	Nine Points of Contrast Between Boss and Leader	25
EMPLOYEE MORALE		25
I.	Some Ways to Develop and Maintain Good Employee Morale	25
II.	Some Indicators of Good Morale	26
MOTIVATION		26
EMPLOYEE PARTICIPATION		27
I.	WHAT IS PARTICIPATION	27
II.	WHY IS IT IMPORTANT?	27
III.	HOW MAY SUPERVISORS OBTAIN IT?	28
STEPS IN HANDLING A GRIEVANCE		28
DISCIPLINE		29
I.	THE DISCIPLINARY INTERVIEW	29
II.	PLANNING THE INTERVIEW	29
III.	CONDUCTING THE INTERVIEW	30

PRINCIPLES AND PRACTICES, OF
ADMINISTRATION, SUPERVISION AND MANAGEMENT

Most people are inclined to think of administration as something that only a few persons are responsible for in a large organization. Perhaps this is true if you are thinking of Administration with a capital *A*, but administration with a lower case *a* is a responsibility of supervisors at all levels each working day.

All of us feel we are pretty good supervisors and that we do a good job of administering the workings of our agency. By and large, this is true, but every so often it is good to check up on ourselves. Checklists appear from time to time in various publications which psychologists say tell whether or not a person will make a good wife, husband, doctor, lawyer, or supervisor.

The following questions are an excellent checklist to test yourself as a supervisor and administrator.

Remember, Administration gives direction and points the way but administration carries the ideas to fruition. Each is dependent on the other for its success. Remember, too, that no unit is too small for these departmental functions to be carried out. These statements apply equally as well to the Chief Librarian as to the Department Head with but one or two persons to supervise.

GENERAL ADMINISTRATION: General Responsibilities of Supervisors

1. Have I prepared written statements of functions, activities, and duties for my organizational unit?

2. Have I prepared procedural guides for operating activities?

3. Have I established clearly in writing, lines of authority and responsibility for my organizational unit?

4. Do I make recommendations for improvements in organization, policies, administrative and operating routines and procedures, including simplification of work and elimination of non-essential operations?

5. Have I designated and trained an understudy to function in my absence?

6. Do I supervise and train personnel within the unit to effectively perform their assignments?

7. Do I assign personnel and distribute work on such a basis as to carry out the organizational unit's assignment or mission in the most effective and efficient manner?

8. Have I established administrative controls by:

    a. Fixing responsibility and accountability on all supervisors under my direction for the proper performance of their functions and duties.

b. Preparations and submitting periodic work load and progress reports covering the operations of the unit to my immediate superior.

c. Analysis and evaluation of such reports received from subordinate units.

d. Submission of significant developments and problems arising within the organizational unit to my immediate superior.

e. Conducting conferences, inspections, etc., as to the status and efficiency of unit operations.

9. Do I maintain an adequate and competent working force?

10. Have I fostered good employee-department relations, seeing that established rules, regulations, and instructions are being carried out properly?

11. Do I collaborate and consult with other organizational units performing related functions to insure harmonious and efficient working relationships?

12. Do I maintain liaison through prescribed channels with city departments and other governmental agencies concerned with the activities of the unit?

13. Do I maintain contact with and keep abreast of the latest developments and techniques of administration (professional societies, groups, periodicals, etc.) as to their applicability to the activities of the unit?

14. Do I communicate with superiors and subordinates through prescribed organizational channels?

15. Do I notify superiors and subordinates in instances where bypassing is necessary as soon thereafter as practicable?

16. Do I keep my superior informed of significant developments and problems?

SEVEN BASIC FUNCTIONS OF THE SUPERVISOR

I. PLANNING
This means working out goals and means to obtain goals. <u>What</u> needs to be done, <u>who</u> will do it, <u>how</u>, <u>when</u>, and <u>where</u> it is to be done.

SEVEN STEPS IN PLANNING

A. Define job or problem clearly.
B. Consider priority of job.
C. Consider time-limit—starting and completing.
D. Consider minimum distraction to, or interference with, other activities.
E. Consider and provide for contingencies—possible emergencies.
F. Break job down into components.

G. Consider the 5 W's and H:
   - WHY..........is it necessary to do the job? (Is the purpose clearly defined?)
   - WHAT........needs to be done to accomplish the defined purpose?
     ....is needed to do the job? (Money, materials, etc.)
   - WHO..........is needed to do the job?
     ....will have responsibilities?
   - WHERE......is the work to be done?
   - WHEN........is the job to begin and end? (Schedules, etc.)
   - HOW..........is the job to bed done? (Methods, controls, records, etc.)

II. ORGANIZING

This means dividing up the work, establishing clear lines of responsibility and authority and coordinating efforts to get the job done.

III. STAFFING

The whole personnel function of bringing in and <u>training</u> staff, getting the right man and fitting him to the right job—the job to which he is best suited.

In the normal situation, the supervisor's responsibility regarding staffing normally includes providing accurate job descriptions, that is, duties of the jobs, requirements, education and experience, skills, physical, etc.; assigning the work for maximum use of skills; and proper utilization of the probationary period to weed out unsatisfactory employees.

IV. DIRECTING

Providing the necessary leadership to the group supervised. Important work gets done to the supervisor's satisfaction.

V. COORDINATING

The all-important duty of inter-relating the various parts of the work.
The supervisor is also responsible for controlling the coordinated activities. This means measuring performance according to a time schedule and setting quotas to see that the goals previously set are being reached. Reports from workers should be analyzed, evaluated, and made part of all future plans.

VI. REPORTING

This means proper and effective communication to your superiors, subordinates, and your peers (in definition of the job of the supervisor). Reports should be read and information contained therein should be used, not be filed away and forgotten. Reports should be written in such a way that the desired action recommended by the report is forthcoming.

VII. BUDGETING
This means controlling current costs and forecasting future costs. This forecast is based on past experience, future plans and programs, as well as current costs.

You will note that these seven functions can fall under three topics:

| Planning) Organizing) | Make a plan | Staffing) Directing) Controlling) | Get things done | Reporting) Budgeting) | Watch it work |

PLANNING TO MEET MANAGEMENT GOALS

I. WHAT IS PLANNING?

    A. Thinking a job through before new work is done to determine the best way to do it
    B. A method of doing something
    C. Ways and means for achieving set goals
    D. A means of enabling a supervisor to deliver with a minimum of effort, all details involved in coordinating his work

II. WHO SHOULD MAKE PLANS?

Everybody!
All levels of supervision must plan work. (Top management, heads of divisions or bureaus, first line supervisors, and individual employees.) The higher the level, the more planning required.

III. WHAT ARE THE RESULTS OF POOR PLANNING?

    A. Failure to meet deadline
    B. Low employee morale
    C. Lack of job coordination
    D. Overtime is frequently necessary
    E. Excessive cost, waste of material and manhours

IV. PRINCIPLES OF PLANNING

    A. Getting a clear picture of your objectives. What exactly are you trying to accomplish?
    B. Plan the whole job, then the parts, in proper sequence.
    C. Delegate the planning of details to those responsible for executing them.
    D. Make your plan flexible.
    E. Coordinate your plan with the plans of others so that the work may be processed with a minimum of delay.
    F. Sell your plan before you execute it.
    G. Sell your plan to your superior, subordinate, in order to gain maximum participation and coordination.
    H. Your plan should take precedence. Use knowledge and skills that others have brought to a similar job.
    I. Your plan should take account of future contingencies; allow for future expansion.
    J. Plans should include minor details. Leave nothing to chance that can be anticipated.
    K. Your plan should be simple and provide standards and controls. Establish quality and quantity standards and set a standard method of doing the job. The controls will indicate whether the job is proceeding according to plan.
    L. Consider possible bottlenecks, breakdowns, or other difficulties that are likely to arise.

V. Q. WHAT ARE THE YARDSTICKS BY WHICH PLANNING SHOULD BE MEASURED?
   A. Any plan should:
   — Clearly state a definite course of action to be followed and goal to be achieved, with consideration for emergencies.
   — Be realistic and practical.
   — State what's to be done, when it's to be done, where, how, and by whom.
   — Establish the most efficient sequence of operating steps so that more is accomplished in less time, with the least effort, and with the best quality results.
   — Assure meeting deliveries without delays.
   — Establish the standard by which performance is to be judged.

   Q. WHAT KINDS OF PLANS DOES EFFECTIVE SUPERVISION REQUIRE?
   A. Plans should cover such factors as:
   — Manpower: right number of properly trained employees on the job
   — Materials: adequate supply of the right materials and supplies
   — Machines: full utilization of machines and equipment, with proper maintenance
   — Methods: most efficient handling of operations
   — Deliveries: making deliveries on time
   — Tools: sufficient well-conditioned tools
   — Layout: most effective use of space
   — Reports: maintaining proper records and reports
   — Supervision: planning work for employees and organizing supervisor's own time

MANAGEMENT PRINCIPLES

I. MANAGEMENT
   Q. What do we mean by management?
   A. Getting work done through others.

   Management could also be defined as planning, directing, and controlling the operations of a bureau or division so that all factors will function properly and all persons cooperate efficiently for a common objective.

II. MANAGEMENT PRINCIPLES

   A. There should be a hierarchy—wherein authority and responsibility run upward and downward through several levels—with a broad base at the bottom and a single head at the top.

   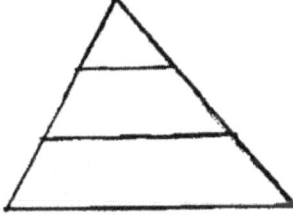

   B. Each and every unit or person in the organization should be answerable ultimately to the manager at the apex. In other words, *The buck stops here!*

C. Every necessary function involved in the bureau's objectives is assigned to a unit in that bureau.

D. Responsibilities assigned to a unit are specifically clear-cut and understood.

E. Consistent methods of organizational structure should be applied at each level of the organization.

F. Each member of the bureau from top to bottom knows: to whom he reports and who reports to him.

G. No member of one bureau reports to more than one supervisor. No dual functions.

H. Responsibility for a function is matched by authority necessary to perform that function. Weight of authority.

I. Individuals or units reporting to a supervisor do not exceed the number which can be feasibly and effectively coordinated and directed. Concept of *span of control*.

J. Channels of command (management) are not violated by staff units, although there should be staff services to facilitate and coordinate management functions.

K. Authority and responsibility should be decentralized to units and individuals who are responsible for the actual performance of operations.
Welfare – down to Welfare Centers
Hospitals – down to local hospitals

L. Management should exercise control through attention to policy problems of exceptional performance, rather than through review of routine actions of subordinates.

M. Organizations should never be permitted to grow so elaborate as to hinder work accomplishments.

III. ORGANIZATION STRUCTURE

Types of Organizations
The purest form is a leader and a few followers, such as:

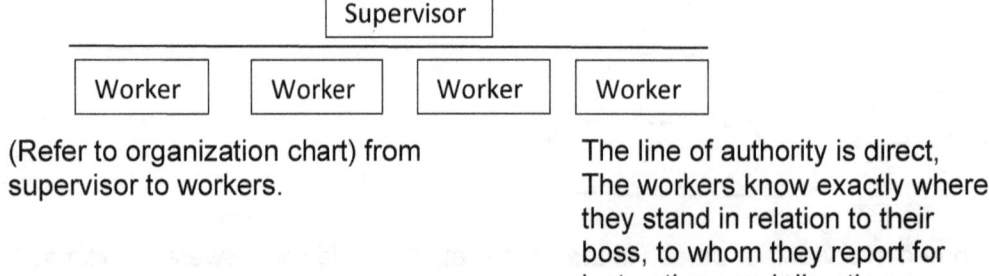

(Refer to organization chart) from supervisor to workers.

The line of authority is direct, The workers know exactly where they stand in relation to their boss, to whom they report for instructions and direction.

Unfortunately, in our present complex society, few organizations are similar to this example of a pure line organization. In this era of specialization, other people are often needed in the simplest of organizations. These specialists are known as staff. The sole purpose for their existence (staff) is to assist, advise, suggest, help or counsel line organizations. Staff has no authority to direct line people—nor do they give them direct instructions.

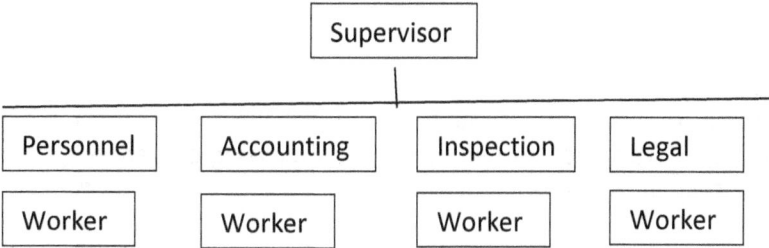

Line Functions
1. Directs
2. Orders
3. Responsibility for carrying out activities from beginning to end
4. Follows chain of command
5. Is identified with what it does
6. Decides when and how to use staff advice
7. Line executes

Staff Functions
1. Advises
2. Persuades and sells
3. Staff studies, reports, recommends but does not carry out
4. May advise across department lines
5. May find its ideas identified with others
6. Has to persuade line to want its advice
7. Staff: Conducts studies and research. Provides advice and instructions in technical matters. Serves as technical specialist to render specific services.

Types and Functions of Organization Charts
An organization chart is a picture of the arrangement and inter-relationship of the subdivisions of an organization.

A. Types of Charts:
   1. Structural: basic relationships only
   2. Functional: includes functions or duties
   3. Personnel: positions, salaries, status, etc.
   4. Process Chart: work performed
   5. Gantt Chart: actual performance against planned
   5. Flow Chart: flow and distribution of work

B. Functions of Charts:
   1. Assist in management planning and control
   2. Indicate duplication of functions
   3. Indicate incorrect stressing of functions
   4. Indicate neglect of important functions
   5. Correct unclear authority
   6. Establish proper span of control

C. Limitations of Charts:
1. Seldom maintained on current basis
2. Chart is oversimplified
3. Human factors cannot adequately be charted

D. Organization Charts should be:
1. Simple
2. Symmetrical
3. Indicate authority
4. Line and staff relationship differentiated
5. Chart should be dated and bear signature of approving officer
6. Chart should be displayed, not hidden

ORGANIZATION

There are four basic principles of organization:
1. Unity of command
2. Span of control
3. Uniformity of assignment
4. Assignment of responsibility and delegation of authority

I. UNITY OF COMMAND

Unity of command means that each person in the organization should receive orders from one, and only one, supervisor. When a person has to take orders from two or more people, (a) the orders may be in conflict and the employee is upset because he does not know which he should obey, or (b) different orders may reach him at the same time and he does not know which he should carry out first.

Equally as bad as having two bosses is the situation where the supervisor is bypassed. Let us suppose you are a supervisor whose boss bypasses you (deals directly with people reporting to you). To the worker, it is the same as having two bosses; but to you, the supervisor, it is equally serious. Bypassing on the part of your boss will undermine your authority, and the people under you will begin looking to your boss for decisions and even for routine orders.

You can prevent bypassing by telling the people you supervise that if anyone tries to give them orders, they should direct that person to you.

II. SPAN OF CONTROL

Span of control on a given level involves:
A. The number of people being supervised
B. The distance
C The time involved in supervising the people. (One supervisor cannot supervise too many workers effectively.)

Span of control means that a supervisor has the right number (not too many and not too few) of subordinates that he can supervise well.

III. UNIFORMITY OF ASSIGNMENT

In assigning work, you as the supervisor should assign to each person jobs that are similar in nature. An employee who is assigned too many different types of jobs will waste time in going from one kind of work to another. It takes time for him to get to top production in one kind of task and, before he does so, he has to start on another.
When you assign work to people, remember that:

A. Job duties should be definite. Make it clear from the beginning what they are to do, how they are to do it, and why they are to do it. Let them know how much they are expected to do and how well they are expected to do it.
B. Check your assignments to be certain that there are no workers with too many unrelated duties, and that no two people have been given overlapping responsibilities. Your aim should be to have every task assigned to a specific person with the work fairly distributed and with each person doing his part.

IV. ASSIGNMENT OF RESPONSIBILITY AND DELEGATION OF AUTHORITY

A supervisor cannot delegate his final responsibility for the work of his department. The experienced supervisor knows that he gets his work done through people. He can't do it all himself. So he must assign the work and the responsibility for the work to his employees. Then they must be given the authority to carry out their responsibilities.

By assigning responsibility and delegating authority to carry out the responsibility, the supervisor builds in his workers initiative, resourcefulness, enthusiasm, and interest in their work. He is treating them as responsible adults. They can find satisfaction in their work, and they will respect the supervisor and be loyal to the supervisor.

PRINCIPLES OF ORGANIZATION

I. DEFINITION

Organization is the method of dividing up the work to provide the best channels for coordinated effort to get the agency's mission accomplished.

II. PURPOSE OF ORGANIZATION

A. To enable each employee within the organization to clearly know his responsibilities and relationships to his fellow employees and to organizational units
B. To avoid conflicts of authority and overlapping of jurisdiction.
C. To ensure teamwork.

III. BASIC CONSIDERATIONS IIN ORGANIZATIONAL PLANNING

A. The basic plans and objectives of the agency should be determined, and the organizational structure should be adapted to carry out effectively such plans and objectives.
B. The organization should be built around the major functions of the agency and not individuals or groups of individuals.

C. The organization should be sufficiently flexible to meet new and changing conditions which may be brought about from within or outside the department.
D. The organizational structure should be as simple as possible and the number of organizational units kept at a minimum.
E. The number of levels of authority should be kept at a minimum. Each additional management level lengthens the chain of authority and responsibility and increases the time for instructions to be distributed to operating levels and for decisions to be obtained from higher authority.
F. The form of organization should permit each executive to exercise maximum initiative within the limits of delegated authority.

IV. BASES FOR ORGANIZATION

A. Purpose (Examples: education, police, sanitation)
B. Process (Examples: accounting, legal, purchasing)
C. Clientele (Examples: welfare, parks, veteran)
D. Geographic (Examples: borough offices, precincts, libraries)

V. ASSIGNMENTS OF FUNCTIONS

A. Every function of the agency should be assigned to a specific organizational unit. Under normal circumstances, no single function should be assigned to more than one organizational unit.
B. There should be no overlapping, duplication, or conflict between organizational elements.
C. Line functions should be separated from staff functions, and proper emphasis should be placed on staff activities.
D. Functions which are closely related or similar should normally be assigned to a single organizational unit.
E. Functions should be properly distributed to promote balance, and to avoid overemphasis of less important functions and underemphasis of more essential functions.

VI. DELEGATION OF AUTHORITY AND RESPONSIBILITY

A. Responsibilities assigned to a specific individual or organizational unit should carry corresponding authority, and all statements of authority or limitations thereof should be as specific as possible.
B. Authority and responsibility for action should be decentralized to organizational units and individuals responsible for actual performance to the greatest extent possible, without relaxing necessary control over policy or the standardization of procedures. Delegation of authority will be consistent with decentralization of responsibility but such delegation will not divest an executive in higher authority of his overall responsibility.
C. The heads of organizational units should concern themselves with important matters and should delegate to the maximum extent details and routines performed in the ordinary course of business.
D. All responsibilities, authorities, and relationships should be stated in simple language to avoid misinterpretation.
E. Each individual or organizational unit charged with a specific responsibility will be held responsible for results.

VII. EMPLOYEE RELATIONSHIPS

   A. The employees reporting to one executive should not exceed the number which can be effectively directed and coordinated. The number will depend largely upon the scope and extent of the responsibilities of the subordinates.
   B. No person should report to more than one supervisor. Every supervisor should know who reports to him, and every employee should know to whom he reports. Channels of authority and responsibility should not be violated by staff units.
   C. Relationships between organizational units within the agency and with outside organizations and associations should be clearly stated and thoroughly understood to avoid misunderstanding.

DELEGATING

I. WHAT IS DELEGATING?
   Delegating is assigning a job to an employee, giving him the authority to get that job done, and giving him the responsibility for seeing to it that the job is done.

   A. What To Delegate
      1. Routine details
      2. Jobs which may be necessary and take a lot of time, but do not have to be done by the supervisor personally (preparing reports, attending meetings, etc.)
      3. Routine decision-making (making decisions which do not require the supervisor's personal attention)

   B. What Not To Delegate
      1. Job details which are *executive functions* (setting goals, organizing employees into a good team, analyzing results so as to plan for the future)
      2. Disciplinary power (handling grievances, preparing service ratings, reprimands, etc.)
      3. Decision-making which involves large numbers of employees or other bureaus and departments
      4. Final and complete responsibility for the job done by the unit being supervised

   C. Why Delegate?
      1. To strengthen the organization by developing a greater number of skilled employees
      2. To improve the employee's performance by giving him the chance to learn more about the job, handle some responsibility, and become more interested in getting the job done
      3. To improve a supervisor's performance by relieving him of routine jobs and giving him more time for *executive functions* (planning, organizing, controlling, etc.) which cannot be delegated

II. TO WHOM TO DELEGATE
    People with abilities not being used. Selection should be based on ability, not on favoritism.

REPORTS

I. DEFINITION
A report is an orderly presentation of factual information directed to a specific reader for a specific purpose

II. PURPOSE
The general purpose of a report is to bring to the reader useful and factual information about a condition or a problem. Some specific purposes of a report may be:

   A. To enable the reader to appraise the efficiency or effectiveness of a person or an operation
   B. To provide a basis for establishing standards
   C. To reflect the results of expenditures of time, effort, and money
   D. To provide a basis for developing or altering programs

III. TYPES

   A. Information Report: Contains facts arranged in sequence
   B. Summary (Examination) Report: Contains facts plus an analysis or discussion of the significance of the facts. Analysis may give advantages and disadvantages or give qualitative and quantitative comparisons
   C. Recommendation Report: Contains facts, analysis, and conclusion logically drawn from the facts and analysis, plus a recommendation based upon the facts, analysis, and conclusions

IV. FACTORS TO CONSIDER BEFORE WRITING REPORT

   A. <u>Why</u> write the report?: The purpose of the report should be clearly defined.
   B. <u>Who</u> will read the report?: What level of language should be used? Will the reader understand professional or technical language?
   C. <u>What</u> should be said?: What does the reader need or want to know about the subject?
   D. <u>How</u> should it be said?: Should the subject be presented tactfully? Convincingly? In a stimulating manner?

V. PREPARATORY STEPS

   A. Assemble the facts: Find out who, why, what, where, when, and how.
   B. Organize the facts: Eliminate unnecessary information
   C. Prepare an outline: Check for orderliness, logical sequence
   D. Prepare a draft: Check for correctness, clearness, completeness, conciseness, and tone
   E. Prepare it in final form: Check for grammar, punctuation, appearance

VI. OUTLINE FOR A RECOMMENDATION REPORT

   Is the report:
   A. Correct in information, grammar, and tone?
   B. Clear?
   C. Complete?

D. Concise?
E. Timely?
F. Worth its cost?

Will the report accomplish its purpose?

MANAGEMENT CONTROLS

I. CONTROL
    What is control? What is controlled? Who controls?

    The essence of control is action which adjusts operations to predetermined standards, and its basis is information in the hands of managers. Control is checking to determine whether plans are being observed and suitable progress toward stated objectives is being made, and action is taken, if necessary, to correct deviations.

    We have a ready-made model for this concept of control in the automatic systems which are widely used for process control in the chemical land petroleum industries. A process control system works this way. Suppose, for example, it is desired to maintain a constant rate of flow of oil through a pipe at a predetermined or set-point value. A signal, whose strength represents the rate of flow, can be produced in a measuring device and transmitted to a control mechanism. The control mechanism, when it detects any deviation of the actual from the set-point signal, will reposition the value regulating flow rate.

II. BASIS FOR CONTROL

    A process control mechanism thus acts to adjust operations to predetermined standards and does so on the basis of information it receives. In a parallel way, information reaching a manager gives him the opportunity for corrective action and is his basis for control. He cannot exercise control without such information, and he cannot do a complete job of managing without controlling.

III. POLICY

    What is policy?

    Policy is simply a statement of an organization's intention to act in certain ways when specified types of circumstances arise. It represents a general decision, predetermined and expressed as a principle or rule, establishing a normal pattern of conduct for dealing with given types of business events—usually recurrent. A statement is therefore useful in economizing the time of managers and in assisting them to discharge their responsibilities equitably and consistently.

    Policy is not a means of control, but policy does generate the need for control.

    Adherence to policies is not guaranteed nor can it be taken on faith. It has to be verified. Without verification, there is no basis for control. Policy and procedures, although closely related and interdependent to a certain extent, are not synonymous. A policy may be adopted, for example, to maintain a materials inventory not to exceed one million dollars.

A procedure for inventory control could interpret that policy and convert it into methods for keeping within that limit, with consideration, too, of possible but foreseeable expedient deviation.

IV. PROCEDURE

What is procedure?

A procedure specifically prescribes:
A. What work is to be performed by the various participants
B. Who are the respective participants
C. When and where the various steps in the different processes are to be performed
D. The sequence of operations that will insure uniform handling of recurring transactions
E. The paper that is involved, its origin, transition, and disposition

Necessary appurtenances to a procedure are:
A. Detailed organizational chart
B. Flow charts
C. Exhibits of forms, all presented in close proximity to the text of the procedure

V. BASIS OF CONTROL – INFORMATION IN THE HANDS OF MANAGERS

If the basis of control is information in the hands of managers, then reporting is elevated to a level of very considerable importance.

Types of reporting may include:
A. Special reports and routine reports
B. Written, oral, and graphic reports
C. Staff meetings
D. Conferences
E. Television screens
F. Non-receipt of information, as where management is by exception
G. Any other means whereby information is transmitted to a manager as a basis for control action

FRAMEWORK OF MANAGEMENT

I. ELEMENTS

   A. Policy: It has to be verified, controlled.

   B. Organization is part of the giving of an assignment. The organizational chart gives to each individual in his title, a first approximation of the nature of his assignment and orients him as being accountable to a certain individual. Organization is not in a true sense a means of control. Control is checking to ascertain whether the assignment is executed as intended and acting on the basis of that information.

   C. Budgets perform three functions:
      1. They present the objectives, plans, and programs of the organization in financial terms.

2. They report the progress of actual performance against these predetermined objectives, plans, and programs.
3. Like organizational charts, delegations of authority, procedures, and job descriptions, they define the assignments which have flowed from the Chief Executive. Budgets are a means of control in the respect that they report progress of actual performance against the program. They provide information which enables managers to take action directed toward bringing actual results into conformity with the program.

D. Internal Check provides in practice for the principle that the same person should not have responsibility for all phases of a transaction. This makes it clearly an aspect of organization rather than of control. Internal Check is static, or built-in.

E. Plans, Programs, Objectives
People must know what they are trying to do. Objectives fulfill this need. Without them, people may work industriously and yet, working aimlessly, accomplish little. Plans and Programs complement Objectives, since they propose how and according to what time schedule the objectives are to be reached.

F. Delegations of Authority
Among the ways we have for supplementing the titles and lines of authority of an organizational chart are delegations of authority. Delegations of authority clarify the extent of authority of individuals and in that way serve to define assignments. That they are not means of control is apparent from the very fact that wherever there has been a delegation of authority, the need for control increases. This could hardly be expected to happen if delegations of authority were themselves means of control.

II. MANAGER'S RESPONSIBILITY

Control becomes necessary whenever a manager delegates authority to a subordinate because he cannot delegate and then simply sit back and forget4 about it. A manager's accountability to his own superior has not diminished one whit as a result of delegating part of his authority to a subordinate. The manager must exercise control over actions taken under the authority so delegated. That means checking serves as a basis for possible corrective action.

Objectives, plans, programs, organizational charts, and other elements of the managerial system are not fruitfully regarded as either controls or means of control. They are pre-established standards or models of performance to which operations are adjusted by the exercise of management control. These standards or models of performance are dynamic in character for they are constantly altered, modified, or revised. Policies, organizational set-up, procedures, delegations, etc. are constantly altered but, like objectives and plans, they remain in force until they are either abandoned or revised. All of the elements (or standards or models of performance), objectives, plans, and programs, policies, organization, etc. can be regarded as a *framework of management*.

III. CONTROL TECHNIQUES

Examples of control techniques:
A. Compare against established standards
B. Compare with a similar operation
C. Compare with past operations
D. Compare with predictions of accomplishment

IV. WHERE FORECASTS FIT

Control is after-the-fact while forecasts are before. Forecasts and projections are important for setting objectives and formulating plans.

Information for aiming and planning does not have to be before-the-fact. It may be an after-the-fact analysis proving that a certain policy has been impolitic in its effect on the relation of the company or department with customer, employee, taxpayer, or stockholder; or that a certain plan is no longer practical, or that a certain procedure is unworkable.

The prescription here certainly would not be in control (in these cases, control would simply bring operations into conformity with obsolete standards) but the establishment of new standards, a new policy, a new plan, and a new procedure to be controlled too.

Information is, of course, the basis for all communication in addition to furnishing evidence to management of the need for reconstructing the framework of management.

PROBLEM SOLVING

The accepted concept in modern management for problem solving is the utilization of the following steps:

A. Identify the problem
B. Gather data
C. List possible solutions
D. Test possible solutions
E. Select the best solution
F. Put the solution into actual practice

Occasions might arise where you would have to apply the second step of gathering data before completing the first step.

You might also find that it will be necessary to work on several steps at the same time.

I. IDENTIFY THE PROBLEM

Your first step is to define as precisely as possible the problem to be solved. While this may sound easy, it is often the most difficult part of the process.

It has been said of problem solving that you are halfway to the solution when you can write out a clear statement of the problem itself.

Our job now is to get below the surface manifestations of the trouble and pinpoint the problem. This is usually accomplished by a logical analysis, by going from the general to the particular; from the obvious to the not-so-obvious cause.

Let us say that production is behind schedule. WHY? Absenteeism is high. Now, is absenteeism the basic problem to be tackled, or is it merely a symptom of low morale among the workforce? Under these circumstances, you may decide that production is not the problem; the problem is *employee morale*.

In trying to define the problem, remember there is seldom one simple reason why production is lagging, or reports are late, etc.

Analysis usually leads to the discovery that an apparent problem is really made up of several subproblems which must be attacked separately.

Another way is to limit the problem, and thereby ease the task of finding a solution, and concentrate on the elements which are within the scope of your control.

When you have gone this far, write out a tentative statement of the problem to be solved.

II. GATHER DATA

In the second step, you must set out to collect all the information that might have a bearing on the problem. Do not settle for an assumption when reasonable fact and figures are available.

If you merely go through the motions of problem-solving, you will probably shortcut the information-gathering step. Therefore, do not stack the evidence by confining your research to your own preconceived ideas.

As you collect facts, organize them in some form that helps you make sense of them and spot possible relationships between them. For example, plotting cost per unit figures on a graph can be more meaningful than a long column of figures.

Evaluate each item as you go along. Is the source material absolutely, reliable, probably reliable, or not to be trusted.

One of the best methods for gathering data is to go out and look the situation over carefully. Talk to the people on the job who are most affected by this problem.

Always keep in mind that a primary source is usually better than a secondary source of information.

III. LIST POSSIBLE SOLUTIONS

This is the creative thinking step of problem solving. This is a good time to bring into play whatever techniques of group dynamics the agency or bureau might have developed for a joint attack on problems.

Now the important thing for you to do is: Keep an open mind. Let your imagination roam freely over the facts you have collected. Jot down every possible solution that occurs to you. Resist the temptation to evaluate various proposals as you go along. List seemingly absurd ideas along with more plausible ones. The more possibilities you list during this step, the less risk you will run of settling for merely a workable, rather than the best, solution.

Keep studying the data as long as there seems to be any chance of deriving additional ideas, solutions, explanations, or patterns from it.

IV. TEST POSSIBLE SOLUTIONS

Now you begin to evaluate the possible solutions. Take pains to be objective. Up to this point, you have suspended judgment but you might be tempted to select a solution you secretly favored all along and proclaim it as the best of the lot.

The secret of objectivity in this phase is to test the possible solutions separately, measuring each against a common yardstick. To make this yardstick try to enumerate as many specific criteria as you can think of. Criteria are best phrased as questions which you ask of each possible solution. They can be drawn from these general categories:

- Suitability – Will this solution do the job?
  Will it solve the problem completely or partially?
  Is it a permanent or a stopgap solution?

- Feasibility - Will this plan work in actual practice?
  Can we afford this approach?
  How much will it cost?

- Acceptability - Will the boss go along with the changes required in the plan?
  Are we trying to drive a tack with a sledge hammer?

V. SELECT THE BEST SOLUTION

This is the area of executive decision.

Occasionally, one clearly superior solution will stand out at the conclusion of the testing process. But often it is not that simple. You may find that no one solution has come through all the tests with flying colors.

You may also find that a proposal, which flunked miserably on one of the essential tests, racked up a very high score on others.

The best solution frequently will turn out to be a combination.

Try to arrange a marriage that will bring together the strong points of one possible solution with the particular virtues of another. The more skill and imagination that you apply, the greater is the likelihood that you will come out with a solution that is not merely adequate and workable, but is the best possible under the circumstances.

VI. PUT THE SOLUTION INTO ACTUAL PRACTICE

As every executive knows, a plan which works perfectly on paper may develop all sorts of bugs when put into actual practice.

Problem-solving does not stop with selecting the solution which looks best in theory. The next step is to put the chosen solution into action and watch the results. The results may point towards modifications.

If the problem disappears when you put your solution into effect, you know you have the right solution.

If it does not disappear, even after you have adjusted your plan to cover unforeseen difficulties that turned up in practice, work your way back through the problem-solving solutions.

> Would one of them have worked better?
> Did you overlook some vital piece of data which would have given you a different slant on the whole situation? Did you apply all necessary criteria in testing solutions? If no light dawns after this much rechecking, it is a pretty good bet that you defined the problem incorrectly in the first place.

You came up with the wrong solution because you tackled the wrong problem.

Thus, step six may become step one of a new problem-solving cycle.

COMMUNICATION

I. WHAT IS COMMUNICATION?
We communicate through writing, speaking, action, or inaction. In speaking to people face-to-face, there is opportunity to judge reactions and to adjust the message. This makes the supervisory chain one of the most, and in many instances the most, important channels of communication.

In an organization, communication means keeping employees informed about the organization's objectives, policies, problems, and progress. Communication is the free interchange of information, ideas, and desirable attitudes between and among employees and between employees and management.

II. WHY IS COMMUNICATION NEEDED?

A. People have certain social needs
B. Good communication is essential in meeting those social needs
C. While people have similar basic needs, at the same time they differ from each other
D. Communication must be adapted to these individual differences

An employee cannot do his best work unless he knows why he is doing it. If he has the feeling that he is being kept in the dark about what is going on, his enthusiasm and productivity suffer.

Effective communication is needed in an organization so that employees will understand what the organization is trying to accomplish; and how the work of one unit contributes to or affects the work of other units in the organization and other organizations.

III. HOW IS COMMUNICATION ACHIEVED?

Communication flows downward, upward, sideways.

A. Communication may come from top management down to employees. This is downward communication.

   Some means of downward communication are:
   1. Training (orientation, job instruction, supervision, public relations, etc.)
   2. Conferences
   3. Staff meetings
   4. Policy statements
   5. Bulletins
   6. Newsletters
   7. Memoranda
   8. Circulation of important letters

   In downward communication, it is important that employees be informed in advance of changes that will affect them.

B. Communications should also be developed so that the ideas, suggestions, and knowledge of employees will flow upward to top management.

   Some means of upward communication are:
   1. Personal discussion conferences
   2. Committees
   3. Memoranda
   4. Employees suggestion program
   5. Questionnaires to be filled in giving comments and suggestions about proposed actions that will affect field operations.

   Upward communication requires that management be willing to listen, to accept, and to make changes when good ideas are present. Upward communication succeeds when there is no fear of punishment for speaking out or lack of interest at the top. Employees will share their knowledge and ideas with management when interest is shown and recognition is given.

C. The advantages of downward communication:
   1. It enables the passing down of orders, policies, and plans necessary to the continued operation of the station.
   2. By making information available, it diminishes the fears and suspicions which result from misinformation and misunderstanding.
   3. It fosters the pride people want to have in their work when they are told of good work.
   4. It improves the morale and stature of the individual to be *in the know*.

5. It helps employees to understand, accept, and cooperate with changes when they know about them in advance.

D. The advantages of upward communication:
1. It enables the passing upward of information, attitudes, and feelings.
2. It makes it easier to find out how ready people are to receive downward communication.
3. It reveals the degree to which the downward communication is understood and accepted.
4. It helps to satisfy the basic social needs.
5. It stimulates employees to participate in the operation of their organization.
6. It encourage employees to contribute ideas for improving the efficiency and economy of operations.
7. It helps to solve problem situations before they reach the explosion point.

IV. WHY DOES COMMUNICATION FAIL?

A. The technical difficulties of conveying information clearly
B. The emotional content of communication which prevents complete transmission
C. The fact that there is a difference between what management needs to say, what it wants to day, and what it does say
D. The fact that there is a difference between what employees would like to say, what they think is profitable or safe to say, and what they do say

V. HOW TO IMPROVE COMMUNICATION

As a supervisor, you are a key figure in communication. To improve as a communicator, you should:
A. Know: Knowing your subordinates will help you to recognize and work with individual differences.
B. Like: If you like those who work for you and those for whom you work, this will foster the kind of friendly, warm, work atmosphere that will facilitate communication.
C. Trust: Showing a sincere desire to communicate will help to develop the mutual trust and confidence which are essential to the free flow of communication.
D. Tell: Tell your subordinates and superiors *what's doing*. Tell your subordinates *why* as well as *how*.
E. Listen: By listening, you help others to talk and you create good listeners. Don't forget that listening implies action.
F. Stimulate: Communication has to be stimulated and encouraged. Be receptive to ideas and suggestions and motivate your people so that each member of the team identifies himself with the job at hand.
G. Consult: The most effective way of consulting is to let your people participate, insofar as possible, in developing determinations which affect them or their work.

VI. HOW TO DETERMINE WHETHER YOU ARE GETTING ACROSS

A. Check to see that communication is received and understood
B. Judge this understanding by actions rather than words
C. Adapt or vary communication, when necessary
D. Remember that good communication cannot cure all problems

VII. THE KEY ATTITUDE

Try to see things from the other person's point of view. By doing this, you help to develop the permissive atmosphere and the shared confidence and understanding which are essential to effective two-way communication.

Communication is a two-way process:
A. The basic purpose of any communication is to get action.
B. The only way to get action is through acceptance.
C. In order to get acceptance, communication must be humanly satisfying as well as technically efficient.

HOW ORDERS AND INSTRUCTIONS SHOULD BE GIVEN

I. CHARACTERISTICS OF GOOD ORDERS AND INSTRUCTIONS

    A. Clear
Orders should be definite as to
—What is to be done
—Who is to do it
—When it is to be done
—Where it is to be done
—How it is to be done

    B. Concise
Avoid wordiness. Orders should be brief and to the point.

    C. Timely
Instructions and orders should be sent out at the proper time and not too long in advance of expected performance.

    D. Possibility of Performance
Orders should be feasible:
1. Investigate before giving orders
2. Consult those who are to carry out instructions before formulating and issuing them

    E. Properly Directed
Give the orders to the people concerned. Do not send orders to people who are not concerned. People who continually receive instructions that are not applicable to them get in the habit of neglecting instructions generally.

    F. Reviewed Before Issuance
Orders should be reviewed before issuance:
1. Test them by putting yourself in the position of the recipient
2. If they involve new procedures, have the persons who are to do the work review them for suggestions.

    G. Reviewed After Issuance
Persons who receive orders should be allowed to raise questions and to point out unforeseen consequences of orders.

H. Coordinated
Orders should be coordinated so that work runs smoothly.

I. Courteous
Make a request rather than a demand. There is no need to continually call attention to the fact that you are the boss.

J. Recognizable as an Order
Be sure that the order is recognizable as such.

K. Complete
Be sure recipient has knowledge and experience sufficient to carry out order. Give illustrations and examples.

A DEPARTMENTAL PERSONNEL OFFICE IS RESPONSIBLE FOR THE FOLLOWING FUNCTIONS

1. Policy
2. Personnel Programs
3. Recruitment and Placement
4. Position Classification
5. Salary and Wage Administration
6. Employee performance Standards and Evaluation
7. Employee Relations
8. Disciplinary Actions and Separations
9. Health and Safety
10. Staff Training and Development
11. Personnel Records, Procedures, and Reports
12. Employee Services
13. Personnel Research

SUPERVISION

I. LEADERSHIP

All leadership is based essentially on authority. This comes from two sources: It is received from higher management or it is earned by the supervisor through his methods of supervision. Although effective leadership has always depended upon the leader's using his authority in such a way as to appeal successfully to the motives of the people supervised, the conditions for making this appeal are continually changing. The key to today's problem of leadership is flexibility and resourcefulness on the part of the leader in meeting changes in conditions as they occur.

Three basic approaches to leadership are generally recognized:

A. The Authoritarian Approach
   1. The methods and techniques used in this approach emphasize the *I* in leadership and depend primarily on the formal authority of the leader. This authority is sometimes exercised in a hardboiled manner and sometimes in a benevolent

manner, but in either case the dominating role of the leader is reflected in the thinking, planning, and decisions of the group.
2. Group results are to a large degree dependent on close supervision by the leader. Usually, the individuals in the group will not show a high degree of initiative or acceptance of responsibility and their capacity to grow and develop probably will not be fully utilized. The group may react with resentment or submission, depending upon the manner and skill of the leader in using his authority.
3. This approach develops as a natural outgrowth of the authority that goes with the leader's job and his feeling of sole responsibility for getting the job done. It is relatively easy to use and does not require must resourcefulness.
4. The use of this approach is effective in times of emergencies, in meeting close deadline as a final resort, in settling some issues, in disciplinary matters, and with dependent individuals and groups.

B. The Laissez-Faire or Let 'em Alone Approach
1. This approach generally is characterized by an avoidance of leadership responsibility by the leader. The activities of the group depend largely on the choice of its members rather than the leader.
2. Group results probably will be poor. Generally, there will be disagreements over petty things, bickering, and confusion. Except for a few aggressive people, individuals will not show much initiative and growth and development will be retarded. There may be a tendency for informal leaders to take over leadership of the group.
3. This approach frequently results from the leader's dislike of responsibility, from his lack of confidence, from failure of other methods to work, from disappointment or criticism. It is usually the easiest of the three to use and requires both understanding and resourcefulness on the part of the leader.
4. This approach is occasionally useful and effective, particularly in forcing dependent individuals or groups to rely on themselves, to give someone a chance to save face by clearing his own difficulties, or when action should be delayed temporarily for good cause.

C. The Democratic Approach
1. The methods and techniques used in this approach emphasize the *we* in leadership and build up the responsibility of the group to attain its objectives. Reliance is placed largely on the earned authority of the leader.
2. Group results are likely to be good because most of the job motives of the people will be satisfied. Cooperation and teamwork, initiative, acceptance of responsibility, and the individual's capacity for growth probably will show a high degree of development.
3. This approach grows out of a desire or necessity of the leader to find ways to appeal effectively to the motivation of his group. It is the best approach to build up inside the person a strong desire to cooperate and apply himself to the job. It is the most difficult to develop, and requires both understanding and resourcefulness on the part of the leader.
4. The value of this approach increases over a long period where sustained efficiency and development of people are important. It may not be fully effective in all situations, however, particularly when there is not sufficient time to use it properly or where quick decisions must be made.

All three approaches are used by most leaders and have a place in supervising people. The extent of their use varies with individual leaders, with some using one approach predominantly. The leader who uses these three approaches, and varies their use with time and circumstance, is probably the most effective. Leadership which is used predominantly with a democratic approach requires more resourcefulness on the part of the leader but offers the greatest possibilities in terms of teamwork and cooperation.

The one best way of developing democratic leadership is to provide a real sense of participation on the part of the group, since this satisfies most of the chief job motives. Although there are many ways of providing participation, consulting as frequently as possible with individuals and groups on things that affect them seems to offer the most in building cooperation and responsibility. Consultation takes different forms, but it is most constructive when people feel they are actually helping in finding the answers to the problems on the job.

There are some requirements of leaders in respect to human relations which should be considered in their selection and development. Generally, the leader should be interested in working with other people, emotionally stable, self-confident, and sensitive to the reactions of others. In addition, his viewpoint should be one of getting the job done through people who work cooperatively in response to his leadership. He should have a knowledge of individual and group behavior, but, most important of all, he should work to combine all of these requirements into a definite, practical skill in leadership.

II. NINE POINTS OF CONTRAST BETWEEN *BOSS* AND *LEADER*

   A. The boss drives his men; the leader coaches them.
   B. The boss depends on authority; the leader on good will.
   C. The boss inspires fear; the leader inspires enthusiasm.
   D. The boss says I; the leader says *We*.
   E. The boss says *Get here on time*; the leader gets there ahead of time.
   F. The boss fixes the blame for the breakdown; the leader fixes the breakdown.
   G. The boss knows how it is done; the leader shows how.
   H. The boss makes work a drudgery; the leader makes work a game.
   I. The boss says *Go*; the leader says *Let's go*.

EMPLOYEE MORALE

Employee morale is the way employees feel about each other, the organization or unit in which they work, and the work they perform.

I. SOME WAYS TO DEVELOP AND MAINTAIN GOOD EMPLYEE MORALE

   A. Give adequate credit and praise when due.
   B. Recognize importance of all jobs and equalize load with proper assignments, always giving consideration to personality differences and abilities.
   C. Welcome suggestions and do not have an *all-wise* attitude. Request employees' assistance in solving problems and use assistants when conducting group meetings on certain subjects.
   D. Properly assign responsibilities and give adequate authority for fulfillment of such assignments.

E. Keep employees informed about matters that affect them.
F. Criticize and reprimand employees privately.
G. Be accessible and willing to listen.
H. Be fair.
I. Be alert to detect training possibilities so that you will not miss an opportunity to help each employee do a better job, and if possible with less effort on his part.
J. Set a good example.
K. Apply the golden rule.

II. SOME INDICATIONS OF GOOD MORALE

A. Good quality of work
B. Good quantity
C. Good attitude of employees
D. Good discipline
E. Teamwork
F. Good attendance
G. Employee participation

MOTIVATION

DRIVES

A drive, stated simply, is a desire or force which causes a person to do or say certain things. These are some of the most usual drives and some of their identifying characteristics recognizable in people motivated by such drives:

A. Security (desire to provide for the future)
Always on time for work
Works for the same employer for many years
Never takes unnecessary chances
Seldom resists doing what he is told

B. Recognition (desire to be rewarded for accomplishment)
Likes to be asked for his opinion
Becomes very disturbed when he makes a mistake
Does things to attract attention
Likes to see his name in print

C. Position (desire to hold certain status in relation to others)
Boasts about important people he knows
Wants to be known as a key man
Likes titles
Demands respect
Belongs to clubs, for prestige

D. Accomplishment (desire to get things done)
   Complains when things are held up
   Likes to do things that have tangible results
   Never lies down on the job
   Is proud of turning out good work

E. Companionship (desire to associate with other people)
   Likes to work with others
   Tells stories and jokes
   Indulges in horseplay
   Finds excuses to talk to others on the job

F. Possession (desire to collect and hoard objects)
   Likes to collect things
   Puts his name on things belonging to him
   Insists on the same location

Supervisors may find that identifying the drives of employees is a helpful step toward motivating them to self-improvement and better job performance. For example: An employee's job performance is below average. His supervisor, having previously determined that the employee is motivated by a drive for security, suggests that taking training courses will help the employee to improve, advance, and earn more money. Since earning more money can be a step toward greater security, the employee's drive for security would motivate him to take the training suggested by the supervisor. In essence, this is the process of charting an employee's future course by using his motivating drives to positive advantage.

EMPLOYEE PARTICIPATION

I. WHAT IS PARTICIPATION

Employee participation is the employee's giving freely of his time, skill, and knowledge to an extent which cannot be obtained by demand.

II. WHY IS IT IMPORTANT?

The supervisor's responsibility is to get the job done through people. A good supervisor gets the job done through people who work willingly and well. The participation of employees is important because:

A. Employees develop a greater sense of responsibility when they share in working out operating plans and goals.
B. Participation provides greater opportunity and stimulation for employees to learn, and to develop their ability.
C. Participation sometimes provides better solutions to problems because such solutions may combine the experience and knowledge of interested employees who want the solutions to work.
D. An employee or group may offer a solution which the supervisor might hesitate to make for fear of demanding too much.

E. Since the group wants to make the solution work, they exert pressure in a constructive way on each other.
F. Participation usually results in reducing the need for close supervision.

II. HOW MAY SUPERVISORS OBTAIN IT?

Participation is encouraged when employees feel that they share some responsibility for the work and that their ideas are sincerely wanted and valued. Some ways of obtaining employee participation are:

A. Conduct orientation programs for new employees to inform them about the organization and their rights and responsibilities as employees.
B. Explain the aims and objectives of the agency. On a continuing basis, be sure that the employees know what these aims and objectives are.
C. Share job successes and responsibilities and give credit for success.
D. Consult with employees, both as individuals and in groups, about things that affect them.
E. Encourage suggestions for job improvements. Help employees to develop good suggestions. The suggestions can bring them recognition. The city's suggestion program offers additional encouragement through cash awards.

The supervisor who encourages employee participation is not surrendering his authority. He must still make decisions and initiate action, and he must continue to be ultimately responsible for the work of those he supervises. But, through employee participation, he is helping his group to develop greater ability and a sense of responsibility while getting the job done faster and better.

STEPS IN HANDLING A GRIEVANCE

1. Get the Facts
    a. Listen sympathetically
    b. Let him talk himself out
    c. Get his story straight
    d. Get his point of view
    e. Don't argue with him
    f. Give him plenty of time
    g. Conduct the interview privately
    h. Don't try to shift the blame or pass the buck

2. Consider the Facts
    a. Consider the employee's viewpoint
    b. How will the decision affect similar cases
    c. Consider each decision as a possible precedent
    d. Avoid snap judgments—don't jump to conclusions

3. Make or Get a Decision
    a. Frame an effective counter-proposal
    b. Make sure it is fair to all
    c. Have confidence in your judgment
    d. Be sure you can substantiate your decision

4. Notify the Employee of Your Decision
   Be sure he is told; try to convince him that the decision is fair and just.

5. Take Action When Needed and If Within Your Authority
   Otherwise, tell employee that the matter will be called to the attention of the proper person or that nothing can be done, and why it cannot.

6. Follow through to see that the desired result is achieved.

7. Record key facts concerning the complaint and the action taken.

8. Leave the way open to him to appeal your decision to a higher authority.

9. Report all grievances to your superior, whether they are appealed or not.

DISCIPLINE

Discipline is training that develops self-control, orderly conduct, and efficiency.

To discipline does not necessarily mean to punish.

To discipline does mean to train, to regulate, and to govern conduct.

I. THE DISCIPLINARY INTERVIEW

Most employees sincerely want to do what is expected of them. In other words, they are self-disciplined. Some employees, however, fail to observe established rules and standards, and disciplinary action by the supervisor is required.

The primary purpose of disciplinary action is to improve conduct without creating dissatisfaction, bitterness, or resentment in the process.

Constructive disciplinary action is more concerned with causes and explanations of breaches of conduct than with punishment. The disciplinary interview is held to get at the causes of apparent misbehavior and to motivate better performance in the future.

It is important that the interview be kept on an impersonal a basis as possible. If the supervisor lets the interview descend to the plane of an argument, it loses its effectiveness.

II. PLANNING THE INTERVIEW

Get all pertinent facts concerning the situation so that you can talk in specific terms to the employee.

Review the employee's record, appraisal ratings, etc.

Consider what you know about the temperament of the employee. Consider your attitude toward the employee. Remember that the primary requisite of disciplinary action is fairness.

Don't enter upon the interview when angry.

Schedule the interview for a place which is private and out of hearing of others.

III. CONDUCTING THE INTERVIEW

A. Make an effort to establish accord.
B. Question the employee about the apparent breach of discipline. Be sure that the question is not so worded as to be itself an accusation.
C. Give the employee a chance to tell his side of the story. Give him ample opportunity to talk.
D. Use understanding—listening except where it is necessary to ask a question or to point out some details of which the employee may not be aware. If the employee misrepresents facts, make a plain, accurate statement of the facts, but don't argue and don't engage in personal controversy.
E. Listen and try to understand the reasons for the employee's (mis)conduct. First of all, don't assume that there has been a breach of discipline. Evaluate the employee's reasons for his conduct in the light of his opinions and feelings concerning the consistency and reasonableness of the standards which he was expected to follow. Has the supervisor done his part in explaining the reasons for the rule? Was the employee's behavior unintentional or deliberate? Does he think he had real reasons for his actions? What new facts is he telling? Do the facts justify his actions? What causes, other than those mentioned, could have stimulated the behavior?
F. After listening to the employee's version of the situation, and if censure of his actions is warranted, the supervisor should proceed with whatever criticism is justified. Emphasis should be placed on future improvement rather than exclusively on the employee's failure to measure up to expected standards of job conduct.
G. Fit the criticism to the individual. With one employee, a word of correction may be all that is required.
H. Attempt to distinguish between unintentional error and deliberate misbehavior. An error due to ignorance requires training and not censure.
I. Administer criticism in a controlled, even tone of voice, never in anger. Make it clear that you are acting as an agent of the department. In general, criticism should refer to the job or the employee's actions and not to the person. Criticism of the employee's work is not an attack on the individual.
J. Be sure the interview does not destroy the employee's self-confidence. Mention his good qualities and assure him that you feel confident that he can improve his performance.
K. Wherever possible, before the employee leaves the interview, satisfy him that the incident is closed, that nothing more will be said on the subject unless the offense is repeated.

FINANCIAL MANAGEMENT

Contents

Introduction vi

I. The Necessity of Financial Planning 1

What is Financial Management? 1
Tools of Financial Planning 1

II. Understanding Financial Statements: A Health Checkup for Your Business 3

The Balance Sheet 3
The Statement of Income 6

III. Financial Ratio Analysis 9

Balance Sheet Ratio Analysis 9
Income Statement Ratio Analysis 11
Management Ratios 11

IV. Forecasting Profits 15

Facts Affecting Pro Forma Statements 15
The Pro Forma Income Statement 16
Comparison with Actual Monthly Performance 16
Break-Even Analysis 18

V. Cash Flow Management: Budgeting and Controlling Costs 24

The Cash Flow Statement 24

VI. Pricing Policy 33

Establishing Selling Prices 33
A Pricing Example 34
The Retailer's Mark-Up 35
Pricing Policies and Profitability Goals 36

VII. Forecasting and Obtaining Capital 38

Types and Sources of Capital 38
Borrowing Working Capital 39
Borrowing Growth Capital 40
Borrowing Permanent Equity Capital 41
Applying for Capital 44

VIII. Financial Management Planning 46

Long-Term Planning 46

FINANCIAL MANAGEMENT

I. The Necessity of Financial Planning

There is one simple reason to understand and observe financial planning in your business—to avoid failure. Eight of ten new businesses fail primarily because of the lack of good financial planning.

Financial planning affects how and on what terms you will be able to attract the funding required to establish, maintain, and expand your business. Financial planning determines the raw materials you can afford to buy, the products you will be able to produce, and whether or not you will be able to market them efficiently. It affects the human and physical resources you will be able to acquire to operate your business. It will be a major determinant of whether or not you will be able to make your hard work profitable.

This manual provides an overview of the essential components of financial planning and management. Used wisely, it will make the readerthe small business owner/manager familiar enough with the fundamentals to have a fighting chance of success in today's highly competitive business environment.

A clearly conceived, well documented financial plan, establishing goals and including the use of Pro Forma Statements and Budgets to ensure financial control, will demonstrate not only that you know what you want to do, but that you know how to accomplish it. This demonstration is essential to attract the capital required by your business from creditors and investors.

What Is Financial Management?

Very simply stated, financial management is the use of financial statements that reflect the financial condition of a business to identify its relative strengths and weaknesses. It enables you to plan, using projections, future financial performance for capital, asset, and personnel requirements to maximize the return on shareholders' investment.

Tools of Financial Planning

This manual introduces the tools required to prepare a financial plan for your business's development, including the following:

- Basic Financial Statementsthe Balance Sheet and Statement of Income

- Ratio Analysis—a means by which individual business performance is compared to similar businesses in the same category

- The Pro Forma Statement of Income—a method used to forecast future profitability

- Break-Even Analysis—a method allowing the small business person to calculate the sales level at which a business recovers all its costs or expenses

- The Cash Flow Statement – also known as the Budget identifies the flow of cash into and out of the business

- Pricing formulas and policies – used to calculate profitable selling prices for products and services

- Types and sources of capital available to finance business operations

- Short- and long-term planning considerations necessary to maximize profits

The business owner/manager who understands these concepts and uses them effectively to control the evolution of the business is practicing sound financial management thereby increasing the likelihood of success.

II. Understanding Financial Statements: A Health Checkup for Your Business

Financial Statements record the performance of your business and allow you to diagnose its strengths and weaknesses by providing a written summary of financial activities. There are two primary financial statements: the Balance Sheet and the Statement of Income.

The Balance Sheet

The Balance Sheet provides a picture of the financial health of a business at a given moment, usually at the close of an accounting period. It lists in detail those material and intangible items the business owns (known as its assets) and what money the business owes, either to its creditors (liabilities) or to its owners (shareholders' equity or net worth of the business).

Assets include not only cash, merchandise inventory, land, buildings, equipment, machinery, furniture, patents, trademarks, and the like, but also money due from individuals or other businesses (known as accounts or notes receivable).

Liabilities are funds acquired for a business through loans or the sale of property or services to the business on credit. Creditors do not acquire business ownership, but promissory notes to be paid at a designated future date.

Shareholders' equity (or net worth or capital) is money put into a business by its owners for use by the business in acquiring assets.

At any given time, a business's assets equal the total contributions by the creditors and owners, as illustrated by the following formula for the Balance Sheet:

Assets	=	**Liabilities**	+	**Net Worth**
(Total funds invested in assets of the business)		(Funds supplied to the business by its creditors)		(Funds supplied to the business by its owners)

This formula is a basic premise of accounting. If a business owes more money to creditors than it possesses in value of assets owned, the net worth or owner's equity of the business will be a negative number.

The Balance Sheet is designed to show how the assets, liabilities, and net worth of a business are distributed at any given time. It is usually prepared at regular intervals; e.g., at each month's end, but especially at the end of each fiscal (accounting) year.

By regularly preparing this summary of what the business owns and owes (the Balance Sheet), the business owner/manager can identify and analyze trends in the financial strength of the business. It permits timely modifications, such as gradually decreasing the amount of money the business owes to creditors and increasing the amount the business owes its owners.

All Balance Sheets contain the same categories of assets, liabilities, and net worth. Assets are arranged in decreasing order of how quickly they can be turned into cash (liquidity). Liabilities are listed in order of how soon they must be repaid, followed by retained earnings (net worth or owner's equity), as illustrated in Figure *2-1,* the sample Balance Sheet for ABC Company.

The categories and format of the Balance Sheet are established by a system known as Generally Accepted Accounting Principles (GAAP). Hie system is applied to all companies, large or small, so anyone reading the Balance Sheet can readily understand the story it tells.

Balance Sheet Categories

Assets and liabilities are broken down into categories as described on page 8.

Figure 2-1

ABC Company
December 31, 20___
Balance Sheet

Cash	$1,896	Notes Payable, Bank	$2,000
Accounts Receivable	1,456	Accounts Payable	2,240
Inventory	6,822	Accruals	940
Total Current Assets	$10,174	Total Current Liabilities	$5,180
Equipment and Fixtures	1,168	Total Liabilities	5,180
Prepaid Expenses	1,278	Net Worth*	7,440
Total Assets	$12,620	Total Liabilities and New Worth	$12,620

*Assets – Liabilities = New Worth

Assets: An asset is anything the business owns that has monetary value.

- Current Assets include cash, government securities, marketable securities, accounts receivable, notes receivable (other than from officers or employees), inventories, prepaid expenses, and any other item that could be converted into cash within one year in the normal course of business.

- Fixed Assets are those acquired for long-term use in a business such as land, plant, equipment, machinery, leasehold improvements, furniture, fixtures, and any other items with an expected useful business life measured in years (as opposed to items that will wear out or be used up in less than one y ar and are usually expensed when they are purchased). These assets are typically not for resale and are recorded in the Balance Sheet at their net cost *less* accumulated depreciation.

- Other Assets include intangible assets, such as patents, royalty arrangements, copyrights, exclusive use contracts, and notes receivable from officers and employees.

Liabilities: Liabilities are the claims of creditors against the assets of the business (debts owed by the business).

- Current Liabilities are accounts payable, notes payable to banks, accrued expenses (wages, salaries), taxes payable, the current portion (due within one year) of long-term debt, and other obligations to creditors due within one year.

- Long-Term Liabilities are mortgages, intermediate and long-term bank loans, equipment loans, and any other obligation for money due to a creditor with a maturity longer than one year.

- Net Worth is the assets of the business minus its liabilities.

Net worth equals the owner's equity. This equity is the investment by the owner plus any profits or minus any losses that have accumulated in the business.

The Statement of Income

The second primary report included in a business's Financial Statement is the Statement of Income. The Statement of Income is a measurement of a company's sales and expenses over a specific period of time. It is also prepared at regular intervals (again, each month and fiscal year end) to show the results of operating during those accounting periods. It too follows Generally Accepted Accounting Principles (GAAP) and contains specific revenue and expense categories regardless of the nature of the business.

Statement of Income Categories

- The Statement of Income categories are calculated as described below:

- Net Sales (gross sales less returns and allowances)

- Less Cost of Goods Sold (cost of inventories)

- Equals Gross Margin (gross profit on sales before operating expenses)

- Less Selling and Administrative Expenses (salaries, wages, payroll taxes and benefits, rent, utilities, maintenance expenses, office supplies, postage, automobile/vehicle expenses, insurance, legal and accounting expenses, depreciation)

- Equals Operating Profit (profit before other non-operating income or expense)

- Plus Other Income (income from discounts, investments, customer charge accounts)

- Less Other Expenses (interest expense)

- Equals Net Profit (Loss) Before Tax (the figure on which your tax is calculated)

- Less Income Taxes (if any are due)

- Equals Net Profit *(Loss) After Tax*

For an example of a Statement of Income, see Figure 2-2 the statement of ABC Company.

Figure 2–2
ABC Company
December 31, 20____
Income Statement

Net Sales		$68,116
Cost of Goods Sold		47,696
Gross Profit on Sales		$20,420
Expenses		
Wages	$6,948	
Delivery Expenses	954	
Bad Debts Allowances	409	
Communications	204	
Depreciation Allowance	409	
Insurance	613	
Taxes	1,021	
Advertising	1,566	
Interest	409	
Other Charges	749	
Total Expenses		$13,282
Net Profit		7,138
Other Income		886
Total Net Income		$8,024

Calculating the Cost of Goods Sold

Calculation of the Cost of Goods Sold category in the Statement of Income (or Profit-and-Loss Statement as it is sometimes called) varies depending on whether the business is retail, wholesale, or manufacturing. In retailing and wholesaling, computing the cost of goods sold during the accounting period involves beginning and ending inventories. This, of course, includes purchases made during the accounting period. In manufacturing it involves not only finished-goods inventories, but also raw materials inventories, goods-in-process inventories, direct labor, and direct factory overhead costs. Regardless of the calculation for Cost of Goods Sold, deduct the Cost of Goods Sold from Net Sales to get Gross Margin or Gross Profit. From Gross Profit, deduct general or indirect overhead, such as selling expenses, office expenses, and interest expenses, to calculate your Net Profit. This is the final profit after all costs and expenses for the accounting period have been deducted.

III. Financial Ratio Analysis

The Balance Sheet and the Statement of Income are essential, but they are only the starting point for successful financial management. Apply Ratio Analysis to Financial Statements to analyze the success, failure, and progress of your business.

Ratio Analysis enables the business owner/manager to spot trends in a business and to compare its performance and condition with the average performance of similar businesses in the same industry. To do this compare your ratios with the average of businesses similar to yours and compare your own ratios for several successive years, watching especially for any unfavorable trends that may be starting. Ratio analysis may provide the all-important early warning indications that allow you to solve your business problems before your business is destroyed by them.

Balance Sheet Ratio Analysis

Important Balance Sheet Ratios measure liquidity and solvency (a business's ability to pay its bills as they come due) and leverage (the extent to which the business is dependent on creditors' funding). They include the following ratios:

Liquidity Ratios.

These ratios indicate the ease of turning assets into cash. They include the Current Ratio, Quick Ratio, and Working Capital.

Current Ratios. The Current Ratio is one of the best known measures of financial strength. It is figured as shown below:

$$\text{Current Ratio} = \frac{\text{Total Current Assets}}{\text{Total Current Liabilities}}$$

The main question this ratio addresses is: "Does your business have enough current assets to meet the payment schedule of its current debts with a margin of safety for possible losses in current assets, such as inventory shrinkage or collectable accounts?" A generally acceptable current ratio is 2 to 1. But whether or not a specific ratio is satisfactory depends on the nature of the business and the characteristics of its current assets and liabilities. The minimum acceptable current ratio is obviously 1:1, but that relationship is usually playing it too close for comfort.

If you decide your business's current ratio is too low, you may be able to raise it by:

- Paying some debts.

- Increasing your current assets from loans or other borrowings with a maturity of more than one year.

- Converting noncurrent assets into current assets.

- Increasing your current assets from new equity contributions.

- Putting profits back into the business.

Quick Ratios. The Quick Ratio is sometimes called the "acid-test" ratio and is one of the best measures of liquidity. It is figured as shown below:

$$\text{Quick Ratio} = \frac{\text{Cash + Government Securities + Receivables}}{\text{Total Current Liabilities}}$$

The Quick Ratio is a much more exacting measure than the Current Ratio. By excluding inventories, it concentrates on the really liquid assets, with value that is fairly certain. It helps answer the question: "If all sales revenues should disappear, could my business meet its current obligations with the readily convertible 'quick' funds on hand?"

An acid-test of 1:1 is considered satisfactory unless the majority of your "quick assets" are in accounts receivable, and the pattern of accounts receivable collection lags behind the schedule for paying current liabilities.

Working Capital. Working Capital is more a measure of cash *flow* than a ratio. The result of this calculation must be a positive number. It is calculated as shown below:

$$\text{Working Capital} = \text{Total Current Assets} - \text{Total Current Liabilities}$$

Bankers look at Net Working Capital over time to determine

a company's ability to weather financial crises. Loans are often tied to minimum working capital requirements.

A general observation about these three Liquidity Ratios is that the higher they are the better, especially if you are relying to any significant extent on creditor money to finance assets.

Leverage Ratio

This Debt/Worth or Leverage Ratio indicates the extent to which the business is reliant on debt financing (creditor money versus owner's equity):

$$\text{Debt/Worth Ratio} = \frac{\text{Total Liabilities}}{\text{Net Worth}}$$

Generally, the higher this ratio, the more risky a creditor will perceive its exposure in your business, making it correspondingly harder to obtain credit.

Income Statement Ratio Analysis

The following important State of Income Ratios measure profitability:

Gross Margin Ratio

This ratio is the percentage of sales dollars left after subtracting the cost of goods sold from net sales. It measures the percentage of sales dollars remaining (after obtaining or manufacturing the goods sold) available to pay the overhead expenses of the

company.

Comparison of your business ratios to those of similar businesses will reveal the relative strengths or weaknesses in your business. The Gross Margin Ratio is calculated as follows:

$$\text{Gross Margin Ratio} = \frac{\text{Gross Profit}}{\text{Net Sales}}$$
(Gross Profit = Net Sales - Cost of Goods Sold)

Net Profit Margin Ratio

This ratio is the percentage of sales dollars left after subtracting the Cost of Goods sold and all expenses, except income taxes. It provides a good opportunity to compare your company's "return on sales" with the performance of other companies in your industry. It is calculated before income tax because tax rates and tax liabilities vary from company to company for a wide variety of reasons, making comparisons after taxes much more difficult. The Net Profit Margin Ratio is calculated as follows:

$$\text{Net Profit Margin Ratio} = \frac{\text{Net Profit Before Tax}}{\text{Net Sales}}$$

Management Ratios

Other important ratios, often referred to as Management Ratios, are also derived from Balance Sheet and Statement of Income information.

Inventory Turnover Ratio

This ratio reveals how well inventory is being managed. It is important because the more times inventory can be turned in a given operating cycle, the greater the profit. The Inventory Turnover Ratio is calculated as follows:

$$\text{Inventory Turnover Ratio} = \frac{\text{Net Sales}}{\text{Average Inventory at Cost}}$$

Accounts Receivable Turnover Ratio

This ratio indicates how well accounts receivable are being collected. If receivables are not collected reasonably in accordance with their terms, management should rethink its collection policy. If receivables are excessively slow in being converted to cash, liquidity could be severely impaired. The Accounts Receivable Turnover Ratio is calculated as follows:

$$\frac{\text{Net Credit Sales/Year}}{365 \text{ Days/Year}} = \text{Daily Credit Sales}$$

$$\text{Accounts Receivable Turnover (in days)} = \frac{\text{Accounts Receivable}}{\text{Daily Credit Sales}}$$

Return on Assets Ratio

This measures how efficiently profits are being generated from the assets employed in the business when compared with the ratios of firms hi a similar business. A low ratio in comparison with industry averages indicates an inefficient use of business assets. The Return on Assets Ratio is calculated as follows:

$$\text{Return on Assets} = \frac{\text{Net Profit Before Tax}}{\text{Total Assets}}$$

Return on Investment (ROI) Ratio.

The ROI is perhaps the most important ratio of all. It is the percentage of return on funds invested in the business by its owners. In short, this ratio tells the owner whether or not all the effort put into the business has been worthwhile. If the ROI is less than the rate of return on an alternative, risk-free investment such as a bank savings account or certificate of deposit, the owner may be wiser to sell the company, put the money in such a savings instrument, and avoid the daily struggles of small business management. The ROI is calculated as follows:

$$\text{Return on Investment} = \frac{\text{Net Profit before Tax}}{\text{Net Worth}}$$

These Liquidity, Leverage, Profitability, and Management Ratios* allow the business owner to identify trends in a business and to compare its progress with the performance of others through data published by various sources. The owner may thus determine the business's relative strengths and weaknesses.

NOTES

NOTES

IV. Forecasting Profits

Forecasting, particularly on a short--term basis (one year to three years), is essential to planning for business success. This process, estimating future business performance based on the actual results from prior periods, enables the business owner/manager to modify the operation of the business on a timely basis. This allows the business to avoid losses or major financial problems should some future results from operations not conform with reasonable expectations. Forecasts--or Pro Forma Income Statements and Cash Flow Statements as they are usually called--also provide the most persuasive management tools to apply for loans or attract investor money. As a business expands, there will inevitably be a need for more money than can be internally generated from profits.

Facts Affecting Pro Forma Statements

Preparation of Forecasts (Pro Forma Statements) requires assembling a wide array of pertinent, verifiable facts affecting your business and its past performance. These include:

- Data from prior financial statements, particularly:
    a. Previous sales levels and trends
    b. Past gross percentages
    c. Average past general, administrative, and selling expenses necessary to generate your former sales volumes
    d. Trends in the company's need to borrow (supplier, trade credit, and bank credit) to support various levels of inventory and trends in accounts receivable required to achieve previous sales volumes

- Unique company data, particularly:
    a. Plant capacity
    b. Competition
    c. Financial constraints
    d. Personnel availability

- Industry-wide factors, including:
    a. Overall state of the economy
    b. Economic status of your industry within the economy
    c. Population growth
    d. Elasticity* of demand for the product or service your business provides
    e. Availability of raw materials

---

*Demand is said to be "elastic" if it decreases as prices increase, a demonstration that consumers can do without or with less of the goods or service. If demand for something is relatively steady as prices increase, it is "inelastic."

Once these factors are identified, they may be used in Pro Formas, which estimate the level of sales, expense, and profitability that seem possible in a future period of operations.

The Pro Forma Income Statement

In preparing the Pro Forma Income Statement, the estimate of total sales during a selected period is the most critical "guesstimate." Employ business experience from past financial statements. Get help from management and salespeople in developing this all-important number.

Then assume, for example, that a 10 percent increase in sales volume is a realistic and attainable goal. Multiply last year's net sales by 1.10 to get this year's estimate of total net sales. Next, break down this total, month by month, by looking at the historical monthly sales volume. From this you can determine what percentage of total annual sales fell on the average in each of those months over a minimum of the past three years. You may find that 75 percent of total annual sales volume was realized during the six months from July through December in each of those years and that the remaining 25 percent of sales was spread fairly evenly over the first six months of the year.

Next, estimate the cost of goods sold by analyzing operating data to determine on a monthly basis what percentage of sales has gone into cost of goods sold in the past. This percentage can then be adjusted for expected variations in costs, price trends, and efficiency of operations.

Operating expenses (sales, general and administrative expenses, depreciation, and interest), other expenses, other income, and taxes can then be estimated through detailed analysis and adjustment of what they were in the past and what you expect them to be in the future.

Comparison with Actual Monthly Performance

Putting together this information month by month for a year into the future will result in your business's Pro Forma Statement of Income. Use it to compare with the actual monthly results from operations by using the SBA form 1099 (4-82) Operating Plan Forecast (Profit and Loss Projection]. Obtain this form from your local SBA office. You will find it helpful to refer to the SBA Guidelines for Profit and Loss Projection. Preparation of the information is summarized below and on the back of the form 1099.

Revenue (Sales)

- List the departments within the business. For example, if your business is appliance sales and service, the departments would include new appliances, used appliances, parts, in-shop service, on-site service.

- In the "Estimate" columns, enter a reasonable projection of monthly sales for each department of the business. Include cash and on-account sales. In the "Actual" columns, enter the actual sales for the month as they become available.
- Exclude from the Revenue section any revenue not strictly related to the business.

Cost of Sales
- Cite costs by department of the business, as above.
- In the "Estimate" columns, enter the cost of sales estimated for each month for each department. For product inventory, calculate the cost of the goods sold for each department (beginning inventory plus purchases and transportation costs during the month minus the inventory). Enter "Actual" costs each month as they accrue.

Gross Profit
- Subtract the total cost of sales from the total revenue.

Expenses
Salary Expenses: Base pay plus overtime.
- Payroll Expenses: Include paid vacations, sick leave, health insurance, unemployment insurance, Social Security taxes.

- Outside Services: Include costs of subcontracts, overflow work farmed-out, special or one-time services.

- Supplies: Services and items purchased for use in the business, not for resale.

- Repairs and Maintenance: Regular maintenance and repair, including periodic large expenditures, such as painting or decorating.

- Advertising: Include desired sales volume, classified directory listing expense, etc.

- Car, Delivery and Travel: Include charges if personal car is used in the business. Include parking, tolls, mileage on buying trips, repairs, etc.

- Accounting and Legal: Outside professional services.

- Rent: List only real estate used in the business.

- Telephone.

- Utilities: Water, heat, light, etc.

- Insurance: Fire or liability on property or products, worker's compensation.

- Taxes: Inventory, sales, excise, real estate, others.

- Interest.

- Depreciation: Amortization of capital assets.

- Other Expenses (specify each): Tools, leased equipment, etc.

- Miscellaneous (unspecified): Small expenditures without separate accounts.

Net Profit
- To find net profit, subtract total expenses from gross profit.

The Pro Forma Statement of Income, prepared on a monthly basis and culminating in an annual projection for the next business fiscal year, should be revised not less than quarterly. It must reflect the actual performance achieved in the immediately preceding three months to ensure its continuing usefulness as one of the two most valuable planning tools available to management.

Should the Pro Forma reveal that the business will likely not generate a profit from operations, plans must immediately be developed to identify what to do to at least break even-nincrease volume, decrease expenses, or put more owner capital in to pay some debts and reduce interest expenses.

Break-Even Analysis

"Break-Even" means a level of operations at which a business neither makes a profit nor sustains a loss. At this point, revenue is just enough to cover expenses. Break-Even Analysis enables you to study the relationship of volume, costs, and revenue.

Break-Even requires the business owner/manager to define a sales leveleither in terms of revenue dollars to be earned or in units to be sold within a given accounting periodat which the business would earn a before tax net profit of zero. This may be done by employing one of various formula calculations to the business estimated sales volume, estimated fixed costs, and estimated variable costs.

Generally, the volume and cost estimates assume the following conditions:

- A change in sales volume will not affect the selling price per unit;

- Fixed expenses (rent, salaries, administrative and office expenses, interest, and depreciation) will remain the same at all volume levels; and

- Variable expenses (cost of goods sold, variable labor costs, including overtime wages and sales commissions) will increase or decrease in direct proportion to any increase or decrease in sales volume.

Two methods are generally employed in Break-Even Analysis, depending on whether the break-even point is calculated in terms of soles doJJar volume or in number of units that must be sold.

Break-Even Point in Sales Dollars

The steps for calculating the first method are shown below:

1. Obtain a list of expenses incurred by the company during its past fiscal year.

2. Separate the expenses listed in Step 1 into either a variable or a fixed expense classification. (See Figure 4-1 under "Classification of Expenses.")

3. Express the variable expenses as a percentage of sales. In the condensed income statement (Figure 4-1) of the Small Business Specialities Co., net sales were $1,200,000. In Step 2, variable expenses were found to amount to $720,000. Therefore, variable expenses are 60 percent of net sales ($720,000 divided by $1,200,000). This means that 60 cents of every sales dollar is required to cover variable expenses. Only the remainder, 40 cents of every dollar, is available for fixed expenses and profit.

4. Substitute the information gathered in the preceding steps in the following basic break-even formula to calculate the break-even point.

Figure 4-1

THE SMALL-BUSINESS SPECIALTIES CO.
Condensed Income Statement
For year ending Dec. 31, 20—

Net sales (60,000 units @ $20 per unit)		$1,200,000
Less cost of goods sold:		
Direct material	$195,000	
Direct labor	215,000	
Manufacturing expenses (Schedule A)	300,000	
Total		710,000
Gross profit		490,000
Less operating expenses:		
Selling expenses (Schedule B)	$200,000	
General and administrative expenses (Schedule C)	210,000	
Total		410,000
Net Income		$ 80,000

Supporting Schedules of Expenses Other Than Direct Material and Labor

	Total	Schedule A manufacturing expenses	Schedule B selling expenses	Schedule C general and administrative expenses
Rent	$ 60,000	$ 30,000	$ 8,000	$ 22,000
Insurance	11,000	9,000	1,000	1,000
Commissions	120,000	....	120,000	....
Property tax	12,000	10,000	1,000	1,000
Telephone	7,000	1,000	5,000	1,000
Depreciation	80,000	70,000	5,000	5,000
Power	100,000	100,000	....	....
Light	60,000	30,000	10,000	20,000
Officers' salaries	260,000	50,000	50,000	160,000
Total	$ 710,000	$ 300,000	$ 200,000	$ 210,000

Classification of Expenses

	Total	Variable	Fixed
Direct material	$ 195,000	195,000	....
Direct labor	215,000	215,000	....
Manufacturing expenses	300,000	100,000	$200,000
Selling expenses	200,000		50,000
General and administrative expenses	210,000	60,000	150,000
Total	$1,120,000	$720,000	$400,000

where: S = F + V (Sales at the break-even point)
F = Fixed expenses
V = Variable expenses expressed as a percentage of sales.

This formula means that when sales revenues equal the fixed expenses and variable expenses incurred in producing the sales revenues, there will be no profit or loss. At this point, revenue from sales is just sufficient to cover the fixed and the variable expenses. In this formula "S" is the break-even point.

For the Small Business Specialties Co., the break-even point (using the basic formula and data from Figure 3-2) may be calculated as follows:

$$S = F + V$$
$$S = \$400,000 + 0.60S$$
$$10S = \$4,000,000 + 6S^*$$
$$10S - 6S = \$4,000,000$$
$$4S = \$4,000,000$$
$$S = \$1,000,000$$

Proof that this calculation is correct follows:

Sales at break-even point per calculation	$1,000,000
Less variable expenses (60 percent of sales)	600,000
Marginal income	400,000
Less fixed expenses	400,000
Equals neither profit nor loss	$ 0

---

*Both sides of the equation were multiplied by 10 to eliminate decimal fractions.

Modification: Break-Even Point to Obtain Desired Net Income.

The first break-even formula can be modified to show the dollar sales required to obtain a certain amount of desired net income. To do this, let "S" mean the soles required to obtain a certain amount *of net* income, say $80,000. The formula then reads:

$$S = F + V + \text{Desired Net Income}$$
$$S = \$400,000 + 0.60S + \$80,000$$
$$10S = \$4,000,000 + 6S + 800,000^*$$
$$4S = \$4,800,000$$
$$S = \$1,200,000$$

Break-Even Point in Units to be Sold

You may want to calculate the break-even point in terms of units to be sold instead of sales dollars. If so, a second formula (in which "S" means units to be sold to break even) may be used:

$$\text{Break-even Sales} = \frac{\text{Fixed expenses}}{\text{Unit sales price - Unit variable expenses}}$$
(S = Units)

$$S = \frac{\$400,000}{\$20 - \$12} = \frac{\$400,000}{\$8}$$

$$S = 50,000 \text{ units}$$

The Small Business Specialties Co. must sell 50,000 units at $20 per unit to break even under the assumptions contained in this illustration. The sale of 50,000 units at $20 each equals $1 million, the break-even sales volume in dollars calculated in the basic formula. This formula indicates there is $8 per unit of sales that can be used to cover the $400,000 fixed expense. Then $400 000 divided by $8 gives the number of units required to break even.

Modification: Break-Even Point in Units to be Sold to Obtain Desired Net Income. The second formula can be modified to show the number of units required to obtain a certain amount of net income. In this case, let S mean the number of units required to obtain a certain amount of net income, again say $80,000. The formula then reads as follows:

$$S = \frac{\text{Fixed expenses + Net income}}{\text{Unit sales price - Unit variable expense}}$$

$$S = \frac{\$400,000 + \$80,000}{\$20 - \$12} = \frac{\$480,000}{\$8}$$

$$S = 60,000 \text{ units}$$

Break-even Analysis may also be represented graphically by charting the sales dollars or sales units required to break even as in Figure 4-2.

Remember: Increased sales do not necessarily mean increased profits. If you know your company's break-even point, you will know how to price your product to make a profit. If you cannot make an acceptable profit, alter or sell your business before you lose your retained earnings.

Figure 4-2

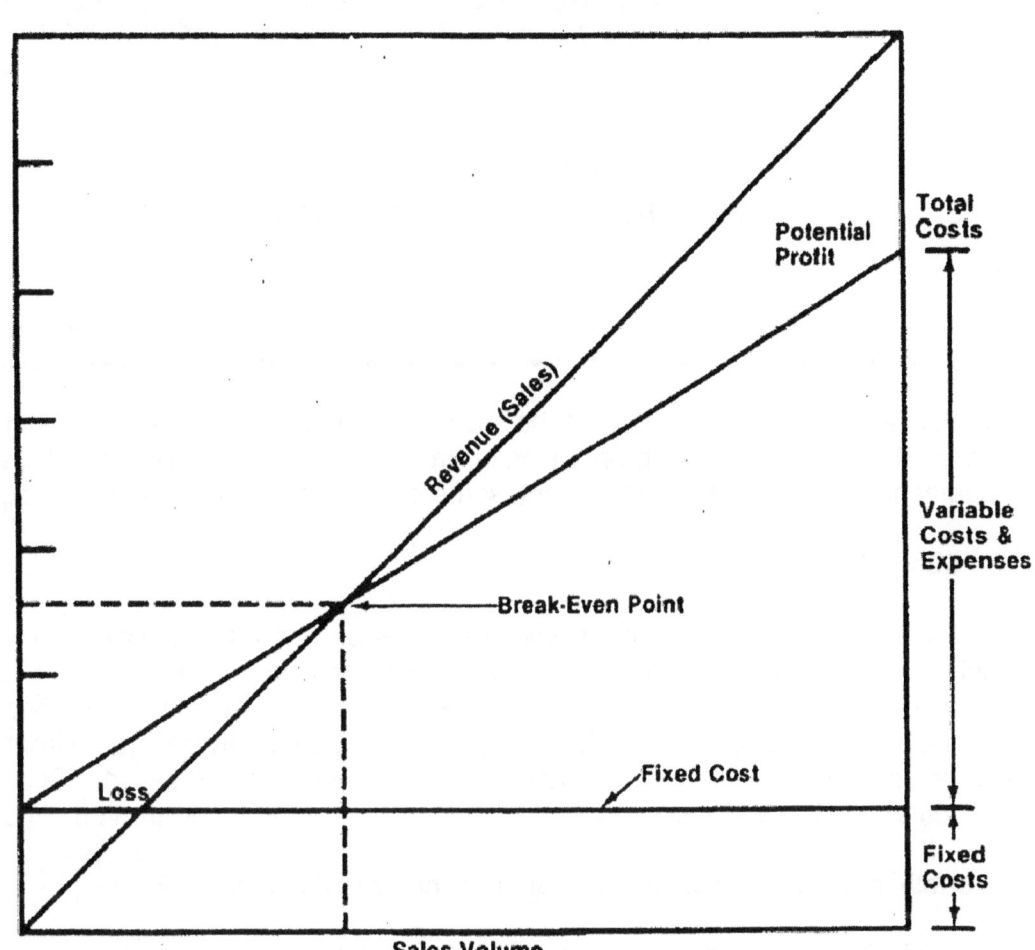

V. Cash Flow Management: Budgeting and Controlling Costs

If there is anything more important to the successful financial management of a business than the thorough, thoughtful preparation of Pro Forma Income Statements, it is the preparation of the Cash Flow Statement, sometimes called the Cash Flow Budget.

The Cash Flow Statement

The Cash Flow Statement identifies when cash is expected to be received and when it must be spent to pay bills and debts. It shows how much cash will be needed to pay expenses and when it will be needed. It also allows the manager to identify where the necessary cash* will come from. For example, will it be internally generated from sales and the collection of accounts receivableor must it be borrowed? (The Cash Flow Projection deals only with actual cash transactions; depreciation and amortization of good

will or other non-cash expense items are not considered in this Pro Forma.)

The Gash Flow Statement, based on management estimates of sales and obligations, identifies when money will be flowing into and out of the business. It enables management to plan for shortfalls in cash resources so short term working capital loans may be arranged in advance. It allows management to schedule purchases and payments in a way that enables the business to borrow as little as possible. Because all sales are not cash sales, management must be able to forecast when accounts receivable will become "cash in the bank" and when expenseswhether regular or seasonalmust be "paid so cash shortfalls will not interrupt normal business operations.

The Cash Flow Statement may also be used as a Budget, permitting the manager increased control of the business through continuous comparison of actual receipts and disbursements against forecast amounts. This comparison helps the small business owner identify areas for timely improvement in financial management.

By closely watching the timing of cash receipts and disbursements, cash balance on hand, and loan balances, management can readily identify such things as deficiencies in collecting receivables, unrealistic trade credit or loan repayment schedules. Surplus cash that may be invested on a short-term basis or used to reduce debt and interest expenses temporarily can be recognized. In short, it is the most valuable tool management has at its disposal to refine the day-to-day operation of a business. It is an important financial tool bank lenders evaluate when a business needs a loan, for it demonstrates not only how large a loan is required but also when and how it can be repaid.

A Cash Flow Statement or Budget can be prepared for any period of time. However, a one-year budget matching the fiscal year of your business is recommended. As in the preparation and use of the Pro Forma Statement of Income, the projected Cash Flow Statement should be prepared on a monthly basis for the next year. It should be revised not less than quarterly to reflect actual performance in the preceding three months of operations to check its projections.

In preparing the Cash Flow Statement or Budget start with the sales budget. Other budgets are related directly or indirectly to this budget. The following is a sales forecast hi units:

Sales Budget – Units
For the Year Ended December 31, 20__

Territory	Total	1st Quarter	2nd Quarter	3rd Quarter	4th Quarter
East	26,000	5,000	6,000	7,000	8,000
West	11,000	2,000	2,500	3,000	3,500
	37,000	7,000	8,500	10,000	11,500

Assume you sell a single product and the sales price for it is $10. Your sales budget in terms of dollars would look like this:

Sales Budget – Dollars
For the Year Ended December 31, 20__

Territory	Total	1st Quarter	2nd Quarter	3rd Quarter	4th Quarter
East	$260,000	$50,000	$80,000	$70,000	$80,000
West	110,000	20,000	25,000	30,000	35,000
	$370,000	$70,000	$85,000	$100,000	$115,000

Say the estimated per unit cost of the product is $1.50 for direct material, $2.50 for direct labor, and $1.00 for manufacturing overhead. By applying unit costs to the sales budget in units, you would come out with this budget:

Cost of Goods Sold Budget
For the Year Ended December 31, 20__

	Total	1st Quarter	2nd Quarter	3rd Quarter	4th Quarter
Direct material	$ 55,500	$10,500	$12,750	$15,000	$17,250
Direct labor	92,500	17,500	21,250	25,000	28,750
Mfg. overhead	37,000	7,000	8,500	10,000	11,500
	$185,000	$35,000	$42,500	$50,000	$57,500

Later on, before a cash budget can be compiled, you will need to know the estimated cash requirements for selling expenses. Therefore, you prepare a budget for selling expenses and another for cash expenditures for selling expenses (total selling expenses less depreciation):

	Total	1st Quarter	2nd Quarter	3rd Quarter	4th Quarter
Commissions	$46,500	$ 8,750	$10,625	$12,500	$14,375
Rent	9,250	1,750	2,125	2,500	2,875
Advertising	9,250	1,750	2,125	2,500	2,875
Telephone	4,625	875	1,062	1,250	1,437
Depreciation office	900	225	225	225	225
Other	22,250	4,150	5,088	6,025	6,983
	$92,500	$17,500	$21,250	$25,000	$28,750

Selling Expenses Budget – Cash Requirements
For the Year Ended December 31, 20___

	Total	1st Quarter	2nd Quarter	3rd Quarter	4th Quarter
Total selling expenses	$92.500	$17,500	$21.250	$25.000	$28.750
Less: depreciation expense-office	900	225	225	225	225
Cash requirements	$91.600	$17.275	$21.025	$24.775	$28.525

Basic information for an estimate of administrative expenses for the coming year is easily compiled. Again, from that budget you can estimate cash requirements for those expenses to be used subsequently in preparing the cash budget.

Administrative Expenses Budget
For the Year Ended December 31, 20___

	Total	1st Quarter	2nd Quarter	3rd Quarter	4th Quarter
Salaries	$22,200	$4,200	$5,100	$ 6,000	$ 6,900
Insurance	1,850	350	425	500	575
Telephone	1,850	350	425	500	575
Supplies	3,700	700	850	1,000	1,150
Bad debt expenses	3,700	700	850	1.000	1,150
Other expenses	3,700	700	850	1,000	1,150
	$37,000	$7,000	$8,500	$10,000	$11,500

Administrative Expenses Budget – Cash Requirements
For the Year Ended December 31, 20___

	Total	1st Quarter	2nd Quarter	3rd Quarter	4th Quarter
Estimated adm. expenses	$37,000	$7,000	$8,500	$10,000	$11,500
Less: bad debt expenses	3,700	700	850	1,000	1,150
Cash requirements	$33,300	$6,500	$7,650	$ 9,000	$10,350

Now, from the information budgeted so far, you can proceed to prepare the budget income statement. Assume you plan to borrow $10,000 at the end of the first quarter. Although payable at maturity of the note, the interest appears in the last three quarters of the year. The statement will resemble the following:

Budgeted Income Statement
For the Year Ended December 31, 20___

	Total	1st Quarter	2nd Quarter	3rd Quarter	4th Quarter
Sales	$370,000	$70,000	$85,000	$100,000	$115,000
Cost of goods sold	185,000	35,000	42,500	50,000	57,500
Gross Margin	$185,000	$35,000	$42,500	$50,000	$57,500
Operating expenses:					
Selling	$92,500	$17,500	$21,250	$25,000	$28,750
Administrative	37,000	7,000	8,500	10,000	11,500
Total	$129,500	$24,500	$29,750	$35,000	$40,250
Net income from operations	$55,500	$10,500	$12,750	$15,000	$17,250
Interest expense	450		150	150	150
Net income before income taxes	$55,050	$10,500	$12,600	$14,850	$17,100
Federal income tax	27,525	5,250	6,300	7,425	8,550
Net income	$27,525	$5,250	$6,300	$7,425	$8,550

Estimating that 90 percent of your account sales is collected in the quarter in which they are made, that 9 percent is collected in the quarter following the quarter in which the sales were made, and that 1 percent of account sales is uncollectible, your accounts receivable budget of collections would look like this:

Budget of Collections of Accounts Receivable
For the Year Ended December 31, 20___

	Total (net)	1st Quarter	2nd Quarter	3rd Quarter	4th Quarter
4th Quarter Sales 19-0	$6,000	$6,000			
1st Quarter Sales 19-1	69,300	63,000	$6,300		
2nd Quarter Sales 19-1	84,150		76,500	$7,650	
3rd Quarter Sales 19-1	99,000			90,000	$9,000
4th Quarter Sales 19-1	103,500				103,500
	$361,950	$69,000	$82,800	$97,650	$112,500

Going back to the sales budget in units, now prepare a production budget in units. Assume you have 2,000 units in the opening inventory and want to have on hand at the end of each quarter the following quantities: 1st quarter, 3,000 units; 2nd quarter, 3,500 units; 3rd quarter, 4,000 units; and 4th quarter, 4,500 units.

Production Budget – Units
For the Year Ended December 31, 20__

	1st Quarter	2nd Quarter	3rd Quarter	4th Quarter
Sales requirements	7,000	8,500	10,000	11,500
Add: ending inventory requirements	3,000	3,500	4,000	4,500
Total requirements	10,000	12,500	14,000	16,000
Less: beginning inventory	2,000	3,000	3,500	4,000
Production requirements	8,000	9,000	10,500	112,000

Next, based on the production budget, prepare a budget to show the purchases needed during each of the four quarters. Expressed in terms of dollars, you do this by taking the production and inventory figures and multiplying them by the cost of material (previously estimated at $1.50 per unit). You could prepare a similar budget expressed in units.

Budget of Direct Materials Purchases
For the Year Ended December 31, 20__

	1st Quarter	2nd Quarter	3rd Quarter	4th Quarter
Required for production	$12,000	$13,500	$15,750	$18,000
Required for ending inventory	4,500	5,250	6,000	6,750
Total	$16,500	$18,750	$21,750	$24,750
Less: beginning inventory	3,000	4,500	5,250	6,000
Required purchases	$13,500	$14,250	$16,500	$18,750

Now suppose you pay 50 percent of your accounts in the quarter of the purchase and 50 percent in the following quarter. Carryover payables from last year were $5,000. Further, you always take the purchase discounts as a matter of good business policy. Since net purchases (less discount) were figured into the $1.50 cost estimate, purchase discounts do not appear in the budgets. Thus your payment on purchases budget will come out like this:

Payment on Purchases Budget
For the Year Ended December 31, 20__

	Total	1st Quarter	2nd Quarter	3rd Quarter	4th Quarter
4th Quarter Sales 19-0	$ 5,000	$ 5,000			
1st Quarter Sales 19-1	13,500	6,750	$ 6,750		
2nd Quarter Sales 19-1	14,250		7,125	$ 7,125	
3rd Quarter Sales 19-1	16,500			8,250	$ 8,250
4th Quarter Sales 19-1	9,375				9,375
Payments by Quarters	$58,625	$11,750	$13,875	$15,375	$17,625

Taking the data for quantities produced from the production budget in units, calculate the direct labor requirements on the basis of units to be produced. (The number and cost of labor hours necessary to produce a given quantity can be set forth in supplemental schedules.)

Direct Labor Budget – Cash Requirements
For the Year Ended December 31, 20___

	Total	1st Quarter	2nd Quarter	3rd Quarter	4th Quarter
Quantity	39,500	8,000	9,000	10,500	12,000
Direct labor cost	$98,750	$20,000	$22,500	$26,250	$30,000

Now outline the items that comprise your factory overhead, and prepare a budget like the following:

Manufacturing Overhead Budget
For the Year Ended December 31, 20___

	Total	1st Quarter	2nd Quarter	3rd Quarter	4th Quarter
Heat and power	$10,000	$1,000	$2,500	$3,000	$3,500
Factory supplies	5,300	1,000	1,500	1,800	1,000
Property taxes	2,000	500	500	500	500
Depreciation	2,800	700	700	700	700
Rent	8,000	2,000	2,000	2,000	2,000
Superintendent	9,400	2,800	1,800	2,500	4,300
	$39,500	$8,000	$9,000	$10,500	$12,000

Figure the cash payments for manufacturing overhead by subtracting depreciation, which requires no cash outlay, from the totals above, and you will have the following breakdown:

Manufacturing Overhead Budget – Cash Requirements
For the Year Ended December 31, 20___

	Total	1st Quarter	2nd Quarter	3rd Quarter	4th Quarter
Productions units	39,500	8,000	9,000	10,500	12,000
Mfg. overhead expenses	$39,500	$8,000	$9,000	$10,500	$12,000
Less: depreciation	2,800	700	700	700	700
Cash requirements	$36,700	$7,300	$8,300	$9,800	$11,300

Now comes the all important cash budget. You put it together by using the Collection of Accounts Receivable Budget; Selling Expenses Budget – Cash Requirements; Administrative Expenses Budget – Cash Requirements; Payment of Purchases Budget; Direct Labor Budget – Cash Requirements; and Manufacturing Budget – Cash Requirements.

Take $15,000 as the beginning balance, and assume that dividends of $20,000 are to be paid in the fourth quarter.

Cash Budget
For the Year Ended December 31, 20__

	Total	1st Quarter	2nd Quarter	3rd Quarter	4th Quarter
Beginning cash balance	$ 15,000	$15,000	$ 3,850	$ 13,300	$ 25,750
Cash collections	361,950	69,000	82,800	97,650	112,500
Total	$376,950	$84,000	$86,650	$110,950	$138,250
Cash payments					
Purchases	$ 58,625	$11,750	$13,875	$ 15,375	$ 17,625
Direct labor	98,750	20,000	22,500	26,250	30,000
Mfg. overhead	38,700	7,300	8,300	9,800	11,300
Selling expense	91,600	17,275	21,025	24,775	28,525
Adm. expenses	33,300	6,300	7,650	9,000	10,350
Federal income tax	27,525	27,525			
Dividends	20,000				20,000
Interest expenses	450				450
Loan repayment	10,000				10,000
Total	$376,950	$90,150	$73,350	$ 85,200	$128,250
Cash deficiency		($6,150)			
Bank loan received	10,000	10,000			
Ending cash balance	$ 10,000	$ 3,850	$13,300	$ 25,750	$ 10,000

Now you are ready to prepare a budget balance sheet. Take the account balances of last year and combine them with the transactions reflected in the various budgets you have compiled. You will come out with a sheet resembling this:

Budgeted Balance Sheet
December 31, 20__
Assets

	20__	20__
Current assets:		
Cash	$ 10,000	$ 15,000
Accounts receivable	11,500	6,666
Less: allowance for doubtful accounts	(1,150)	(666)
Inventory:		
Raw materials	6,750	3,000
Finished goods	22,500	10,000
Total current assets	$ 49,600	34,000
Fixed assets:		
Land	$ 50,000	$ 50,000
Building	148,000	148,000
Less: allowance for depreciation	(37,000)	(33,000)
Total fixed assets	$161,100	$164,700
Total assets	$210,600	$198,700

Liabilities and Shareholders' Equity

Current liabilities:		
Account payable	$ 9,375	$ 5,000
Shareholders' equity:		
Capital stock (10,000 shares; $10 par value)	$100,000	$110,000
Retained earnings	101,225	93,700
	$201,225	$193,700
Total liabilities and shareholders' equity	$210,600	$198,700

depending upon the size of your company, the budget reports can be prepared to correspond with the organizational structure of the company.

Two typical budget reports* are shown below to demonstrate various forms these reports may take.

Report of Actual and Budgeted Sales
For the Year Ended December 31, 20__

	Actual sales $	Budgeted sales $	Variations from budget (under) Quarterly $	Cumulative $
1st Quarter				
2nd Quarter				
3rd Quarter				
4th Quarter				

Budgeted Report on Selling Expenses
For the Year Ended December 31, 20__

Budget This Month	Actual This Month	Variation This Month	Budget Year to Date	Actual Year to Date	Variations Year to Date	Remarks

Remember, the Cash Flow Statement used as the business's Budget allows the owner/manager to anticipate problems rather than react to them after they occur. It permits comparison of actual receipts and disbursements against projections to identify errors in the forecast. If cash flow is analyzed monthly, the manager can correct the cause of the error before it harms profitability.

VI. Pricing Policy

Identifying the actual cost of doing business requires careful and accurate analysis. No one is expected to calculate the cost of doing business with complete accuracy. However, failure to calculate all actual costs properly to ensure an adequate profit margin is a frequent and often overlooked cause of business failure.

Establishing Selling Prices

The costs of raw materials, labor, indirect overhead, and research and development must be carefully studied *before* setting the selling price of items offered by your business. These factors must be regularly re-evaluated, as costs fluctuate.

Regardless of the strategies employed to maximize profitability, the method of costing products offered for resale is basic. It involves four major categories:

- Direct Material Costs

- Direct Labor Costs

- Overhead Expenses

- Profit Desired

Combining these factors allows you to calculate an item's minimum sales price, which is described below:

1. Calculate your Direct Material Costs. Direct material costs are the total cost of all raw materials used to produce the item for sale. Divide this total cost by the number of items produced from these raw materials to derive the Total Direct Materials Cost Per Item.

2. Calculate your Direct Labor Costs. Direct labor costs are the wages paid to employees to produce the item. Divide this total direct labor cost by the total number of items produced to get the Total Direct Labor Cost Per Item.

3. Calculate your Total Overhead Expenses. Overhead expenses include rent, gas and electricity, telephone, packing and shipping, delivery and freight charges, cleaning expenses, insurance, office supplies, postage, repairs and maintenance, and the manager's salary. In other words, all operating expenses incurred during the same time period that you used for calculating the costs above (one year, one quarter, or one month). Divide the Total Overhead Expense by the number of items produced for sale during that same time period to get the Total Overhead Expense Per Item.

4. Calculate Total Cost Per Item. Add the Total Direct Material Cost Per Item, the Total Direct Labor Cost Per Item, and the Total Overhead Expense Per Item to derive the Total Cost Per Item.

5. Calculate the Profit Per Item. Now, calculate the profit you determine appropriate for each category of item offered for sale based on the sales and profit strategy you have set for your business.

6. Calculate the Total Price Per Item. Add the Profit Figure Per Item to the Total Cost Per Item.

A Pricing Example

You produce skirts that take 1 1/2 yards of fabric per skirt, and you can manufacture three skirts per day. The fabric costs $2.00 per yard. The normal work week is five days. If you complete three skirts per day, your week's production is 15 skirts.

1. Calculate Direct Materials Cost

Materials	Cost
Fabric for 1 week's production: 15 skirts x 1 1/2 yds. each = 22 1/2 yds. x $2 per yd.	$45.00
Linings, interfacings, etc.: $.50 per skirt x 15 skirts	7.50
Zippers, buttons, snaps: $.50 per skirt x 15 skirts	7.50
Belts, ornaments, etc.: $.75 per skirt x 15 skirts	11.25
Thread, seam binding, etc.: One week's supply	5.00
Total Direct Materials Cost:	$76.25 per week

$$\frac{\text{Total Direct Materials Cost per week}}{15 \text{ skirts per week}} = \$5.08 \text{ Direct Materials Cost per skirt}$$

2. Calculate Direct Labor Costs

Wages paid to employees = $100.00 per week

$$\frac{\text{Total Direct Labor Cost per week}}{15 \text{ skirts}} = \$6.67 \text{ Direct Labor Cost per skirt}$$

3. Calculate Overhead Expenses Per Month

Overhead Expenses	Monthly Expenses
Owner's Salary	$400.00
Rent	100.00
Electricity	24.00
Telephone	12.00
Insurance	15.00
Cleaning	20.00
Packing Materials and Supplies	15.00
Delivery and Freight	20.00
Office Supplies, Postage	10.00
Repairs and Maintenance	15.00
Payroll Taxes	5.00
Total Monthly Overhead Expenses:	$636.00

15 skirts per week $\times$ 4 weeks in one month = 60 skirts per month.

$$\frac{\text{Total Monthly Overhead Expenses}}{60 \text{ skirts per month}} = \$10.60 \text{ Overhead Cost per skirt}$$

4. **Calculate the Total Cost per Skirt** by adding the total individual costs per skirt calculated in the three preceding steps.

Total Direct Material Cost per Skirt	$5.08
Total Direct Labor Cost per Skirt	6.67
Total Overhead Expense per Skirt	10.60
TOTAL COST PER SKIRT	$22.35

5. Assume you want to make a profit of $5.00 per skirt.

6. **Calculate the Total Price Per Item:**

Total Cost per Skirt	$22.35
Total Profit per Skirt	5.00
Total Selling Price Per Skirt	$27.35

The Retailer's Mark-Up

A word of caution is in order regarding the popular but misunderstood pricing method known as retailers mark-up. Retail mark-up means the amount added to the price of an item to arrive at the retail sales price, either in dollars or as a percentage of the cost. For example, if a single item costing $8.00 is sold for $12.00 it carries a mark-up of $4.00 or 50 percent. If a group of items costing $6,000 is offered for $10,000, the mark-up is $4,000 or 66 2/3 percent. While in these illustrations the mark-up percentage appears generally to equal the gross margin percentages, the mark-up is **not** the same as the gross margin. Adding mark-up to the price merely to simplify pricing will almost always adversely affect profitability.

To demonstrate, assume a manager determines from past records that the business's operating expenses average 29 percent of sales. She decides that she is entitled to a profit of 3 percent. So she prices her goods at a 32 percent gross margin, in order to earn a 3 percent profit after all operating expenses are paid. What she fails to realize, however, is that once the goods are displayed, some may be lost through pilferage. Others may have to be marked down later in order to sell them, or employees may purchase some of them at a discount. Therefore, the total reductions (mark-downs, shortages, discounts) in the sales price realized from selling all the inventory actually add up to an annual average of six percent of total sales. To correctly calculate the necessary mark-up required to yield a 32 percent gross margin,

these reductions to inventory must be anticipated and added into its selling price. Using the formula:

$$\text{Initial Mark-up} = \frac{\text{Desired Gross Margin} + \text{Retail Reductions}}{100 \text{ Percent} + \text{Retail Reductions}}$$

$$\frac{32 \text{ percent} + 6 \text{ percent}}{100 \text{ percent} + 6 \text{ percent}} = \frac{38 \text{ percent}}{106 \text{ percent}} = 35.85 \text{ percent}$$

To obtain the desired gross margin of 32 percent, therefore, the retailer must initially mark up his inventory by nearly 36 percent.

Pricing Policies and Profitability Goals

Break-Even Analysis, discussed in Chapter IV, and Return on Investment, described in Chapter III, should be reviewed at this time. Remember, all costs (direct and indirect), the break-even point, desired profit, and the methods of calculating sales price from these factors must be thoroughly studied when you establish pricing policies and profitability goals. They should be understood before you offer items for sale because an omission or error in these calculations could make the difference between success and failure.

Selling Strategy

Proper product pricing is only one facet of overall planning for profitability. A second major factor to be determined once costs, break-even point, and profitability goals have been analyzed, is the selling strategy. Three sales planning approaches are used (often concurrently) by businesses to develop final pricing policies, as they strive to compete successfully.

In the first, employed as a short-term strategy in the earliest stages of a business, the owner/manager sells products at such low prices that the business only breaks even (no profit), while trying to attract future steady customers. As volume grows, the owner/manager gradually builds in the profit margin necessary to achieve the targeted Return on Investment.

"Loss leaders" are a second strategy practiced in both developing and mature business. While a few items are sold at a loss, most goods are priced for healthy profits. The hope is that while customers are in the store to purchase the low-price items, they will also buy enough other goods to make the seller's overall profitability higher than if he had not used "come-ons." The seller wants to maximize total profit and can sacrifice profit on a few items to achieve that goal.

The third strategy recognizes that maximum profit does not result only from selling goods at relatively high profit margins. The relationship of volume, price, cost of merchandise, and operational expenses determines profitability. Price increases may result in fewer sales and decreased profits. Reductions in prices, if sales volume is substantially increased, may produce satisfactory profits.

There is no arbitrary rule about this. It is perfectly possible for two stores, with different pricing structures to exist side by side and both be successful. It is the owner/manager's responsibility to identify and understand the market factors that affect his or her unique business circumstances. The level of service (delivery, availability of credit, store hours, product advice, and the like) may permit a business to charge higher prices in order to cover the costs of such services. Location, too, often permits a business to charge more, since customers are often willing to pay a premium for convenience.

The point is that many considerations go into setting selling prices. Some small businesses do not seek to compete on price at all, finding an un- or under-occupied market niche, which can be a more certain path to success. What is important is that all factors that affect pricing must be recognized and analyzed for their costs as well as their benefits.

VII. Forecasting and Obtaining Capital

Forecasting the need for capital, whether debt or equity, has already been discussed in Chapter V. This chapter looks at the types and uses of external capital and the usual sources of such capital.

Types and Sources of Capital

The capital to finance a business has two major forms: debt and equity. Creditor money (debt) comes from trade credit, loans made by financial institutions, leasing companies, and customers who have made prepayments on larger-frequently manufactured-orders. Equity is money received by the company in exchange for some portion of ownership. Sources include the entrepreneur's own money; money from family, friends, or other non-professional investors; or money from venture capitalists, Small Business Investment Companies (SBICs), and Minority Enterprise Small Business Investment Companies (MESBICs) both funded by the SBA.

Debt capital, depending upon its sources (e.g., trade, bank, leasing company, mortgage company) comes into the business for short or intermediate periods. Owner or equity capital remains in the company for the life of the business (unless replaced by other equity) and is repaid only when and if there is a surplus at liquidation of the business-**after** all creditors are repaid.

Acquiring such funds depends entirely on the business's ability to repay with interest (debt) or appreciation (equity). Financial performance (reflected in the Financial Statements discussed in Chapter II) and realistic, thorough management planning and control (shown by Pro Formas and Cash Flow Budgets), are the determining factors in whether or not a business can attract the debt and equity funding it needs to operate and expand.

Business capital can be further classified as equity capital, working capital, and growth capital. Equity capitol is the cornerstone of the financial structure of any company. As you will recall from Chapter II, equity is technically the part of the Balance Sheet reflecting the ownership of the company. It represents the total value of the business, all other financing being debt that must be repaid. Usually, you cannot get equity capital at least not during the early stages of business growth.

Working capital is required to meet the continuing operational needs of the business, such as "carrying" accounts receivable, purchasing inventory, and meeting the payroll. In most businesses, these needs vary during the year, depending on activities (inventory build-up, seasonal hiring or layoffs, etc.) during the business cycle.

Growth capital is not directly related to cyclical aspects of the business. Growth capital is required when the business is expanding or being altered in some significant and costly way that is expected to result in higher and increased cash flow. Lenders of growth capital frequently depend on anticipated increased profit for repayment over an extended period of time, rather than expecting to be repaid from seasonal increases in liquidity as is the case of working capital lenders.

Every growing business needs all three types: equity, working, and growth capital. You should not expect a single financing program maintained for a short period of time to eliminate future needs for additional capital.

As lenders and investors analyze the requirements of your business, they will distinguish between the three types of capital in the following way: 1) fluctuating needs (working capital); 2) needs to be repaid with profits over a period of a few years (growth capital); and 3) permanent needs (equity capital).

If you are asking for a working capital loan, you will be expected to show how the loan can be repaid through cash (liquidity) during the businesses next full operating cycle, generally a one year cycle. If you seek growth capital, you will be expected to show how the capital will be used to increase your business enough to be able to repay the loan within several years (usually not more than seven). If you seek equity capital, it must be raised from investors who will take the risk for dividend returns or capital gains, or a specific share of the business.

Borrowing Working Capital

Chapter II defined working capital as the difference between current assets and current liabilities. To the extent that a business does not generate enough money to pay trade debt as it comes due, this cash must be borrowed.

Commercial banks obviously are the largest source of such loans, which have the following characteristics: 1) The loans are short-term but renewable; 2) they may fluctuate according to seasonal needs or follow a fixed schedule of repayment (amortization); 3)

they require periodic full repayment ("clean up"); 4) they are granted primarily only when the ratio of net current assets comfortably exceeds net current liabilities; and 5) they are sometimes unsecured but more often secured by current assets (e.g., accounts receivable and inventory). Advances can usually be obtained for as much as 70 to 80 percent of quality (likely to be paid) receivables and to 40 to 50 percent of inventory. Banks grant unsecured credit only when they feel the general liquidity and overall financial strength of a business provide assurance for repayment of the loan.

You may be able to predict a specific interval, say three to five months, for which you need financing. A bank may then agree to issue credit for a specific term/Most likely, you will need working capital to finance outflow peaks in your business cycle. Working capital then supplements equity. Most working capital credits are established on a one-year basis.

Although most unsecured loans fall into the one-year line of credit category, another frequently used type, the amortizing loan, calls for a fixed program of reduction, usually on a monthly or quarterly basis. For such loans your bank is likely to agree to terms longer than a year, as long as you continue to meet the principal reduction schedule.

It is important to note that while a loan from a bank for working capital can be negotiated only for a relatively short term, satisfactory performance can allow the arrangement to be continued indefinitely.

Most banks will expect you to pay off your loans once a year (particularly if they are unsecured) in perhaps 30 or 60 days. This is known as "the annual clean up," and it should occur when the business has the greatest liquidity. This debt reduction normally follows a seasonal sales peak when inventories have been reduced and most receivables have been collected.

You may discover that it becomes progressively more difficult to repay debt or "clean up" within the specified time. This difficulty usually occurs because: 1) Your business is growing and its current activity represents a considerable increase over the corresponding period of the previous year; 2) you have increased your short-term capital requirement because of new promotional programs or additional operations; or 3) you are experiencing a temporary reduction in profitability and cash flow.

Frequently, such a condition justifies obtaining both working capital and amortizing loans. For example, you might try to arrange a combination of a $15,000 open line of credit to handle peak financial requirements during the business cycle and $20,000 in amortizing loans to be repaid at, say $4,000 per quarter. In appraising such a request, a commercial bank will insist on justification based on past experience and future projections. The bank will want to know: How the $15,000 line of credit will be self-liquidating during the year (with ample room for the annual clean up); and how your business will produce increased profits and resulting cash flow to meet the schedule of amortization on the $20,000 portion in spite of increasing your business's interest expense.

Borrowing Growth Capital

Lenders expect working capital loans to be repaid through cash generated in the short-term operations of the business, such as, selling goods or services and collecting receivables. Liquidity rather than overall profitability supports such borrowing programs. Growth capital loans are usually scheduled to be repaid over longer periods with profits from business activities extending several years into the future. Growth capital loans are, therefore, secured by collateral such as machinery and equipment, fixed assets which guarantee that lenders will recover their money should the business be unable to make repayment.

For a growth capital loan you will need to demonstrate that the growth capital will be used to increase your cash flow through increased sales, cost savings, and/or more efficient production. Although your building, equipment, or machinery will probably be your collateral for growth capital funds, you will also be able to use them for general business purposes, so long as the activity you use them for promises success. Even if you borrow only to acquire a single piece of new equipment, the lender is likely to insist that all your machinery and equipment be pledged.

Instead of bank financing a particular piece of new equipment, it may be possible to arrange a lease. You will not actually own the equipment, but you will have exclusive use of it over a specified period. Such an arrangement usually has tax advantages. It lets you use funds that would be tied up in the equipment, if you had purchased it. It also affords the opportunity to make sure the equipment meets your needs before you purchase it.

Major equipment may also be purchased on a time payment plan, sometimes called a Conditional Sales Purchase. Ownership of the property is retained by the seller until the buyer has made all the payments required by the contract. (Remember, however, that time payment purchases usually require substantial down payments and even leases require cash advances for several months of lease payments.)

Long-term growth capital loans for more than five but less than fifteen years are also obtainable. Real estate financing with repayment over many years on an established schedule is the best example. The loan is secured by the land and/or buildings the money was used to buy. Most businesses are best financed by a combination of these various credit arrangements.

When you go to a bank to request a loan, you must be prepared to present your company's case persuasively. You should bring your financial plan consisting of a Cash Budget for the next twelve months, Pro Forma Balance Sheets, and Income Statements for the next three to five years. You should be able to explain and amplify these statements and the underlying assumptions on which the figures are based. Obviously, your assumptions must be convincing and your projections supportable. Finally, many banks prefer statements audited by an outside accountant with the accountant's signed opinion that the statements were prepared in accordance with generally accepted accounting principles and that they fairly present the financial condition of your business.

If borrowing growth capital is necessary and no private conventional source can be found, the U.S. Small Business Administration (SBA) may be able to guarantee up to 90 percent of a local bank loan. By law, SBA cannot consider a loan application without evidence that the loan could not be obtained elsewhere on reasonable terms without SBA assistance. Even for such guaranteed loans, however, the borrower must demonstrate the ability to repay.

Borrowing Permanent Equity Capital

Permanent capital sometimes comes from sources other than the business owner/manager. Considered ownership contributions, they are different from "stockholders equity" in the traditional sense of the phrase. Small Business Investment Companies (SBIC's) licensed and financed by the Small Business Administration are authorized to provide venture capital to small business concerns. This captital may be in the form of secured and/or unsecured loans or debt securities represented by common and preferred stock.

Venture capital, another source of equity capital, is extremely difficult to define; however, it is high risk capital offered with the principal objective of earning capital gains for the investor. While venture capitalists are usually prepared to wait longer than the average investor for a profitable return, they usually expect in excess of 15 percent return on their investment. Often they expect to take an active part in determining the objectives of the business. These investors may also assist the small business owner/manager by providing experienced guidance in marketing, product ideas, and additional financing alternatives as the business develops. Even though turning to venture capital may create more bosses, their advice could be as valuable as the money they lend. Be aware, however, that venture capitalists are looking for businesses with real potential for growth and for future sales in the millions of dollars.

Figure 7-1
Financing Sources for Your Business

Equity (Sell part of company)
- Family, friends, and other non-professional investors
- Venture Capitalists
- Small Business Investment Companies (SBICs and MESBICs)

Personal Loans
   •Banks
        ——Unsecured loans (rare)
        ——Loans secured by:
     Real Estate
     Stocks and Bonds
   •Finance Companies
        ——Loans secured by:
     Real Estate
     Personal Assets
   •Credit Unions
        ——Unsecured "signature"
        ——Loans Loans secured by:
     Real Estate (some credit unions]
     Personal Assets
   •Savings and Loan Associations
        ——Unsecured loans (rare)
        ——Loans secured by Real Estate
   •Mortgage Brokers and Private Investors
        ——Loans secured by Real Estate
   •Life Insurance Companies
        ——Policy loans (borrow against cash value)

Business Loans Loons

   •Banks (short-term)
        ——Unsecured loans (for established,
       financially sound companies only)
        ——Loans secured by:
     Accounts Receivable
     Inventory
     Equipment
    Banks [long-term)
        ——Loans secured by:
     Real Estate
        ——Loans guaranteed by:

Small Business Administration (SBA)
Farmers Home Administration (FmHA)
- Commercial Finance Companies
    ____Loans secured by:
    Real Estate
    Equipment
    Inventory
    Accounts Receivable
- Life Insurance Companies
    ____Loans secured by commercial Real Estate
    (worth at least $150,000)
- Small Business Administration (SBA)
    ____Loans secured by:
    All available business assets
    All available personal assets
- Suppliers
    ____Trade Credit
- Customers
    ____Prepayment on orders

Leasing
- Banks
- Leasing Companies
    ____Loans secured by:
    Equipment
Sales of Receivables (called "factoring")

Applying for Capital

Below is the minimum information you must make available to lenders and investors:

1. Discussion of the Business
   - Name, address, and telephone number.
   - Type of business you are in now or want to expand or start.

2. Amount of Money You Need to Borrow
   - Ask for *all* you will need. Don't ask for a part of the total and think you can come back for more later. This could indicate to the lender that you are a poor planner.

3. How You Will Use the Money
   - List each way the borrowed money will be used.
   - Itemize the amount of money required for each purpose.

4. Proposed Terms of the *Loan*
   - Include a payback schedule. Even though the lender has the final say in setting the terms of the loan, if you suggest terms, you will retain a negotiating position.
5. Financial Support Documents
   - Show where the money will come from to repay the loan through the following projected statements:

     _____Profit and Loss Statements (one year for working capital loan requests and three to five years for growth capital requests)

     _____Cash Flow Statements (one year for working capital loan requests and three to five years for growth capital requests)

6. Financial History of the Business
   - Include the following financial statements for the last three years:
     _____Balance Sheet
     _____Profit and Loss Statement
     _____Accounts Receivable and Accounts Payable Listings and Agings

7. Personal Financial Statement of the Owner(s)
   - Personal Assets and Liabilities
   - Resume(s)

8. Other Useful Information Includes
   - Letters of Intent from Prospective Customers
   - Leases or Buy/Sell Agreements Affecting Your Business
   - Reference Letters

Although it is not required, it is useful to calculate the ratios described in Chapter III for your business over the past three years. Use this information to prove the strong financial health and good trends in your business's development and to demonstrate that you use such management tools to plan and control your business's growth.

VIII. Financial Management Planning

Studies overwhelmingly identify bad management as the leading cause of business failure. Bad management translates to poor planning by management.

All too often, the owner is so caught up in the day-to-day tasks of getting the product out the door and struggling to collect receivables to meet the payroll that he or she does not plan. There never seems to be time to prepare Pro Formas or Budgets. Often new managers understand their products but not the financial statements or the bookkeeping records, which they feel are for the benefit of the IRS or the bank. Such overburdened owner/managers can scarcely identify what will affect their businesses next week, let alone over the coming months and years. But, you may ask, "What should I do? How can I, as a small business owner/manager, avoid getting bogged down? How can I ensure success?"

Success may be ensured only by focusing on all factors affecting a business's performance. Focusing on planning is essential to survival.

Short-term planning is generally concerned with profit planning or budgeting. Long-term planning is generally strategic, setting goals for sales growth and profitability over a minimum of three to five years.

The tools for short- and long-term plans have been explained in the previous chapters: Pro Forma Income Statements, Cash Flow Statements or Budgets, Ratio Analysis, and pricing considerations. The business's short-term plan should be prepared on a monthly basis for a year into the future, employing the Pro Forma Income Statement and the Cash Flow Budget.

Long-Term Planning

The long-term or strategic plan focuses on Pro Forma Statements of Income prepared for annual periods three to five years into the future. You may be asking yourself, "How can I possibly predict what will affect my business that far into the future?" Granted, it's hard to imagine all the variables that will affect your business in the next year, let alone the next three to five years. The key, however, is controlcontrol of your business's future course of expansion through the use of the financial tools explained in the preceding chapters.

First determine a rate of growth that is desirable and reasonably attainable. Then employ Pro Formas and Cash Flow Budgets to calculate the capital required to finance the inventory, plant, equipment, and personnel needs necessary to attain that growth in sales volume. The business owner/manager must anticipate capital needs in time to make satisfactory arrangements for outside funds if internally generated funds from retained earnings are insufficient.

Growth can be funded in only two ways: with profits or by borrowing. If expansion outstrips the capital available to support higher levels of accounts receivable, inventory, fixed assets, and operating expenses, a business's development will be slowed or stopped entirely by its failure to meet debts as they become payable. Such insolvency will result in the business's assets being liquidated to meet the demands of the creditors. The only way to avoid this "outstripping of capital" is by planning to control growth. Growth must be understood to be controlled. This understanding requires knowledge of past financial performance and of the future requirements of the business.

These needs must be forecast in writingusing the Pro Forma Income Statement in particularfor three to five years in the future. After projecting reasonable sales volumes and profitability, use the Cash Flow Budget to determine (on a quarterly basis for the next three to five years) how these projected sales volumes translate into the flow of cash in and out of the business during normal operations. Where additional inventory, equipment, or other physical assets are necessary to support the sales forecast, you must determine whether or not the business will generate enough profit to sustain the growth forecast.

Often, businesses simply grow too rapidly for internally generated cash to sufficiently support the growth. If profits are inadequate to carry the growth forecast, the owner/manager must either make arrangements for working growth capital to borrowed, or slow growth to allow internal cash to "catch up" and keep pace with the expansion. Because arranging financing and obtaining additional equity capital takes time, this need must be anticipated well in advance to avoid business interruption.

To develop effective long-term plans, you should do the following steps:

1. Determine your personal objectives and how they affect your willingness and ability to pursue financial goals for your business. This consideration, often overlooked, will help you determine whether or not your business goals fit your personal plans. For example, suppose you hope to become a millionaire by age 45 through your business but your long-term strategic plan reveals that only modest sales growth and very slim profit margins on that volume are attainable in your industry. You must either adjust your personal goals or get into a different business. Long-range planning enables you to be realistic about the future of your personal and business expectations.

2. Set goals and objectives for the company (growth rates, return on investment, and direction as the business expands and matures). Express these goals in specific numbers, for example, sales growth of 10 percent a year, increases in gross and net profit margins of 2 to 3 percent a year, a return on investment of not less than 9 to 10 percent a year. Use these long-range plans to develop forecasts of sales and profitability and compare actual results from operations to these forecasts. If after these goals are established actual performance continuously falls short of target, the wise business owner will reassess both the realism of expectations and the desirability of continuing to pursue the enterprise.

3. Develop long-range plans that enable you to attain your goals and objectives. Focus on the strengths and weaknesses of your business and on internal and external factors that will affect the accomplishment of your goals. Develop strategies based upon careful analysis of all relevant factors (pricing strategies, market potential, competition, cost of borrowed and equity capital as compared to using only profits for expansions, etc.) to provide direction for the future of your business.

4. Focus on the financial, human, and physical requirements necessary to fulfill your plan by developing forecasts of sales, expenses, and retain earnings over the next three to five years.

5. Study methods of operation, product mix, new market opportunities, and other such factors to help identify ways to improve your company's productivity and profitability.

6. Revise, revise. Always use your most recent financial statements to adjust your short- and long-term plans. Compare your company's financial performance regularly with current industry data to determine how your results compare with others in your industry. Learn where your business may have performance weaknesses. Don't be afraid to modify your plans if your expectations have been either too aggressive or too conservative.

Planning is a perpetual process. It is the key to prosperity for your business.

www.ingramcontent.com/pod-product-compliance
Lightning Source LLC
Chambersburg PA
CBHW081805300426
44116CB00014B/2242